THE REPUBLIC OF THE USHAKOVKA

Admiral Kolchak and the Allied
Intervention in Siberia
1918–20

R.M. Connaughton

London and New York

First published 1990
by Routledge
11 New Fetter Lane, London EC4P 4EE
29 West 35th Street, New York, NY 10001

© 1990 R.M. Connaughton

Typeset in 10/12 Palatino by Megaron, Cardiff, Wales
Printed in Great Britain by Richard Clay Ltd, Bungay, Suffolk

British Library Cataloguing in Publication Data
Connaughton, Richard
The Republic of the Ushakovka: Admiral Kolchak and the
allied intervention in Siberia, 1918–20.
1. Russia, (RSFSR). Siberia, Political events. Role of
Kolchak, Aleksandr Vasilevich, 1873–1920
I. Title
957'.0841'0924

ISBN 0–415–05198–3

Library of Congress Cataloging in Publication Data
Connaughton, R. M. (Richard Michael), 1942–
The republic of the Ushakovka: Admiral Kolchak and the allied
intervention in Siberia, 1918–20/Richard Connaughton.
p. cm.
"The second book in a regional trilogy"–Pref.
Continues: The war of the rising sun and tumbling
bear. Includes bibliographical references.
1. Soviet Union–History–Allied intervention, 1918–1920.
2. Kolchak, Aleksandr Vasiliyevich, 1873–1920. 3. Siberia
(R.S.F.S.R.)–History–Revolution, 1917–1921. I. Title.
DK265.4.C66 1990   89–70246
947.084'1–dc20   CIP

For Rosemary Best

CONTENTS

ILLUSTRATIONS

PLATES

MAPS

The author and publishers would like to extend their grateful thanks to Mr Martin Heller for the loan of *K Vítězné Svobodě*, by Rudolf Medek, from which several of the pictures in this book were taken, and to J. C. Lucas for providing the maps.

vii

PREFACE

I set out to write this, the second book in a regional trilogy, by describing the Allied Intervention in Siberia 1918–20 through the means of a biography of Admiral Kolchak. Perhaps I should emphasize that this is an historical story. I have not set out to attempt either an analysis or evaluation of the lessons in international, politico-military and human relations arising from this disastrous Allied Intervention in Russia.

It would not be an unreasonable digression, however, just to touch upon a few aspects of a broader subject deserving a separate and detailed review. It must be admitted that there existed an inevitability of conflict between the emerging ideology of Communist Russia and the West. While the episode is largely unknown in the West, it is indelibly imprinted in the Russian soul and a major factor in the extension of the cold war. Herein therefore lies an important lesson in the potential political and spiritual penalties which can arise as a legacy of intervention in another state's internal affairs.

When Khrushchev visited the United States in 1959 he found the tweaking of the eagle's feathers irresistible. 'We remember the grim days when American soldiers went to our soil headed by their generals to help our White Guards combat the new revolution. All the capitalist countries of Europe and America marched on our country to strangle our new revolution. Never have any of our soldiers been on American soil, but your soldiers were on Russian soil. Those are the facts.' More recently, writing in *Perestroika*, Gorbachev provides a timely reminder that the misguided allied initiative has been neither forgiven nor forgotten. 'It is true to say that post-revolutionary development underwent difficult stages, largely due to the rude meddling of imperial forces in our internal

affairs.' The underlying message to modern-day would-be interventionists is, look before you leap.

The episode was perhaps best summarized in a footnote written
on the relevant official British Foreign Office file by Lord Hardinge,
Permanent Under Secretary of State, to the Foreign Secretary, Lord
Curzon. By March 1920, all British troops had been withdrawn
from Russia, Kolchak was dead and the post of High Commissioner
dissolved. 'So ends a not very creditable enterprise', wrote
Hardinge. When the file crossed Curzon's desk he looked at
Hardinge's note, took out his fountain pen and amended it to read,
'So ends a highly discreditable enterprise.'

This book differs from its predecessor, *The War of the Rising Sun
and Tumbling Bear*, because the scale and scope are significantly
broader. It does, nevertheless, still represent a continuation of the
events of 1904–5 through the period 1918–20 to the final and as
yet unwritten book in the trilogy, the story of the Japanese invasion
of China.

RMC
January 1990

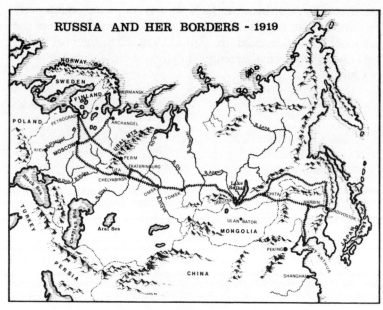

RUSSIA AND HER BORDERS - 1919

Map 1

1

IN THE BEGINNING

The Obovkov ordnance works, St Petersburg, where Alexander Vasilevich Kolchak was born in 1873, would seem an unlikely birthplace for one destined to become the Supreme Ruler of Russia. Yet, despite Russia's apparent disregard of the pursuit of progressive goals, her engineers did enjoy a status at odds with the age. The history of Russia is replete with examples of successive invasion from all directions. Being bereft of natural barriers, the engineers, the heirs of Todleben, grew to be revered as the architects of the artificialities of the state's defence. They provided that essential reassurance for a people totally absorbed in a womb to tomb siege mentality.

Kolchak's father, Vasilii Ivanovich, a Crimea veteran, had spent his career in naval artillery and passed his later years at Obovkov in the rank of Major-General. Kolchak's mother came from an aristocratic Odessa family, but on neither side was there inherited wealth. It was therefore his father's acceptable rank and calling which gave the young Kolchak that essential foot up the social ladder. In 1888, the boy entered Navy School, graduating in 1894.

Rather like 1904, 1894 was one of those important years which, when examined, helps in part in the understanding of the reasons for the allied Intervention in Russia from 1918–22. To put 1894 in perspective, however, it is necessary to begin this historical summary in 1875. Baulked in her endeavours to expand elsewhere, Russia looked eastward towards the lands of China, Korea, and Japan. By 1875, when Russia dispossessed Japan of Sakhalin, the Japanese were the last remaining Asian nation of substance not to have fallen under the colonial domination of one or other of the Western powers. As if to emphasize her determination to be in a strong position to mop up Japan and exploit weaknesses in both

1

China and Korea, Russia expanded and developed Vladivostok – Lord of the East. It was for the Japanese an ominous step, as though an arrow was pointing at the nation's very heart. Vladivostok, with its port closed by ice for three months of the year, was not the ideal strategic city. The only guaranteed line of constant communication would therefore have to be overland, and out of this necessity the single-track Siberian Railway Project was spawned in 1891. In that year, the Tsarevich visited Vladivostok to hammer home the first bolt to inaugurate an undertaking destined to bring Russia and Japan into open conflict. Accompanying the Tsarevich was a squadron of six warships, an unusually large display of power for the traditionally quiet Pacific. Ominously, two of the warships were named *Manchuria* and *Korea*, both areas which had become the economic colonies of Japan.

The Russian squadron visited Japan and it was in the course of being shown the beauties of Lake Biwa that an officer stepped from the crowd and struck the Russian prince across the head with his sword. Had the Russians paused to reflect upon the reason for such a symbolic attack that bruised little more than the Tsarevich's ego, then perhaps the pointless slaughter of 1904–5 might have been avoided. Instead, it convinced the Russian court of Japan's volatility, unpredictability, and pretensions in the area. This growing awareness of Japan's emergence as a regional power drew together a concert of Europe in the form of Russia, France, and Germany to safeguard their interests against the 'Yellow Peril'.

For many years, China had maintained suzerainty over a bankrupt, corrupt, and feudal Korea. China's growing weakness tempted other powers to consider the possibility of attempting to fill what was seen as a possible power vacuum. Russia coveted the economic and strategic benefits to be derived from the occupation of Korea. Such a move would only serve to excite Japan for whom Korea had become a market vital to her own continuing stability. In 1894, after some sparring with China, it was to be Japan who was to make the first step, declaring war on China.

It was a short war barely spanning eight months. The Chinese were trounced on land and at sea. A certain Captain (later Admiral) Togo sank the British-registered steamer *Kowshing* leased to the Chinese as a troopship. When the *Kowshing* went down Togo ordered the Chinese soldiers struggling in the water to be machine-gunned or left to drown. Only the Europeans were plucked from the sea. From the resultant international furore, Japan learnt something of the need for a public relations policy but, more important, the need for regional allies. 'This is a time', declared Prince Ito, 'that we must do all we can to have England on our side.' The Imperial Japanese Navy was trained in the ways of the Royal Navy. There was something the Japanese could admire in the Nelsonian dictum that a nation should possess a navy strong enough to attack the enemy in their own ports. They would go on to emulate Nelson's strategic principle at Port Arthur, Pearl Harbor, and Darwin.

Following the Battle of Sedan in 1870 the Japanese dropped their French military advisers in favour of the Prussian victors. The land campaign was conducted with Germanic thoroughness and China sued for peace. By the Treaty of Shimonoseki of 10 April 1895, the full independence of Korea was recognized, Japan secured Formosa, the Pescadores, and, very significantly, retained the peninsula she had won in battle and upon which rested the ice-free port of Port Arthur. From time immemorial it had been the perennial aspiration of Russian foreign policy to possess an ice-free port which would provide unhindered access to the sea on her southern flank. Now, seemingly, an upstart race of *makaki*, leather-skinned dwarfs, had secured that goal in a matter of months at minimal cost. Japan had now placed herself in arguably the most opportune position to act when the expected fragmentation of the Chinese Empire occurred.

Russia was mortified. Her semi-official newspaper, *Novoe Vremya*, summarized the situation: 'Russia cannot permit the protectorate over Korea which Japan has secured for herself by the conditions of the treaty. If the single port of Port Arthur remains in the possession of Japan, Russia will suffer severely in the material interest and in the prestige of a Great Power.' It was with little difficulty that the Tsar was able to persuade the Kaiser to mobilize his interests to intervene. Although the Germans had one eye on the sick Austro-Hungarian Empire, they nonetheless retained some capacity to find a 'place in the sun' to be there when the race began for the spoils arising from the division of China. Japan was offended by the behaviour of a nation she considered friendly. In 1914, as a *quid pro quo*, Japan seized Germany's Far East colonies. France, as ever the model of international virtue, aligned herself with Russia and Germany. She had substantial colonial interests in Africa and Indo-China, and Asian adventurism could not be tolerated. *Le Temps* regarded Japan's action as 'a serious blow dealt at the immediate adjacent powers', and suggested that a European reaction was 'now a duty towards civilisation'.

The fleets of the three European allies were reinforced and concentrated while ambassadors in Tokyo delivered letters of protest. Japan recognized that she was not sufficiently strong to face Russia, Germany, and France. The Emperor found himself in no position to resist the allies' demands and, accordingly, withdrew from the Treaty of Shimonoseki. 'I have', announced the Emperor, 'yielded to the dictates of magnanimity, and accepted the advice of the three powers.' Stripped of her gains, Japan had only the consolation of £5,000,000 by way of reparations from China. While her enraged nationals were left to riot throughout the land, Japan sent emissaries to England authorized to spend the total Chinese reparations on the best, most modern battle fleet the money would buy. As a result of this move, the Tokyo newspaper *Kokumin* penned this warning: 'It was but yesterday we were robbed because we were weak. Today we are stronger and can fight the robbers. Tomorrow they will learn to leave us alone in peace.'

The course of events set in train in 1894 would rumble on until 1945 and beyond. The Sino-Japanese War heralded a period of a quarter of a century where the history of Asia would be marked by the most extraordinary power struggle involving the world's major powers. In that time, hunter would become hunted and new forces would appear to redress the balance left by the declining fortunes of the old.

When Kolchak passed out of Navy School in 1894 he was assigned to the Seventh Petersburg Naval Battalion. After only a few months had elapsed he was drafted to the new cruiser *Rurik* built especially for the Vladivostok Squadron. On his arrival at Vladivostok Kolchak was transferred as watch officer to the veteran cruiser, the *Kreiser*. In December 1897, the Russian Pacific Squadron anchored off Port Arthur and after three months of political pressure, the Chinese capitulated leasing the port to Russia. To the Europeans this seemed to be the green light they had been waiting for to join the scramble to secure concessions from China. For Japan, it was a bitter moment not to be forgotten.

Russia's fortification of Port Arthur grew apace as did her building of new railways. In 1898, a new line, a branch of the Chinese Eastern, was begun, running from Port Arthur through Mukden to Harbin to connect with the newly aligned Trans-Siberian Railway which took a shorter, more direct route than that planned, through China to reach Vladivostok. Attendant upon this Russian rail-building in Manchuria came the built-in excuse for

Russia to intervene should the railway be interfered with. Nothing was surer to incense and excite the local populace than the iron monsters which offended the *fung shui* (literally wind and water; meaning something like natural harmony) and showed no respect for the multiplicity of what the engineers regarded as haphazard last resting sites. When Kolchak took his leave of Vladivostok in 1899 there were unmistakable signs among the Chinese of disaffection with their government's obsequious manner in the face of Western demands. They objected principally to the subordination of their spiritualism to the whim of Western materialism.

Meanwhile, Kolchak had arrived at Kronstadt, an island fortress on the Gulf of Finland guarding the approaches to St Petersburg. While languishing in Vladivostok he had, in addition to his normal duties, studied the subjects of oceanology and hydrology. These were no random choices, for this was the age of polar exploration promising the exposure of earth's last great frontiers. This was the stuff that then fired the imagination of the masses. It was, after all, a goal of national prestige tempered undoubtedly by the possibilities of pecuniary reward. The young Lieutenant Kolchak became captivated by this prospect of adventure and it was to remain his ambition to discover the South Pole. For the time being, he immersed himself in the study of Antarctic conditions and associated scientific investigation.

The Commander at Kronstadt was Vice-Admiral S. Ossipovich Makarov, perhaps Russia's most respected senior naval officer. He had a reputation as intellectual, inventor and, unusually for senior Russian officers, he was superbly fit. Makarov's abiding extramural interest was polar exploration. His own particular ambition had been to take an ice breaker of his own design to conduct experiments at the North Pole. When Kolchak arrived at Kronstadt, Makarov was preparing the English-built ice-breaker *Yermak* for a polar expedition. Kolchak pleaded in vain to be allowed to join *Yermak* or, failing that, one of the fishery protection patrol ships in the Behring Sea.

It was therefore an utterly frustrated Kolchak who was drafted to join the recently built *Petropavlovsk*, designated flagship of the Pacific Squadron, on its inaugural voyage to Port Arthur. The young Lieutenant never reached his destination, for he was put ashore while his ship was passing through the Suez Canal. His polar reputation had gone before him and fortuitously coincided with the Academy of Sciences' need for volunteers to join an Arctic expedition to be led by the well known but foolhardy Baron Toll. The navy was content to release Kolchak for the expedition. He spent the time in his preparatory studies between the Chief Physical Observatory at St Petersburg and the Pavlovsk Magnetic Observatory. Just prior to the team's departure in 1900 the newspapers announced the murders in Peking of the Japanese Chancellor and German Ambassador.

At the same time that the Russian expedition headed north in search of a large continent Toll believed to exist among the wastes of the frozen north, the vengeful nations of Japan and the West mobilized their troops to intervene in China to raise the siege of Peking. Among the participants were the same nations who would so readily intervene in Russia in 1918–22. It was not until December 1902 that Kolchak returned to St Petersburg, where he discovered that nothing had been heard of Baron Toll who had gone off with a separate group. Kolchak offered to lead an expedition to retrace Toll's steps to find out what had befallen the adventurer. The Academy of Sciences sponsored the second expedition but it was one on which Kolchak's former companions declined to go. In their view it was a risky, dangerous act with little point since Toll and his party were most certainly dead.

While Kolchak was still immersed in his enterprise, the international scene which he was destined to catch up and be carried away by had witnessed the settlement of the Boxer 'rebellion'. On 30 January 1902, Japan and Britain entered into a bilateral agreement whereby it was understood that if either party went to war against a third party, the uncommitted nation would remain neutral. Should the war be extended by the appearance of another party, then the uncommitted country would come to the aid of her ally. In the same year, similar agreements were drawn up between France and Russia, and China and Russia. During the course of the 'rebellion', Russia had predictably entered Manchuria after the railway had been attacked. Following the peace, Russia began slowly to evacuate Manchuria but further progress came to an abrupt halt. Russia refused to continue with the withdrawal unless China agreed to seven conditions which, if granted by the wavering Chinese, would have served to consolidate the Russian position in Manchuria. Encouraged by the support of Great Britain, the United States, and Japan, China rejected the Russian demands as an unwarranted intrusion in her own domestic affairs.

Russia did not budge. By 13 January 1904, a conciliatory Japan agreed to recognize Manchuria as being outside her sphere of interest and sought in return a similar statement of Russia abandoning her interest in Korea. The Tsar had thoughtfully provided his negotiators with the authority to abandon claims on Korea in favour of a free hand in Manchuria. It was a card to be played if the need arose. Since, however, the Tsar's negotiating team was headed by noblemen with financial interests in Korea, this vital concession was not to be introduced. In the judgement of the Russian team, they had nothing to fear from the Japanese and therefore nothing to concede. They saw no prospect of these puny Asiatics wanting to cross swords with mighty Russia. Besides, it was naïvely felt in some quarters that a short victorious war was just the tonic to stem the revolutionary tide at home. Russia had miscalculated. On 8 February 1904, Japan made two co-ordinated pre-emptive attacks in Korea and against the Russian Fleet at Port Arthur. Japan had neglected to indulge in the niceties of a declaration of war, which did not occur until 10 February.

After a year in the northern wilderness, Kolchak returned emaciated from his fruitless search for Baron Toll. It was at Yakutsk that he was to learn of the Japanese attack on Port Arthur and the replacement of Admiral Stark by Admiral Makarov. He signalled the Admiralty requesting to be assigned to the Pacific Fleet subject to the Academy of Sciences being agreeable. Permission was granted and Kolchak secured his dream posting to Port Arthur and the seat of war.

Before leaving for Port Arthur, Kolchak contacted his father and fiancée of four years with the suggestion that all three should make rendezvous at the ancient Siberian city of Irkutsk so that he and his future wife might be married. They met at Glaskov railway station which lay to the west of the city on the other side of the 400-yard wide Angara river. In summer, a pontoon bridge would be laid to the north of the railway station to connect Glaskov suburb to the heart of the city. In deep winter, however, the bridge was superfluous and the trio made their crossing over the thick ice towards the cathedral. There was something ominous in the selection of Irkutsk as the place of marriage for this as yet obscure junior Russian naval officer. A short walk from the cathedral lies the main thoroughfare named the *Bolshaya*. After a few hundred yards in its northward journey, the road narrows to be taken by a bridge over the relatively small Ushakovka river. The confluence with the

Angara lies 500 yards to the north west. On the far bank, to the left of the bridge and raised above the river is Irkutsk gaol. It was in this prison, sixteen years later, that Kolchak spent his last moments, and the woman who shared those last moments was not Sofia Fedorovna whom he married at Irkutsk.

Many Russians fight shy of speaking directly of death, and the euphemism is therefore quite common. To be consigned to the Republic of a named river meant an individual had been killed and the body dumped in the river, frequently through a hole in the ice. It was a clean, efficient, and reliable disposal system. A testimony to its effectiveness is found in the well-documented despatch of the illiterate, turbulent holy man Grigory Rasputin. With Nicholas II absent at the front, the Tsarina became so mesmerized by the drunken, lecherous Rasputin that he became an unwelcome power in the land. In December 1916 a group of Russian noblemen led by Prince Yusupov decided to do away with him. This was no easy task as Rasputin proved to be a most tenacious fellow. He consumed cakes laced with cyanide, survived a shot from one would-be assassin, and fell to the ground only after Yusupov had emptied all six chambers of his revolver into the monk's body. The corpse was thereupon consigned to the 'Republic of the Neva'. Unusually, the Neva gave up Rasputin's body and the resultant autopsy revealed that the monk had died by drowning. The route to, and manner in which, Kolchak entered the Republic of the Ushakovka is the underlying theme of this story, intertwined as it is with political chicanery of the highest order.

In March 1904, Kolchak reported to Admiral Makarov in Port Arthur. Could he, he politely requested, have a destroyer? Makarov studied the thin, gaunt man before him and demurred. The Admiral believed it best for this man of substance to recover his strength aboard a ship requiring less adherence to a spartan routine. Accordingly, Kolchak was assigned to join the five-funnelled cruiser *Askold*. This ship was later captured by the British during the Revolution and recommissioned as HMS *Glory IV*, not to be confused with HMS *Glory*, also operating in Baltic waters. The silhouettes of the two ships produced no confusion. The former *Askold's* profusion of thin funnels led her to be dubbed the 'packet of Woodbines' by the British servicemen.)

The dramatic turning-point in what had been the improving Russian naval fortunes at Port Arthur occurred when the flagship *Petropavlovsk* struck a mine. She sank in a minute, taking with her

635 officers and men. Among those lost was the great hope of the Russian Navy, Admiral Makarov. Subsequent Russian naval commanders at Port Arthur erred on the side of caution. Some success was gained against Japanese warships by the use of mines – weapons which the Russians were adept at using. In time, the still unwell Kolchak was to be granted his wish to command a destroyer, and it was in one of his fields that the Japanese cruiser *Takasago* blew up. For the most part, however, the Pacific Fleet was left to languish in Port Arthur with crew and guns dispersed throughout the land defences. It was from the fort ramparts that Kolchak witnessed the humiliating destruction of the Russian Fleet by Japanese Army artillery. In addition, the vengeful, ill-prepared fleet sent from the Baltic was almost entirely annihilated by Togo at Tsushima.

The Russian Army fared equally badly, losing every battle it fought against the Japanese. With the exception of those under siege at Port Arthur they were forced progressively northward, deep into Manchuria, along their logistic vertebra, the railway. The railway proved to be a mixed blessing. It clearly delineated the Russian tactical opportunities and drew in masses of troops for protection from the attention of the mounted *Hunhutze* brigands. By 1905, railway operations were being conducted extremely efficiently under the direct supervision of the able Minister of Ways and Communications, Prince Khilikov. It had been little short of a logistic miracle to have sustained an army in Manchuria, 5,000 miles from Moscow, supported by only a single-track railway. From this point, the railway system throughout Russia would be expanded and the famous Trans-Siberian Railway planned to be double tracked. Despite these improvements, the system would never again reach the level of efficiency achieved in 1905. The railways sank into what was at first a slow, almost imperceptible decline, gradually deepening during the First World War.

By 1905, however, the Japanese war effort had run out of steam. Japan had fought a total war, committing everything, yet for Russia this had been a limited war, leaving millions of troops uncommitted in the west. Half of the Japanese revenue was being devoted to the war effort. Foreign bankers now looked with suspicion upon Japanese aspirations and would lend no more. Japan had therefore not only run out of money but also manpower, wasted on the battlefields of Manchuria. It was President Teddy Roosevelt who came forward offering to act as the peace broker between the two warring nations. The plenipotentiaries were invited aboard the

Mayflower at Portsmouth, New Hampshire on 6 August 1905 to find a path to peace. Russia played a canny hand, appearing 'more sinned against than sinning'. The tactic worked in winning over American popular opinion. The initial, understandable republican opprobrium raised by the excesses of the Russian autocracy gave way to an alignment between the man in the street and the Christian Russians against the unbelieving, apparently grasping Japanese.

Russia left the peace talks virtually scot-free. She gave up her interest in Korea – which she had been prepared to do before the commencement of war – she agreed to Japan holding Port Arthur (she could do little else), but she did not pay Japan a rouble in indemnity. Had Russia been more heavily penalized at the peace talks it seems probable that the inevitability of the events of 1917 would have been brought forward. None the less, in Russia the humiliation of this defeat was sorely felt and the widespread rioting which broke out in 1905 simmered on until the Great October Socialist Revolution. The fury which erupted in Japan was immeasurable. It had not been an auspicious début for the United States in this her first major appearance on the world's political stage. To the xenophobic Japanese she had failed to be the honest broker, siding instead with Russia. It is from this point that the fatal rivalry developed between Japan and the United States, leading eventually to conflict in the Pacific.

One small but none the less significant act occurred in July 1905 when Japan seized Sakhalin from Russia, the only Russian territory to be conceded throughout the duration of the Russo-Japanese War.[1] The move in order to use the island as a bargaining pawn in the impending peace talks was logical, yet in the action lay the reality that Japan had a need to expand beyond the confines of her insufficiently productive and claustrophobic islands. It was eminently pragmatic for Japan, up until that point preoccupied with securing a presence in Korea and Manchuria, to seize the opportunity to whittle away at Russian territory. Sakhalin had after all once belonged to Japan.

The United States, who had embarked upon her international 'coming-out party' at Portsmouth, became increasingly wary as to long-term Japanese regional aims. Out of this wariness developed a determination to monitor, limit, and if necessary chaperon, Japanese aspirations in the Far East. The European allies broadly fell in line so that when, in 1915, Japan presented her twenty-one demands aimed at the annexation of China, a world coalition was able to frustrate those plans. From the British Embassy in Peking, however, came the lone voice of the Military Attaché:

> If Japan is not given a free hand in some part of the Far East, there is a danger that she might actually go over to the enemy. With Russia a prostrate neutral between them, Japan and Germany would form an extremely strong combination which would threaten the whole of the allies' possessions in Asia and even in Australasia.

When Port Arthur fell to the Japanese in December 1904, Kolchak was a sick and wounded man. Crippled with rheumatism, he was unable to leave the former Russian military hospital where he was held as a prisoner of war until April 1905. When he regained his strength he was moved to Nagasaki. Here the Russian sick and wounded were given the option of either making a complete recovery in Japanese cure centres or returning directly home. Almost without exception they took the latter course, travelling home via the United States to St Petersburg. Kolchak's medical board found him to be a complete invalid and sent him on a four-month cure to a tranquil village resort. It was in such places that worthy army and navy officers, stung by the ignominy of humiliating defeat, had the time to reflect upon their situation. Russia had demonstrated her total unpreparedness to fight a modern war. Her forces had been ill equipped, poorly trained and indifferently led. Both services were in dire need of reform and for the dissolution of the gerontocracy which held almost all the senior service appointments. If these goals could be achieved, the situation on the home front might be stabilized, and internationally Russia might also regain her dignity and credibility as a world force.

In early 1906, Kolchak had been released once more to the Academy of Sciences to document his earlier exploits. While in St Petersburg he and other naval kindred spirits formed themselves into a lobby group aimed at reconstructing the Navy along the lines envisaged by Makarov. The 'St Petersburg Naval Circle' received official recognition, some funding, and offices were provided within the precincts of the Naval Academy. The first step towards the goal of a naval meritocracy was the creation of a Naval General Staff. This step was approved and Commander Kolchak filled one of the very first staff appointments. It was here that his reputation developed through being required frequently to brief the newly elected assembly – the *Duma* – on naval subjects. Having

11

established the foundation for the Staff, the Circle next emphasized the glaringly obvious need for a new ship-building programme. One of the driving forces was Admiral von Essen who, like Kolchak, had been one of Makarov's protégés at Port Arthur. The Admiral's appointment to command the battleship *Sevastopol* while holding the substantive rank of Commander was not achieved without ruffling a good number of career feathers. In association with the equally capable Admiral Grigorovich, this trio, firmly believing that war against Germany would begin in 1915, had mapped out a regenerative ship-building programme to be completed by 1915.

In 1907, the newly appointed Minister of the Navy, Voevodsky, opposed the naval reforms which the weak *Duma* was endeavouring to force through. Kolchak put up a strong and spirited defence, but in vain. He then displayed a personal trait that had been seen before. He walked away from the problem to seek refuge in some other activity. After a short period spent lecturing at the reorganized Naval College, he resigned and returned to his real love – scientific work. From 1908–10, Kolchak prepared and led a two-ship expedition to investigate the north-east sea route from the Atlantic to the Arctic Ocean. When, in 1910, he returned from the Behring Sea to winter at Vladivostok, there were two telegrams awaiting Kolchak's attention. One came from Voevodsky and the other from the new Chief of the Naval Staff, Prince Lieven. Both implored him to return to the Naval General Staff and set his undoubted talent and energies towards accelerating the now resurrected ship-building programme. Kolchak went directly to the Baltic as Head of Section under the Commander-in-Chief, Admiral von Essen. As the sands of time drew Russia closer to ultimate disaster, Kolchak passed through various appointments; he had command of a destroyer, and was a shore-based Operations Captain, until the spring of 1914 when he was apointed to *Rurik*, von Essen's flagship.

Russia was unable to make up the two years lost out of the ship-building programme. The new Baltic ships had not been completed by August 1914 and, reminiscent of 1904, would go to sea with up to 400 dockyard workers aboard. This unpreparedness meant that when war was declared, an act universally welcomed by the Baltic Fleet, it none the less placed great store on the effectiveness of the Russian minelayers. These task forces, sometimes consisting of more than fifty vessels, proved more than equal to the requirement.

Their success was reflected in Kolchak's rapid advancement. In April 1916 he was a Captain, in June 1916 Rear-Admiral and, in July 1916 he was promoted to Vice-Admiral and appointed Commander-in-Chief of the Black Sea.

2

PRELUDE AND DISASTER

In compliance with his orders, Kolchak reported to the *Stavka*, Petrograd[2] before hoisting his flag in the Black Sea. He spent almost two hours being briefed by General Alexeiev on the military and political situation on the Western Front and along the Russian lines. It had been neither an encouraging nor optimistic report but it was no more than could have been expected. In 1900, a British observer in China had coined the now famous phrase that the Russian soldiers were 'lions led by asses', and this view was certainly confirmed by the events of 1904–5.

The principal Russian commanders at the military disaster of Tannenberg in August 1914 were three senior Russians who had survived that epic apogee of Russian military incompetence – the Russo-Japanese War. The overall commander of the North West Front at Tannenberg was General Zhilinski, formerly Chief-of-Staff to Admiral Alexeiev, the Viceroy of the Far East. Between them they interfered with the military planning of the Land Commander, General Kuropatkin, with disastrous consequences. Zhilinski's army commanders were the cavalry Generals Samsonov and Rennenkampf. Neither officer had served with distinction in Manchuria and the ineffectiveness of cavalry in a modern conflict was one of the primary lessons to arise from the Russo-Japanese War. What had distinguished both Samsonov and Rennenkampf was the widely circulated report of their public brawl at Mukden railway station. It was hardly the most auspicious of omens for the prospect of future good inter-formation co-operation. It did indicate however that the army, rather in the same way as the navy, appeared to have been unable to put into practice the lessons learned from their recent conflict with Japan. Trotsky claimed: 'It is no accident that the war (1914–17) did not create one single distinguished military name in Russia.' General Zaleski, a member of the Russian High Command, summed up his peer group as having: 'Much adventurism, much ignorance, much egotism, intrigue, careerism, greed, mediocrity, lack of foresight, very little knowledge, talent or desire to risk life, or even comfort and health'.

Russian unpreparedness, poverty of equipment, indifferent leadership, and growing disillusionment among the rank and file were building up their own shock wave soon to flood and overwhelm the state. For Britain and France it was absolutely vital that Russia should remain in the war against Germany. In 1917, the Russian Army was 9,000,000 strong, of which 7,000,000 were directly employed at the seat of war. Admittedly the army was poorly equipped, but significantly their massive resource of manpower occupied the attention of 160 German divisions. Keeping Russia in the war for $3\frac{1}{2}$ years did impose logistic penalties on Joffre and Haig but the implications for the German High Command were much more severe. The existence of a second front made profound demands on German manpower and *matériel* which, if the front had not existed, might have been employed to tip the fine balance in favour of Germany on the Western Front. The presence of a defended Russian line served also to deny the Germans the raw materials and food of southern Russia. The situation facing the allies was desperate. Britain and France had virtually exhausted their manpower reserves and the latter nation walked the tightrope of the constant threat of general and widespread mutiny. Even localized reluctance to soldier on as seen at the Aisne led to the court martial of 100,000 men. Little wonder the Allied Command asked still more of the Russians but, while their own tally of casualties was grim, the Russian tally was grotesque. They had suffered 2,000,000 dead. They could not be pushed much further.

It was a pessimistic Kolchak who left the *Stavka* for an audience with the Tsar. The blame for the state of the nation at that time can be laid squarely at Tsar Nicholas's feet. He was intolerant of political initiatives, refused to temper the power of the autocracy or heed the advice of his friends to impose change before change imposed itself. The rumblings of discontent were not confined to the streets, and there was more than one hint of a planned palace coup. Had Kolchak hoped to be greeted with a glimmer of optimism he was to be disappointed. The Tsar confided that against his better judgement he had succumbed to French pressure by authorizing the entry of Rumania into the war. 'She is totally unprepared', said the Tsar.

Nicholas then outlined his thoughts of a concept of operations mentioned earlier by General Alexeiev involving military action against Constantinople. The Tsar proposed to Kolchak two possibilities. Firstly that of the land forces, with or without naval support, advancing along the western coast of the Black Sea to the Bosphorus, or, secondly, for the navy to inject a land force directly into the Bosphorus. When Kolchak took his leave of the Tsar he departed for his new headquarters at Sevastopol.

Kolchak spent the day allocated to the change of command attending operational briefings. He heard that the two principal problems facing the Black Sea Fleet were the activities of U-Boats and Raiders. The submarines working out of Varna were becoming increasingly effective. In addition, the *Goeben* and *Breslau* were operating through the Bosphorus against targets on the Black Sea coast, thereby threatening the seaborne supply of the Caucasus Army.

Just after midnight on 7 July 1916, shortly after Admiral Ebergard's flag had been lowered, Kolchak heard that the *Breslau* had steamed into the Black Sea. A task force to be led by the battleship *Imperatritsa Maria* and including a cruiser and six destroyers was ordered to raise steam. Under the flag of the new Commander-in-Chief they slipped their moorings at dawn. At 3 p.m. the *Breslau* was sighted on course for Novorossisk. On seeing the Russian force, the German ship changed direction making best speed for the Bosphorus. *Breslau* did not escape damage or injury to her crew, being hit by the battleship's long range guns. Neither *Breslau* nor *Goeben* returned to the Black Sea while Kolchak was in command.

On the land front in spring 1917 the Russian steamroller had come to a complete standstill. Britain and France dug into their emptying coffers to find £600 million and £160 million respectively as further war loans to bolster the Russian economy thereby preventing, they hoped, the joining of two German armies on the Western Front. On 11 March, the soldiers of Petrograd garrison threw in their hands with the mobs of striking workers that had been roaming the streets since February. The mutiny and disorder were widespread. The *Duma* formed a provisional government in an attempt to restore order while nearby, in parallel, the mutinous soldiers and workers formed their own political action committee, the Petrograd Soviet. In the naval dockyards, the Commander-in-Chief Baltic Fleet, Admiral Wiren, the last Russian naval commander at Port Arthur, was murdered. His body was diced into small pieces before being burned in a wooden box in the public square. Wiren's family also died and, of the Baltic Fleet's total complement of officers, only eight retained their liberty, the remainder having been slaughtered or imprisoned.

The flame of the March riots was fanned as much by the Tsar's heavy-handedness as by the heady, emotive, euphoria of the masses. The effect of all this mayhem and disorder proved to be too much for a nervous Tsar whose life had always been dogged by the threat of some shadowy assassin's gun or bomb. His grandfather and many of his relatives had died in that manner and, indeed, it was the execution of Lenin's brother for complicity in an attempt on the life of Alexander III that did much to harden Lenin's attitude and resolve. Above all, Nicholas was a devoted father and family man, and he decided to abdicate while the fabric of his immediate family still remained intact. For that reason, his son the young Tsarevitch was not considered for the succession which passed instead to the Tsar's brother Mikhail. After a day's quiet reflection Mikhail too abandoned the crown. So, suddenly, a thousand years of Russian monarchy had come to a dramatic end. The Romanovs had been consumed by a leaderless, spontaneous combustion. Even the Bolshevik chiefs were caught off their guard, exiled as they were in various countries or in the remoteness of Siberia. The Tsar moved out of the city, benevolently supported by the Provisional Government, to take residence in a small summer palace to the south of Petrograd. Meanwhile Germany, intent on taking Russia out of the war, transported Lenin and his supporters in a sealed train from Switzerland across Germany to Stockholm. Churchill described this action as 'the most grisly of all weapons. They transported Lenin in a sealed truck like a plague bacillus from Switzerland into Russia.' Others too were drawn into the power vacuum; Trotsky from the United States and Stalin from Siberia.

The effect that these political developments had on the Russian troops facing the Germans was, of course, dramatic. In April, Major-General Alfred Knox, the British Military Attaché, visited the front. He was appalled at what he saw. 'Units have turned into political debating societies; the infantry refuses to allow the guns to shoot at the enemy; parlaying in betrayal of the Allies and the best interests of Russia takes place daily with the enemy.' The incidence of desertion grew until Lenin would say in October: 'The Army voted for peace with its feet.'

To return for the time being to the Black Sea, the advent of spring saw Kolchak still proceeding with his war mission. An effective mine barrage now blocked the Bosphorus. An attempt by the Germans and Turks to clear a passage through the minefield and a foray by Turkish destroyers ended for them in disaster. Training with the assigned division for the intended Russian land operation was well under way when news of the March uprising percolated through to the Black Sea. A message from the President of the *Duma* informed Kolchak that the State Committee of the *Duma* had taken charge, and requested him to ensure that no excesses broke out within his command. Other messages, originating from the German espionage service operating out of Constantinople and broadcast in bad Russian and Bulgarian, gave news of mutinies at the front and the murder of the officers of the Baltic Fleet.

While serving as Commander-in-Chief Black Sea, Kolchak was fortunate also to be double-hatted as the Governor of the Crimea. This situation afforded him greater power than that possessed by the late Admiral Wiren. Also to his advantage was the geography of the Crimea which enabled him to isolate the peninsula, encircling it with its own cordon sanitaire. A proclamation was issued advising against listening to or heeding German disinformation, and the Admiral promised that all authentic information would be made public. The first important news to be confirmed was that of the Tsar's abdication and the end of the Romanov line. True to his word, Kolchak mustered representatives of ships' companies aboard the harbour flagship *George the Victorious*. Admitting that the dynasty had come to an end, he reminded the assembled masses that Russia was still at war and that it was their duty to continue the fight. For the time being the Admiral's argument was found to be most persuasive, and even the dockworkers refused to restrict their working hours to the new eight-hour working day. Then, when all the officers and men had, on Kolchak's instruction, taken the solemn oath of service to the Government, the fleet put to sea to show the flag.

The next important signal to be put on Kolchak's desk was more ominous. It was the first order to be broadcast by the Petrograd Soviet of Workers and Soldiers' Deputies placing limitations on the powers of officers and authorizing the establishment of soldiers' committees. The Admiral chose to ignore this instruction on the grounds that it had not originated from or passed through the Government. Shortly after, however, the Government did advise the setting up of soldiers' committees and this was done at Sevastopol, Odessa, and other Black Sea ports. Initially, the committees were gentle, pliant, respectful groups. Kolchak vetted the chairmen's reports, either endorsing or rejecting their decisions. Favourable articles on Kolchak's Black Sea regime appearing in the right-wing press drew admiring public attention. This state of affairs could not last long. The Crimea could not escape the realities of the political developments to the north, and soon deputations of propagandists arrived from the Baltic intent on disrupting the harmony that existed in the Black Sea Fleet.

In mid-April, Guchkov, the new War Minister, met Kolchak at Odessa. The Minister confirmed the Government's confidence in the Admiral's ability to hold the ring. Kolchak's response was blunt and forthright. His lot, he said, was not helped by what appeared to be a government acting as the mouthpiece of the Petrograd Soviet. Not one to suffer from immodesty, Kolchak told the Minister with some justification that it was only the Commander-in-Chief's inspirational leadership which permitted the maintenance of the status quo. The Minister absorbed what had been said and admired the Admiral's self-confidence. Before he left, he told Kolchak to attend a series of meetings planned at the end of the month at Petrograd and Pskov.

Shortly after arriving at Petrograd, Kolchak called on the War Minister. It was then that Guchkov revealed his intention to transfer Kolchak to command the Baltic Fleet. None too subtly the Minister confided in the Admiral that Maximov, the elected Commander-in-Chief, had proved to be a demagogue, and a further massacre of officers was thought to be imminent. The situation at Kronstadt, where the Commander-in-Chief and officers had also been murdered, had deteriorated to such an extent that it was considered impossible to restore the equilibrium. Kolchak replied that he would naturally do as ordered but said that, in his view, it was only a matter of time before the same would occur in the Black Sea. Returning from Pskov, Kolchak again called on Guchkov and asked for a final decision as to whether he should transfer to the Baltic. Weighed down as he was by more pressing problems, the War Minister shrugged his shoulders: 'It will make very little difference; perhaps you had better return to the Black Sea.'

The message Kolchak brought back to those still loyal to the old order was far from encouraging. He communicated to his off-duty sailors the impression of weak government, the collapse of the fabric of war, and the continuing efforts of Britain and France to provide Russia with financial support by way of war loans. The sailors absorbed the unwelcome news of the Baltic, but what had impressed everyone was the news of the attempted allied offensive which had aimed at allowing Russia to find time to stabilize her front. Stimulated by what they had heard, the sailors insisted that the war effort must continue and that their own representatives should go to the front to bolster the wavering lines. So it was that the 'Black Sea Delegation' went to seek out the land war to persuade their comrades to persevere. It was a noble, brave, but pointless gesture.

The general *malaise* that had beset the army and navy, but had so far spared the Black Sea Fleet, made its unwelcome call in May. The crew of a destroyer refused to put to sea for minelaying duties. At the same time, the local Soviet was reorganized with an emphatic swing to the left as Mensheviks made way for Bolsheviks. Very shortly the same procedures which had caused chaos in the Baltic, namely the election of officers and supervision of the commander, were introduced at Sevastopol. It was at this juncture that Kerensky, the head of the Provisional Government, visited, doing his utmost to rally support. His speeches had little effect but his example, persistence, and dedication persuaded Kolchak to continue in command. Rumours of an officer plot, real or imaginary, to conduct a counter-revolution was the excuse awaited by the Sevastopol Soviet to escalate their action. In mid-afternoon, a signal was flashed between ships ordering all officers to be disarmed and their homes searched. A number of officers committed suicide. The order was carried out in a capable and efficient manner, only Kolchak being spared the ordeal.

The Commander-in-Chief was understandably furious. He ordered the crew of *George the Victorious* up on deck. How dare they disarm their officers; were they not aware what an insult this was to him, the Commander-in-Chief? What exactly had they expected, he demanded. Did they not know that the senior officers were all loyal to the Government and that there was no counter-revolution? 'I myself would not permit, at such a time, any moves to be made, as they would only hasten the day of our destruction.' He had had enough. He would command no more and would telegraph that decision to the Government. That said, Kolchak unbuckled his sword belt, threw his St George's sword over the side into the sea and stormed below in a rage.[3]

Until 2 April 1917, the United States of America had been sitting the war out on the touchline, broadly supporting Great Britain,

France, and their allies. President Wilson took his young nation to war to join those who had been in the field from the beginning. They brought a new vitality to bolster the flagging energies of the allies. Equally important, they introduced new reserves of that precious resource – manpower. America was, therefore, a highly valued and beneficial ally lacking perhaps in just one key area – experience.

The day following Kolchak's dramatic resignation, an American naval war delegation under Admiral Glennon arrived at Sevastopol to learn of the Commander-in-Chief's experience in mine and anti-submarine warfare. Kolchak was embarrassed that he could not meet the team officially but, by chance, they travelled together by train to Petrograd where informal discussions between Kolchak and Glennon whetted the latter's appetite. The interpreter between the two admirals was a Russian naval officer who had served previously under Kolchak in the Baltic. His name was Fedotov White. According to White, Kolchak's whole demeanour throughout the journey was one of caution and anxiety. 'It was obvious that the strain he had been under was beginning to tell and he apparently was not able to control himself.' Those accompanying the Admiral had great difficulty in preventing him from shooting there on the spot a sailor he suspected of being a Bolshevik agent.

In Petrograd Kolchak reported to the Government now installed in the Marinsky Palace. The Admiral was unapologetic. It was, he insisted, entirely the Government's fault. In their desire to appease the revolutionaries they had undermined the authority of his officers, disorganized his command, and placed his commanders in an invidious and hopeless position. 'The model condition of the Black Sea Fleet with respect to the command has been systematic-ally corrupted under my very eyes.' A British military intelligence report confirmed Kolchak's assertion that:

> The Government has been in the hands of the Soviet and has now been thrown even more into their hands....The outlook is extremely bad and the Soviet is in its turn drifting more and more into the direction of the Bolsheviks. The Bolsheviks supported by German money, are organising as they have not organised before. An outbreak at no very distant date is almost a certainty, and the triumph of the Bolsheviks will be the first step towards a separate peace.

When Kerensky heard of the first troubles in the Black Sea Fleet, he sent a special commission to Sevastopol under Zarudny, later to be Justice Minister. While the inquiry was under way, Kolchak took an apartment in Petrograd to await Zarudny's return. Zarudny disputed Kolchak's claims that the trouble in the Black Sea Fleet was of the Government's making. He pleaded with the Admiral:

> It is perfectly clear that all this is the work of German agents. No matter how thoroughly we investigated the matter, it remained clear that the crews had absolutely nothing against you. Therefore, you ought to make a sacrifice and return to the Fleet, because the majority of the better element desire your return.

Kolchak emphasized how sorely he felt the insult, and reiterated his unswerving decision never again to return to the Black Sea Fleet. The Admiral had passed a quiet, contemplative time in Petrograd, hardly seeing anyone. One notable exception had been the Russian aide-de-camp attached to the visiting United States' Navy delegation. Would His Excellency care to meet Admiral Glennon to discuss matters of mutual interest? Glennon pumped Kolchak of all he knew of mine warfare, anti-submarine operations, and assault landing techniques. Both admirals were aware that the sands of time for the old Russia were almost exhausted, and Glennon's invitation to visit the United States to brief a wider audience was not unexpected.

Reluctantly, the Government gave permission for Kolchak to visit the United States. By July, all was ready. Just as he was about to leave, his Flag Captain asked the Admiral whether he would receive a deputation of 'Union of Officers at the Front'? He replied affirmatively and the group was ushered into his office. They wished him *bon voyage* and presented him with a replacement St George's sword. It was an emotional and reflective Kolchak who took his leave of Petrograd bound for England via Bergen. Never again would he return to the capital and much was to happen during his temporary absence.

The erosion of the Provisional Government's power continued. It suffered an attempt by General Kornilov, 'the lionheart with the brain of a sheep',[4] to bring off a military dictatorship and also an earlier but ill-prepared Bolshevik effort at a coup. The Bolshevik pressure, however, was irresistible, coming to a head on 7 November when, with Kerensky out of the capital endeavouring to raise sympathetic army support, the rump of the government had assembled in the Winter Palace. Outside, in the palace grounds, the revolutionaries drew up artillery pieces. The cruiser *Aurora*, crewed by mutinous sailors, slipped her moorings and made towards the Tsar's former palace.

The role and place of the *Aurora* in the Revolution is worthy of mention, particularly in view of the esteem she is afforded in modern Russia. She had been among those in Admiral Rozhdestvenski's fleet which had made the disastrous voyage from the Baltic to Tsushima 1904–5. While passing through the Dogger Bank, the Russian Squadrons fired on the Gamecock fishing fleet out of Hull in the absurd but genuinely held belief that the trawlers were sheltering Japanese torpedo boats. In the resultant panic, the Russian ships shot up one another as well as sinking a number of the 100-ton trawlers. The *Aurora*'s chaplain fell, mortally wounded. The British reaction was predictably one of indignation, not only at this affront to her maritime prestige, but because the Russians had not stopped to rescue the fishermen in the sea. The Tsar refused to apologize for the incident, being prepared only to offer his regrets. The British fleets were mobilized and it was an anxious Admiral 'Jacky' Fisher who was to write to his wife: 'It has nearly been war again.'

The 'Dogger Bank' incident served to polarize an already British-held antipathy towards the Tsar. That he had a German wife did nothing to further his prospects of being granted asylum and a place of safety after his abdication. What was being seen in Russia in 1917 was an extreme manifestation of the emergence of international Communism. The same sympathies and reactions existed to varying degrees throughout Europe and the United States. Was this, pondered foreign governments, the beginning of the promised world revolution? It was certain that, during the course of the vilest war the world had seen, the offer of refuge to the Autocrat of All The Russias would have been political suicide, inviting domestic retaliation. The Tsar and his family therefore remained in limbo in Russia, waiting for disaster to overtake them. After five months in Petrograd, their safety could no longer be guaranteed and they were moved to what was initially a cosy, reasonable exile in Siberia.

The cruiser *Aurora* proved to be an anti-hero for, even after steaming half-way round the world, she had no appetite for battle with the Japanese. Under cover of darkness she fled the scene, to arrive in Manila where she and others of Admiral Enquist's unheroic cruisers were disarmed. In view of her performance on the Dogger Bank, it seemed quite appropriate that on the night of 7 November this undistinguished cruiser's guns should be loaded with blank ammunition. 'The boom and flash of blank', explained Bolshevik Flerovsky, 'are much bigger than from a loaded gun'. Blanks from the ship's forward gun were fired in the direction of the Winter Palace, signalling the commencement of the Bolshevik attack on defences manned by cadets and a women's battalion. Under orders not to retaliate, the Palace fell with little resistance. Kerensky's later attempt to regain power was nipped in the bud in a clash at Tsarkoe Selo but again, with little bloodshed. The Prime Minister slipped away, his Government had disintegrated leaving the allies with no acceptable focal point at which they could negotiate. For the Bolsheviks it had all been surprisingly easy, almost an anti-climax – but the real struggle was yet to come in a bloody civil war which left its mark on international relations that remains today.

Petrograd was an extremely badly located capital. It is well today when hearing or seeing Soviet propaganda aimed against the Interventionists, to reflect upon two facts. First, the reason the allies first set foot on Russian soil was to keep Russia in the war. With Germany pressing, the Russian capital was vulnerable to land, sea and air attack. Second, the allies were invited by no less a person than Trotsky to intervene in the north west where the Bolsheviks had their power base. Away from that power base in the regions remote from direct Bolshevik control there would be many diverse, opportunist attempts at securing regional autonomy. On the first day of the October Revolution, the first such coup occurred when Ataman Alexei Kaledin proclaimed an independent Don Cossack State. His was the first, only serving to confuse and dilute the larger issue, thereby contributing to the prospects for a complete Bolshevik victory.

The Russian decision to withdraw from the war hit the allies like a bombshell. It was not so much that the appeal which went out to all belligerents was addressed to their 'class conscious workers' but rather that the allies had not been forewarned of the momentous decision. Realistic observers in Russia had been saying since the spring that the war-weary, unable and unwilling army had lost its heart and recommended that Russia should be permitted to find her own separate peace to find comfort for her tortured peasantry. The appeal to 'begin negotiations for a just and democratic peace' was addressed to the three mightiest states among those taking part in the war – England, France and Germany. Significantly, that debutante in international affairs, the United States, had been excluded from consideration as a mighty power, emphasizing how rapid her rise to superpower status has been. While deprecating the poor diplomatic form implicit in Russia's failure to consult, Britain's unofficial and philosophical attitude was guided by her Ambassador in Petrograd, Sir George Buchanan. The French were both publicly and privately raging. The image conjured of a mighty German force being released to the Western Front, the easing of the allied blockade on Germany perhaps by her enemy gaining access to the agriculture of the Ukraine and oil of Baku, all served to heighten the sense of betrayal. *Ad hoc* damage control measures were sought out with a grim sense of urgency.

Britain took an uncharacteristic, almost classically Gallic course, endeavouring to have her cake and eat it. She attempted to be conciliatory towards the Bolsheviks but at the same time undertook the financial support of those groups, principally Cossacks, who were being oppressed by the Bolsheviks. The latter course was not favoured by the furious British diplomats in Petrograd, surrounded as they were by the most extreme and hardline of the revolutionaries who had already demonstrated their disdain for diplomatic niceties. The French solution was embodied in the Foch Plan. Marshal Foch sought to counterbalance the loss of the Russian army by introducing new forces to block a perceived German thrust through a defenceless Russia. The Marshal insisted that the United States and Japan should march through Siberia to confront the onslaught of the Central Powers. Fortunately, the allied military staffs were absolved the need to conjure up the logistic miracle required to support the Foch Plan. The proposal was rejected out of hand by both the United States and Japan. What Foch had achieved, however, was to turn the spotlight on an ally who had remained passive from the outbreak of the war – Japan. French Foreign Minister Pichon goaded the Japanese insisting that throughout the war they had been 'greatly enriched and had obtained colossal advantages'. Japan had indeed done little to support her allies' cause. In 1914 she absorbed the German colonies in China, supplied Russia and France with some armaments and provided some low-level naval support in the Mediterranean and Pacific. She persistently refused to make manpower available to help the war effort in either the west or the east. The proffered excuse was that her public, remembering the losses of 1904–5, were against such measures and the army was not structured to undertake an interventionist role. In reality, Japan was biding her time to resurrect in a tangible form her aspirations to dominate China. She had not forgotten the 1895 humiliation of Shimonoseki or again in 1911 when the allies stopped her fulfilling her aim of gaining a mainland presence. Now she awaited war's end when none of the warring powers would have either the inclination or ability to interfere again with what Japan saw as her destiny in China.

However, as Pichon pointed out with justification, the recent events in Russia had transformed the situation in South East Asia. If Germany won the war, he argued, Japan would forfeit her newly won colonies and would see the end of her Far East aspirations. One question uppermost in the allies' minds was that if, as some suspected, the Bolsheviks were in the pay of the Germans, would they release the thousands of prisoners of war in Siberia to mutual advantage?

Japan's hankering to expand to the mainland was conditional upon being unaccompanied and on her own terms. For the Russians – of all political persuasions – this prospect was totally repugnant. Their national loathing of the Germans is well documented but when Trotsky said he preferred Germans as conquerors to the Japanese he justified that statement by saying: 'because the German is more cultured, the people are more educated and there are more workmen, and awakening is possible; while the Japanese are foreign people, we do not know their language, the working class is less conscious'. The Siberians were conscious of Japanese capabilities from their recent war and, as a result, children were taught to regard the men of Nippon as bogymen. Japan's indifference to what was happening in Europe is understandable but recent developments in Russia and the persuasive arguments being developed by the allies now gave her cause to ponder her situation. The Bolshevik success had slowed as it moved eastward but had reached Omsk and caused other subsequent dominos to tumble including Krasnoyarsk and Barnaul. Red intimidation surfaced at Harbin and Vladivostok. If the Revolution were to spread to Pacific Russia then trade with Japan's third most important partner would be severely inhibited. Her own national security would also be at risk. In 1916 she had struck a secret diplomatic deal with the Tsarists to guarantee the integrity of the sensitive areas of Sakhalin and the Kurile Islands. Now in 1917, these secrets were being exposed and disowned by the Bolsheviks. Who could tell what the effects of their pernicious political cancer would be upon Japan's regional neighbours. The diplomatic questions demanding answers were; should she conciliate the Bolsheviks with the aim of some power-sharing agreement or should she exploit the fact of their weakness in Siberia to seize and retain the immensely rich and desirable Amur Basin?

On 22 November, the Bolsheviks passed instructions to the front to begin fraternizing with the Germans. The Commander-in-Chief of the Army, General Dukhonin, refused to comply with the order and, as a result, was replaced by an ensign and hanged for his disobedience. The disintegration of the Russian armed forces accelerated and on 29 November the Bolsheviks advised Russia's former allies that the struggle was over and that on 2 December formal peace negotiations would begin with Germany. The peace emissaries actually met on 22 December at Brest-Litovsk for the first round of peace talks. The Bolsheviks, acutely aware of their military weakness, set about the concurrent task of raising a volunteer army. On 23 December, Britain and France concluded a spheres of influence agreement for the Black Sea region. The aim in allocating to France the Ukraine and Crimea and to Britain the Caucasus was to deny the resources of these territories to the central powers. This plan was to have the effect of drawing both nations into the Russian Civil War. Future military action would not illuminate the usually illustrious military reputation of either nation.

At the same time, the revolutionary government could not resist the urge to stir anti-colonial sentiments in India. Ever since Japan beat Imperial Russia in 1905, the cry 'Asia for the Asians' had spread throughout southern Asia. Lenin's and Stalin's combined appeal to the Indian sub-continent, therefore, to overthrow the British 'robbers and enslavers' was unlikely to please the British Government nor encourage them to seek to find accommodation with the Bolsheviks.

Meanwhile, the peace talks broke down and Germany resumed her advance. Lenin had no means available of stopping the German juggernaut. In early March he had little option but to persuade his comrades of the inescapable need to accede to the harsh terms to be embodied in the Treaty of Brest-Litovsk. The price for keeping alive the hopes and aspirations of the Bolsheviks was high; three thousand million roubles (equivalent in those days to £300 million), the loss of a sizeable portion of Eastern Europe to Germany, the effective loss of the Ukraine with her immense resources, as well as providing Turkey with her share in the Caucasus. This had been a bitter pill for the Bolsheviks and difficult to sell to their followers. They moved the seat of government to Moscow and to Trotsky fell the vital task of reorganizing the army. He assumed the new post of

Chairman of the Supreme Military Soviet and People's Commissar, drawing up an action plan which would bring into being compulsory military training and put an end to the idealistic and unworkable practice of electing Commanders.

Out in the country and in the towns, groups of uncoordinated private armies gathered as the prelude to civil war under the banner which best represented their political persuasion, the Red or the White. There was in this equation, however, one non-Russian group which became immensely important. It would affect Reds, Whites, allies, and opponents, and, in particular, the future role to be played by Admiral Kolchak. At that time, they were an army without a country – they were the Czech connection.

3

THE PALESTINIANS OF EUROPE

When Archduke Franz Ferdinand of Austria was assassinated on that hot summer's afternoon in Sarajevo on 28 June 1914, the state of Czechoslovakia did not exist. The Czechs and Slovaks lived in the region of Bohemia, Moravia and Slovakia embraced by the then fragile borders of the Austro-Hungarian Empire. The Archduke's death provided the stimulus and essential boost to encourage the Czechoslovak national movement to come out of the shadows and on to the international stage. The leader of the revolutionaries was distinguished in both appearance and academic achievement. His name was Thomas Masaryk, and his receding hairline complemented a professorial image. Not only was he Professor of Philosophy at Prague University, he was also a member of the Austro-Hungarian Parliament. For thirty years his aim had been to separate the Slavic people from the Austrians, a nation with whom they had no natural affinity. In order to achieve that aim, Masaryk believed that it was essential to establish both a government in exile and a national army.

The prospect for a national army seemed a fond aspiration as long as the Slavs were constrained by the Habsburg yoke. The men were compulsorily inducted into the army of Austro-Hungary and escorted with reluctance to war. The Czech units were often interspersed among and overseen by troops loyal to the central powers, invariably Germans, Austrians or Magyars. The Slavs had no wish to fight the Russians whose order of battle included people of their own race. Their lack of enthusiasm for the war was reciprocated by a harsh disciplinary regime enforced by their Austrian officers. In Russia, other ethnic Slavs were faring little better because the Tsarists, despite their expansive talk of pan-Slavism, had embarked upon a programme of enforced evacuation

29

towards Siberia. The announcement on 20 August 1914, therefore, of the formation of a Czechoslovak unit called *Družina* as a constituent part of the Russian Army, ran contrary to the norm of Russia's treatment of their own fellow Slavs. There were 70,000 Czechs living at that time in Russia but only 1,000 of the thousands of volunteers were permitted to join the *Družina*. Masaryk's distrust of the Russians merely intensified but, in the *Družina*, he had at the very least the embryo of what he had always dreamed, a Czech national army.

Understandably, Masaryk's dilemma was in deciding which of the warring sides the Czechs should support. Thus far, no hint of a possibility of nationhood within the Austro-Hungarian Empire had been forthcoming. Clearly, the path towards national status was totally dependent upon backing the winner, an issue which at that time was by no means obvious. The decision was not made any easier by a division of opinion within the Czech revolutionary committee, which had the unlikely name of the Mafia. Masaryk decided in favour of Britain and France and began to contact their men of influence. At that time, very little was known in either Britain or France of the Czechs or Slovaks. For centuries their national identities had been submerged within the greater Empire. It is a sad indictment that long after Masaryk had secured his dream of nationhood for his people Chamberlain would describe Czechoslovakia as: 'That small, distant country of which we know so little. . . .' It is therefore not surprising that formal British and French support of the Czech cause would suffer a lingering period of gestation; the next important move was to be made by Russia.

In October 1914, the *Stavka* issued an order permitting other Slavic people to join the Russian Army on condition that they took Russian citizenship. At the same time, Slav prisoners of war were separated from the Austrians and received better treatment although in this area the improvement was barely perceptible. Arrangements were made on the Eastern Front via the Mafia, contacts in England, and the Russian staff for the wholesale desertion of Czech and Slovak troops from the ranks of their enemy. Pre-arranged codes – the singing of patriotic songs for example – were the preliminaries to whole regiments absconding towards the doubtful security of the Russian lines. This system was employed throughout 1915 with varying degrees of success. The desertion of the Twenty-Eighth Regiment was the last straw for the Habsburg Empire. From this point repression within Bohemia was stepped up, and to underline the severity of the situation the use of the heraldic arms of Bohemia was prohibited. The Twenty-Eighth or 'Children of Prague' Regiment of Infantry was escorted from its barracks in 1914 through the streets of Prague by a German regiment with bayonets fixed. Wherever they went the same precaution was taken and, when they took up their position in the front line, they found themselves flanked by German and Magyar regiments. It was some considerable achievement therefore that during the battle of Limanov in December 1915 the Twenty-Eighth, complete with regimental band and colours, was able to shake off the attention of its chaperons and pass over to the Russian side. By the Spring of 1916, there were 100,000 Czechoslovaks in Russian prisoner of war camps.

The *Družina's* strength increased to 1,700 and it earned a well-deserved reputation as an heroic band of fighting men. Despite this improvement in Czech military fortunes, it would be of little consequence without the guidance and direction of an organized political body. Thus, in Paris the Czech National Council came into being. Fund raising became a crucial activity. Money arrived from Britain and France but the emphasis was placed on targeting the United States. A direct appeal was made to the generosity of the 1,500,000 Czechs and Slovaks residing in Bohemian colonies in such cities as New York, Philadelphia, and Chicago. The appeal to America touched the righteous heart of a public possessing a predictable propensity to support the underprivileged. As circumstances would show, this early fond rapport with the United States would reap its own political dividend. The fact that Thomas Masaryk had an American wife was not without relevance.

France, as ever on the lookout for untapped sources of manpower, had observed the bravery of the Czechs serving within her own Foreign Legion. Service in the Legion had not greatly appealed to the Czech volunteers but French law precluded them from forming a national unit within the French Army. In 1916, France too had a significant number of Czech and Slovak prisoners of war in her camps. Masaryk used his newly formed friendship with Prime Minister Briand to try to persuade him to turn these troops against France's enemies in the west. Masaryk's great hope was that this army would fight against the central powers under the Czech flag and be answerable to the Czech National Council. French sponsorship was sought to provide both the strategic environment and essential logistic support. No matter how desirable this proposition might be, it overtaxed the French administrative and legal departments. In consequence, a decision was not immediately forthcoming. With the bit now firmly between the teeth, the Czech National Council put a further imaginative proposal before what was now a thoroughly constipated French bureaucracy. It was a bold plan seeking French assistance to arm and equip the 300,000 Czechs and Slovaks held prisoner in Russia. The French were reminded that these were men with a score to settle and keen to engage the Germans. The plan was to take these trained reinforcements out of Russia through the northern port of Archangel and disembark them in the French channel ports. It was now the height of summer, July 1916. The port of Archangel was open but, from October, would be closed by ice for six months.

For the Czech plan to work depended rather more upon Russia's goodwill. It was well known that Masaryk distrusted the Tsarists and had written as much in his book *Russland und Europa*. The suspicions were mutual. To the Russian hierarchy Masaryk and his followers were recognized for the revolutionaries that they were. The Czechoslovaks had little empathy with a regime with whom they had nothing in common and certainly nothing to respect. At a time when Russia had a surfeit of her own revolutionary upheaval it is understandable that she should be reluctant to support a similar foreign movement. The Czechs never forgave the old regime's intransigence and this was to be a significant factor in their failure to support Kolchak when it appeared that he was reintroducing the old order to Siberia.

The main centre of Czechoslovak population in Russia was in the city of Kiev in the Ukraine. At the same time that Masaryk was exchanging pleasantries in Petrograd, the Kiev Czechs, of their own initiative and with Russian support, drew up a plan to form a Czech army in Russia. It was quite natural therefore that Kiev should become the headquarters of the new Czechoslovak Legion. The *Družina* provided the core of the First Czech 'Hussite' Division and the Second Division was established at Borispol. Volunteers and prisoners of war came flooding in. Although Russia had endorsed the formation of a Czech Army, she made no overt gestures to assist, preoccupied as she was in 1917 with other, more urgent matters. Masaryk's foremost Russian detractor was Kerensky, then filling the post of Minister for War. Even he, however, could not remain unmoved by the evidence of continuing Czech valour and the unfortunate parallels being drawn with his own demoralized

EUROPEAN RUSSIA - 1919

Map 2

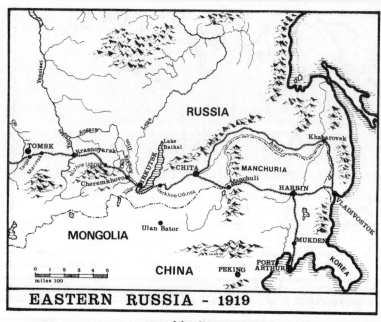

EASTERN RUSSIA - 1919

Map 3

Russian Army. The consistent bravery of the *Družina* reached new peaks when it achieved a stunning victory in July 1917 at Zborov in Galicia. General Brusilov sent a congratulatory signal to Professor Masaryk. This was of course the endorsement the Czechs craved. Not only was it turned into a well-deserved public relations coup but also served to win over Kerensky. From that moment he supported the increased recruitment into the Czech National Army.

Recruiting went on apace. In the United States 2,000 volunteers signed up although only 235 reported for duty. By September 1917, the Czech Army was 40,000 strong and had been accepted as a separate corps within the Russian Army. The Second Division had now outgrown its quarters and moved nearer to Kiev, thus centralizing the Czech Army elements. All was not rosy, however, and talk was in the air of the impending collapse of Kerensky's government and a separate peace being made with the Czechs' enemies. To make matters worse, the Bolsheviks let it be known that they believed any peace settlement should be conditional upon there being no changes to national boundaries.

There existed in Kiev a well-established Ukrainian separatist movement, and in October matters came to a head when rioting broke out in the streets. The Commander of the Kiev military district sought and received Czech assistance to restore order. All along, Masaryk had directed his followers to stay out of Russian politics. When he heard of this development he was furious and ordered his troops to extricate themselves from the unwelcome situation in which they had placed themselves.

The Czechs of the Eastern Army were poorly equipped. They had no equipment establishment as such but relied upon a highly organized, opportune battlefield scavenge among the abandoned equipment of the Russians. Fortunately, there was much to be found, but little hope existed of uniformity or commonality of arms and equipment. Regimental quartermasters were now sent out to locate and bring in abandoned trains on a scale of one per battalion. Masaryk now realized that the rapidly changing circumstances in Russia required an urgent reappraisal of his plans. The possibility of employing the Czech Eastern Army against the Germans in the west or breaking the Austro-Hungarian front to gain freedom of their own country had evaporated. Russia no longer possessed an effective, credible military force and the Germans were now pushing through the Baltic, intent upon seizing resources and also destroying the only remaining organized, disciplined military body standing in their way, the Czech Army. Although it would be revived, the Archangel option had also to all intents and purposes gone. To get there would involve transiting the Bolshevik power base as well as heading by land in the direction of the advancing German Army. Even had they reached the port there would then have been the prospect of a long and difficult sea passage through German-controlled waters. The problems were therefore considerable, not least because the Czechs had not yet achieved their target of seventy trains. The onset of winter and the general confused state in the country made the possibility of the procurement of the necessary supplies extremely doubtful.

December 1917 brought another milestone with the recognition of the Czechs by the allies as a political force in their own right. At the same time, French parochial objections to the formation of a Czech Army of the West were made academic by an enabling government decree. French sensitivities concerning command were put at ease by the appointment of a French General, Maurice Janin, to command the 10,000-strong Czech Army which had become a constituent part of the French Chasseurs. General Janin would play a key role in this unfolding story, for it was he who in effect handed over Admiral Kolchak to the Bolsheviks, thereby acquiescing in the eventual execution of the ruler of Siberia.

The Czech Army of the East, now 70,000 strong, found itself to be the cherry in a political cocktail fast becoming flat and sour. They still enjoyed a reasonable relationship with the Bolsheviks and co-operated in a number of operations. A few Czechs were to be swayed by the romance of the Bolshevik revolution and their concerned commanders saw them change sides. The Kiev inhabitants, however, were distinctly anti-Bolshevik and pro-German, being keen to pursue the dream of a separate Ukrainian state. It was these very people who had been unimpressed by the Czech interference in their recent domestic upheaval. Kiev had therefore become an unhealthy environment for what still remained a very powerful, disciplined, but inescapably foreign army. With the northern exit blocked, the only remaining route available for this army still intent on joining forces with the allies in the west was via Vladivostok, some 6,000 miles distant along the Trans-Siberian Railway. The Czech anabasis has been compared with the march of Xenophon's Ten Thousand struggling to the sea. The essential difference was that Cyrus the Younger was heading homeward while the Czech forces headed off in the opposite direction towards unknown dangers. After adventure and tragedy, the Czechs would dribble into Vladivostok concluding what Lloyd George would suggest to Professor Masaryk had been 'one of the greatest epics in history'.

On 14 March, the Bolshevik Council of People's Ministers approved the redeployment of the Czech Army. Shortly afterwards and after time for quiet reflection, the Bolsheviks had second thoughts as to the wisdom of letting loose the Czech Army on a journey across the breadth of Russia. Was there not, they reasoned, inherent danger in releasing what was arguably the best fighting force available within Russia's boundaries? Could not these soldiers and technicians be encouraged or pressed into the service of the Revolution? Were not their Tsarist commanders still in place? The Bolsheviks agonized over the implications of what they had done. Heaven knows what the Czech Army could achieve in the east after liaising with Ataman Semenov's anti-Bolsheviks or Interventionist forces.

Early March was characterized by skirmishes between the Czechs and Germans. Some sympathy could be extended to the revolutionaries for this complication in their revolution but the situation eased when the Czechs, now in their protected or armoured trains, broke clean along the Trans-Siberian Railway. Professor Masaryk made plans to meet the American leadership, having moved the Czech headquarters from Kiev to Omsk in Siberia. Despite being in possession of bona fide movement orders from the Bolshevik Command each separate region demonstrated its own autonomy by interfering with or delaying the progress of the Czech convoy of trains.

On 26 March, new conditions were laid down for the continuing movement of the Czech Army through Siberia. Bolshevik insistence that the Tsarist officers in command were to be removed coincided with the Czech belief that the time had also come to replace the Russians with their own young thrusting commanders. A few trusted Russians were retained, among them Colonel Kappel, still with a part to play, and the Commander-in-Chief General Shokarov who was to continue until a suitable French general could be found to replace him. In an effort to dilute the effectiveness of the Czech fighting strength each train was limited to 168 rifles and 300 rounds for each rifle and a machine gun with 1,200 rounds. Czech and Slovak ingenuity at squirrelling weapons away and hiding ammunition proved to be a vital precaution, for as they moved from region to region the local Soviet extracted their own tithe of weapons. As the Czechs recommenced their journey eastward they did so not as soldiers but 'as groups of free citizens'.

By April the 'free citizens' had had enough of the continual weakening of their strength. Not only did they refuse to hand over any more of their weapons but also demanded the return of those already forfeited. A strong, undisguised message was sent to Moscow so that it would be understood along the line to the effect that the Czechs would continue to distance themselves from involvement in Russian politics but that any military operations against them would be met with due force.

In early May the exasperation, impatience, and confusion of the Czech Army came to a head when they discovered from the Bolsheviks that Masaryk's deputy, Edward Beneš, with both Bolshevik and allied involvement had formulated a new movement plan. The idea had come from the British who recommended syphoning off those Czechs who had not yet crossed the Urals (later amended by the French to those west of Omsk) through Archangel and Murmansk. Here, they argued, was a trained body of men intent on joining the war. Their resources were tailor-made to plug the Western Front's battered and in some places breached line. In addition, a detachment would be of use to guard the substantial ordnance depots whose supplies were to be denied to both the pushing Germans and renegade Russians. No one had the courtesy to consult with or explain this plan to the Czechs. As far as they were concerned, Masaryk's orders were that they should go to Vladivostok. They were not equipped to travel through the tail end of what had been a harsh northern winter. Now, spread out as they were like a string of pearls over a distance of 5,000 miles, with their forward elements already in Vladivostok reporting the absence of ships, the men of Czechoslovakia felt acutely vulnerable and suspicious. Envoys were despatched to Moscow to seek clarification while a national meeting, a Conference of Legionnaires, was convened to be held in mid-May at a Siberian railway town named Chelyabinsk. The Conference could be more aptly described as a Council of War.

On the morning of 14 May 1918, three trains were standing in the unspectacular station of the unspectacular Siberian town of 70,000 inhabitants named Chelyabinsk. Two trains on the eastbound track facing towards the open Siberian Plain carried the Czech Sixth Regiment which had suffered further delays in its progress towards

Vladivostok. The other train which had also been delayed for a number of days was on the westbound track facing towards the foothills of the Urals. This train was filled with civilian refugees returning to European Russia, that is with the exception of those in the last three carriages. In these carriages were returning Austrian and Hungarian prisoners of war repatriated under the terms of the Treaty of Brest-Litovsk. As can be imagined, there was no love lost between the Czechs and Austro-Hungarians. During the time that the trains were held up at the station, however, some friendships developed between the opposing sides. The intermingling of passengers is one of those inescapable phenomena of life on the Trans-Siberian Railway – particularly for those who are delayed. The great leveller is the ubiquitous small hut, above which appears the word 'kipyatok': invariably, there would be a tap protruding through the wall from which a steady steam vapour rose into the chill air. Here the passengers would congregate with their personal teapots to draw off the inexhaustible supply of boiling water.

The Czechs were supported by a good administrative system, being relatively well provided for. Both refugees and prisoners were short of food and the local Soviet had done nothing to assist. The Czechs generously handed over part of their rations to the prisoners of war. These men were in a particularly poor state and were therefore grateful for this display of generosity. It will be remembered that Russia's record of care for her own troops does not stand close examination. For her enemy, therefore, there was no place for magnanimity and benevolence. The prisoners remained philosophical as they awaited the appearance of an engine to continue their journey westward. They were grateful on two accounts; that they had survived their captivity and now, patently, were homeward bound. Within the group of prisoners was one of Czech nationality, a man named Malík which means 'little finger'. There was nothing little about the influence or impact this renegade Czech would have upon the future course of the Intervention and the progress of his fellow countrymen homeward. Speculation suggested that Malík had succumbed to that Austrian habit of germanizing their Czech subjects. There is no doubt that Malík bore a grudge against the Czechs and boasted that he would kill one before leaving Chelyabinsk.

At mid-morning, an engine arrived and was coupled to the westbound train. The priority did not pass unnoticed by the Czechs. They were not in an aggressive mood and when the engine's whistle blew, a group gathered around the rear carriages to wish the returning former prisoners *bon voyage*. As the train moved slowly off, a loud Hungarian curse was heard, followed immediately by part of a broken stove which poleaxed and severely injured a Czech named Ducháček. The Czechs found this action intolerable, feeling that they had been bitten by those they had fed. Soldiers ran to the still slowly moving engine and brought it to an abrupt halt. The eighty occupants in the last three carriages were ordered out on to the platform and were advised in no uncertain terms that they moved no further until the culprit was identified. The Austro-Hungarians went through the motions of being uncooperative, but, since their paramount aim was to go home, they very shortly pointed out Malík. He was beaten to death there and then.

Before being permitted to proceed, the remainder of the prisoners were taken the two miles to the local office of the Bolshevik Commissar. They readily agreed that it was Malík who had so severely injured Ducháček and volunteered that he had got what he deserved. Only then were the relieved Austro-Hungarians allowed to rejoin their train which steamed off in the early dusk towards the purple silhouette of hills. The Bolshevik Soviet did not release the Czechs who had escorted the prisoners into town. They decided that those who had killed Malík must be tried. The soldiers involved and their ten-man escort were thereupon arrested as a preliminary to facing a Soviet court. The reputation of these courts had preceded them and it was an extremely worried group of Czech soldiers who settled down to await developments.

Meanwhile, at the station, the men's officers became concerned by their absence. Two officers were despatched to demand the release of the Czech soldiers. They too were arrested. For an army which had lived for so long on a short fuse this proved too much. The senior officer present marched two battalions into Chelyabinsk and occupied the main thoroughfares and crossroads. While taking up position, a corporal was shot dead by a Bolshevik patrol. The encircling Czech troops closed in on the Bolsheviks who were disarmed and forfeited the contents of their armoury. The Bolshevik Commissar capitulated, agreeing to release the Czechs on condition that the troops left town at once. This solution was agreeable and the Legionnaires marched back to the station. By now, the concerned delegates attending the Conference of Legionnaires had begun to assemble in one of the station's waiting rooms. Among them was Gustav Bečvář whose message from his battalion was quite clear:

> We are scattered. A few have already reached Vladivostok. The rest of us are distributed perilously along six thousand miles of railway. Nevertheless, our position is not necessarily so precarious as it seems. While we hold the railway, Siberia is ours, and the Bolsheviks will have great difficulty in getting at us in force. We can afford to fight. Indeed, to fight our way through is the only chance for any of us. Where Bolsheviks already hold the line, we must drive them away and link up with our brothers.

Whereas the Chelyabinsk incident had been amicably defused at the local level, the same did not apply when the news reached Moscow. There occurred a surprising and substantial over-reaction which would serve to threaten the whole of the Revolution by the overthrow of Bolshevik power throughout Siberia and the Urals. The two emissaries of the Czech National Council were arrested and made to sign an order to the corps commander to the effect that all weapons were to be handed over to the Soviet authorities. Trotsky then directed that a telegraphic message be sent ordering the Siberian Soviets to detrain the Czech troops and either form them into labour battalions or draft them into the Soviet Red Army.

The Czech delegates in the Chelyabinsk waiting-room had meanwhile unanimously rejected the plan to divide their forces when, on 23 May, the order to disarm arrived from the snubbed Czech National Council. Again unanimously, the Legionnaires decided to ignore the order and passed a resolution expressing their determination to retain their weapons and reach Vladivostok. One of the leading orators, of whom more will be heard, was the representative of a First Division battalion which had been delayed for days at the town of Novonikolaievsk. He was a notable fire-eater, whose youth (he was twenty-seven) and junior rank as a Lieutenant belied his true power and enthusiasm to come to grips with the Bolsheviks. While incarcerated at the railway station he befriended a Tsarist officers' group and, contrary to policy, openly suggested that when the moment was opportune they should jointly rise up and overthrow the Bolsheviks. His name was Rudolf Gajda. The Chelyabinsk meeting broke up on 24 May with delegates dispersing back to their units armed with plans to shoot their way through and out of Siberia.

When the Czech plan to shoot and scoot was revealed to Trotsky it had a violent effect. On 25 May he sent an order to the Soviets along the Trans-Siberian Railway threatening that failure to implement his instructions would be considered treason attracting severe punishment to the offenders.

All Soviets are hereby ordered to disarm the Czechoslovaks immediately. Every armed Czechoslovak found on the railway is to be shot on the spot; every troop train in which even one armed man is found shall be unloaded, and its soldiers shall be interned in a war prisoners' camp.

Trotsky's order was further embellished when relayed by a Central Siberian Soviet conscious of the patchiness of their military strength. If local forces proved inadequate they should 'do everything possible to stop the echelons:[5] side track them, take their locomotives, in urgent cases tear up the railway tracks'.

It is difficult to explain Trotsky's heavy-handed action in fanning what W.H. Chamberlin described as a 'spark that ignited a blaze of civil war over a vast expanse of Russian territory'. It has been the pet thesis of some Soviet historians that the Commissar for War believed the Czech action was encouraged by their accompanying French officers at the behest of the allies and as a curtain raiser to future Japanese intervention in Siberia. Equally, other Soviet historians will have it that Trotsky deliberately provoked the Czechs in order to further the allied cause. It had always been the express intention of the Czechs to leave Russia and to do so without involvement in domestic politics. The trivial Chelyabinsk incident needs to be seen as an isolated, spontaneous act by troops at the end of their tether. The death of but one renegade Czech set against the context where millions had perished thus far in the war seems poor justification for providing the allies with what Lloyd George described as the 'determining factor' to intervene.

Control of the railway also meant control of the communications. Trotsky's unequivocal and uncompromising signals were received by the Czechs at the same time as they were received by the Soviets. Forewarned and forearmed, on 25 May, the plan formulated in Chelyabinsk was put into effect. In pre-emptive moves the Czechs took over the railway lines in their areas. In little more than one week, over a thousand miles of railway were in anti-Bolshevik hands, from Penza (only 400 miles distant from Moscow), to the Urals, and from Chelyabinsk to Krasnoyarsk. The pawn had moved.

The Soviets were taken completely by surprise. They were unprepared and possessed no reliable trained troops. The tactical solution to overturn the simultaneous Czech attacks along the Trans-Siberian was to launch counter moves along the railway – something quite difficult to achieve while that railway remained in Czech hands. An additional bonus for the Czechs was the existence in many Siberian towns of resistance movements which responded to the Czech initiative by rising up enthusiastically against the despised Bolsheviks.

Rarely has such a minor event drawn quite so much into its vortex. It would confirm the fact of allied intervention in Russia leaving as a residue a legacy of distrust between today's Superpowers; it caused the Tsar's death warrant to be signed; it almost caused the Revolution to be overturned, and was a contributory factor in the failure of Admiral Kolchak's counter-revolution, restoring to Russia what some saw as the old order. As George Kennan wrote:

Had the Corps succeeded in making its way peacefully through the vast tinderbox of central Siberia during the Spring of 1918, striking no sparks and raising no crucial issues as it went along, this – rather than what actually occurred – would have been the true wonder.

4

THE GATHERING STORM

A contemporary description of Kolchak, the man and his mannerisms, is provided by Colonel John Ward's observations of the Admiral at an Omsk banquet:

> But as my liaison officer was repeating the names of those present a smart little energetic figure entered the room. With eagle eyes he took in the whole scene at a glance. The other officers had bowed gracefully to all their friends and gallantly kissed the ladies' hands, while around them buzzed the conversation. For an instant the buzz ceased, during which the brown figure with the dark, clear cut face shook hands with an officer friend and departed. The impression on my mind was that I had seen a small, vagrant, lonely, troubled soul without a friend enter unbidden to a feast.

Kolchak did then have one apparent prerequisite of a dictator, namely that he was small in stature. Ward's description is confirmed by something similar in George Stewart's *White Armies of Russia*: 'His smooth-shaven face and smart appearance were more like that of a Western European officer than the traditional bearded and robust Russian soldier.' Among his other traits it was noted that he was impetuous, bad tempered, and excitable; he was a small, well-dressed and energetic man moving about with quick, nervous gestures.

While *en route* to the United States, Kolchak called on the British Director of Naval Intelligence and also on Admiral Jellicoe. The British Admiral was very interested in the Russian's views concerning the mining of the North Sea. In return, Jellicoe was able to satisfy Kolchak's enthusiasm for naval development by allowing him to visit a number of naval flying stations prior to sailing for

Halifax, Nova Scotia. Kolchak's group of five was met by the Russian naval agent and proceeded to the United States via Montreal. They stayed for some weeks at the Naval War College at Newport, Rhode Island, and joined the US flagship *Pennsylvania* for twelve days of manoeuvres, but Kolchak was ill at ease. He decided he had to go home. He had not greatly enjoyed the American experience. While his hosts had been most proper and kind to him personally, the overwhelming public attitude was decidedly anti-Russian. Even when he met the President he was subjected to a detailed interrogation to account for the Russian failure in the Riga operation. The time had come, he thought, to put his talents back into his troubled country. The day he boarded the *Kario Maru* at San Francisco, the news broke of the Bolshevik Revolution and Kerensky's flight. There had been many such similar reports and this one Kolchak chose to ignore.

The Japanese steamer called at Hawaii before docking at Yokohama on 9 November. There to meet him was the grim-faced Russian Naval Attaché, Admiral Dudorov. The visitor confirmed the news that had been reported to the incredulous Kolchak while in San Francisco. Depressed and deflated, the traveller recorded how the unwelcome news had affected him:

> This to me was the heaviest blow, perhaps even worse than the one I received in the Black Sea Fleet. I saw that the work of my whole life had ended precisely as I feared that it might – an eventuality against which I had worked persistently all my life.

'What do you propose to do now?' enquired Dudorov. Kolchak considered the question carefully. To his mind, the peace negotiations at Brest-Litovsk had turned Russia into a German puppet state. He could not, he argued to himself, support a government which had signed away the nation's political independence in a peace settlement that he did not recognize. 'I came to the conclusion that only one thing remained for me to do: to carry on the war, as a representative of the former Russian government which had undertaken certain obligations to the allies.' He told his accompanying officers that they must choose their own courses. Three of the four elected to stay with him.

Kolchak reported to the British Ambassador in Tokyo, Sir Conyngham Greene. The Russian desired to fight on the Western Front and was prepared to do so as a private soldier if that were necessary. He had already rejected in his own mind the possibility of joining the Royal Navy. His seniority would have made it very difficult for him to be assimilated and given a real job. 'That is why I stressed my desire to go into the army, even if it were as a common soldier.' That the British took what might appear to be a melodramatic offer seriously can be seen from the fact that it was handled personally by the Foreign Secretary. Britain was on the lookout for new Russian horses to back and that same week had decided to support Kaledin's Don Cossacks. The Cossack enterprise would last but two months, having been unfunded, suffered from rampant desertion, and culminated in Kaledin blowing his brains out. Kolchak, however, was no Kaledin. He had a fine reputation and was widely respected as a sincere and patriotic Russian.

On 29 December the Foreign Office advised the British Ambassador in Tokyo that they would be pleased to accept Kolchak's offer although, for the time being, the place of his employment had not yet been determined. The reason for this indecision was due to the responsibility for Kolchak's future being passed from the Foreign Office to the War Office. The general staff was at that time drawing up plans to deal with a perceived German and Turkish threat to the Baku oilfields of the Caucasus – within Britain's sphere of influence – threatening to leap from a Caspian springboard into the Near East and central Asia. The planners' solution was to send a military mission led by General Dunsterville from Baghdad to the Caucasus. Here they were to liaise and co-operate with a group of Russians who, like Kolchak, refused to recognize the Brest-Litovsk Treaty. It may be assumed that a role was foreseen for Kolchak in the interface between Dunsterville and the Russian troops.

Kolchak was therefore appointed to the Mesopotamian Front and took the next ship out of Yokohama for Shanghai. In January 1918, Kolchak and two of his naval staff arrived in Shanghai but were obliged to wait three weeks for onward passage to Bombay. While waiting in Shanghai, Kolchak was to receive a significant message and a significant visitor. The Russian Ambassador to China, Prince Kudashev, approached the British Ambassador in Peking to ask whether he might discuss matters pertaining to Siberia with the Russian admiral now apparently under British orders. Kolchak did not relish the prospect of diverting to Peking. His orders were to go to Mesopotamia and now, half-way through that journey, at his own expense, he refused to be swayed unless specifically ordered by the British Government. Sir John Jordan, the British Ambassador in Peking, referred the matter to the Foreign Office. On 10 February, after discussion between the two relevant state departments, confirmation that the Admiral was indeed to proceed to Mesopotamia was relayed through diplomatic channels.

In the meantime, Kolchak had received a Cossack visitor. The man, a Cossack squadron commander, was named Zhevchenko. He advised his host of an insurrection that had broken out against Soviet rule in the area through which the Chinese Eastern Railway ran. The leader was a Cossack Captain by the name of Semenov who had 2,000 troops under command. Was the Admiral sympathetic to this movement, asked the squadron commander? Kolchak replied in the affirmative, but since he had undertaken to support the British enterprise in Mesopotamia he would remain true to his word. On 12 February he sailed for Bombay via Hong Kong and Singapore.

The Admiral's arrival at Hong Kong was inauspicious and certainly the arrangements were inappropriate for such a distinguished and valued volunteer. The Director of Military Intelligence had failed to notify the Hong Kong authorities of the presence of this respected ally. Kolchak found the requirement to report to the police every time he went ashore beneath his dignity. Happily, he was soon on his way to Singapore where, on 11 March, he was greeted by General Ridout, General Officer Commanding Straits Settlements. The General handed the Russian a message from British Intelligence. The changed conditions on the Mesopotamia Front and the insistent pressure from Prince Kudashev had swayed British opinion to the option of Kolchak returning to Russia and ultimately the Far East. 'Your secret presence in Manchuria is most desirable.' The Admiral was exasperated and angry. Was this communication an order or merely advice, he enquired? Why could he not have been diverted when he had passed through Shanghai? He received in reply an imprecise response but there was a recommendation that he should put himself at Kudashev's disposal. Irritated but obedient, Kolchak took an enforced sojourn at the Raffles Hotel prior to taking the next steamer back to Shanghai, from where he travelled by rail to Peking. While on that long journey, Kolchak pencilled a draft letter to a Madame Timireva, 'my good acquaintance of long standing'.

Kolchak did not hold Kudashev in high esteem. He deeply mistrusted his motives and particularly his commercial interests in the Chinese Eastern Railway. This was a Russian business, a subsidiary of the Russo-Asiatic Bank which also had its plethora of self-interested businessmen who had conspired to use the Admiral's undoubted integrity to bolster their own business interests. Kolchak now perceived that instead of fighting as he wished in support of the allied cause, his role had been relegated to nothing more than that of a commercial traveller.

Kudashev did his utmost to disabuse his visitor of this impression. Kolchak's mission was to establish 'an armed force to guarantee law and order in the Far East'. There really was no point in continuing to Mesopotamia, explained the plausible diplomat, because the Russians operating in Persia had now withdrawn. In the south, the volunteer forces of Generals Alexeiev and Kornilov were already in action and something similar was required for the Far East. 'Semenov is operating in Transbaikalia,' continued Kudashev, 'and you should work in the Chinese Eastern Railway Zone. You will have to reach a compromise with Semenov and assume the administration of the funds which are now being distributed haphazardly.' From the very beginning, Semenov was taking arms and money from the Japanese while the British and French had their own separate and uncoordinated detachments. The Chinese also took the opportunity to try to wrest control of the railway from the weakening Russian hand. A railway agreement between the interventionists was still a year away. Mindful of the presence of two governments living in relative harmony in Harbin, one conservative the other Socialist, neither of which had power or authority, led Kudashev to forecast that the Admiral would find complete chaos when he arrived in Harbin.

While in Peking, Kolchak met Lieutenant-General Dmitri Horvath, Managing Director of the railway and also Chairman of Harbin's conservative faction. Horvath was a devious man, well versed in the interests and intrigues of the region. He had held his position since 1903, the year prior to the Russo-Japanese War. That the Managing Director was a military man was not accidental. The Russians controlled the land adjoining the Chinese Eastern Railway in much the same way as a colonial power would. The post of military member of the railway board was currently vacant and Ambassador Kudashev, barred from holding office personally, installed Kolchak as a board member. Other than the predictable French diplomatic protest, there were no further diplomatic objections and the plan was implemented. It was at this stage of events that John F. Stevens, Chairman of the American Railroad

Commission to Russia, had reached agreement with Horvath for the first group of Americans comprising their Russian Railway Service Corps to leave for Siberia. The Corps's role was to improve the railway. This development engendered considerable suspicion in the ranks of the Japanese.

Although Wilson would baulk at putting soldiers into Siberia, the decay and dilapidation of the railway system had prompted his country to persuade the Russians to receive a Railway Advisory Commission. In November 1917, 288 commissioned and uniformed railwaymen embarked aboard the American Army transport vessel *Thomas* at San Francisco. The purpose of these men of the Russian Railway Service Corps was to act as advisers to put the Trans-Siberian back on the rails. In support of this project the American Government granted substantial loans to the Provisional Government and in addition provided 1,500 engines and 30,000 assorted carriages to replace the worn and damaged stock.

The sending of uniformed advisers into a war zone proved for the age to be a highly confusing affair. It seriously confused the Japanese; it also confused and annoyed the US soldiers whom the railmen had preceded (the railmen were better paid); but no one was more confused than the railmen themselves. The volunteers believed that they had enlisted into and were to conduct their duties as members of the United States Army. It was the absence of proper terms and conditions of service that left their employment open to interpretation. The United States Government would insist that the Russian Railway Service Corps was a special, quasi-military unit. So determined was the government to indicate publicly that the railmen were not military that they refused to grant the men honourable discharges. There was no question of pay or other records being involved, but the Government was to fight in the courts for over half a century the rights of the railmen to an honourable discharge. When in 1973 the survivors of the Russian Railway Service Corps won their ultimate victory in the American courts, there were only thirty-three left alive.

On 14 December 1917 when transport *Thomas* arrived at Vladivostok, the city was found to be in a state of disorder and anarchy. The Chairman of the Railway Advisory Commission, John F. Stevens, was dissatisfied with the administrative provision for his men and accordingly the team returned to Japan to await an improvement in the situation. Meanwhile, Stevens gave Wilson food for thought when he insisted that in his view the railway work could not proceed unless it received the protection of the United States Army.

On completion of his discussions in Peking, Kolchak left for Harbin via Mukden. Harbin was of immense strategic significance due to the course of the railway running east–west and connecting Vladivostok to the rest of Siberia. There was the additional junction of the southern Manchurian railway link to Mukden, Dalny and Port Arthur. Otherwise, there was little to distinguish this cosmopolitan city of 80,000, of whom over one-third were Russian. The American General Graves described it as the 'worst city in the world', a view supported by Colonel Ward.

> There are no special features about Harbin. It is just a conglomeration of houses of a more or less Chinese character thrown together in three heaps, the first two attempts of the thrower not getting quite near enough to the target, which was the junction of the Chinese Eastern Railway.

In the city was a hotchpotch of private armies all attracted by the realization that in order to control an area it was first necesssary to control the communications, which meant the railway. General Pleshkov was in command of the armed forces in the railway zone but, despite his large administrative staff, his authority was essentially nominal. Kolchak observed of the General:

> He had begun his work by forming a large staff without having any armed force whatsoever. All these detachments obeyed nobody and nothing. They turned to the staff when necessary with requests for money, supplies and arms; but when it came to receiving any orders from the staff they did not wish to obey.

Command of the largest detachment resided in the hands of a murderous bandit named Ataman Grigori Semenov, described by Ward as:

> a man of medium height with square broad shoulders, an enormous head, the size of which is greatly enhanced by the flat Mongol face, from which gleam two clear, brilliant eyes that rather belong to an animal than a man. The whole pose of the man is at first suspicious, alert, determined, like a tiger ready to spring, to rend and tear but in repose the change is remarkable, and with a quiet smile upon the brown face the body relaxes.

This then is the man with whom Kolchak was to co-operate. Rarely have two men been so completely opposite, the coarse but politically astute facing the refined yet politically naïve.

Japan needed to find a puppet in Manchuria and Siberia to help extend her influence throughout the region. In Semenov they found a convenient and willing ally to whom they half promised the Kingdom of Mongolia once their full aims had been realized. Semenov's was not the only band to receive cash and arms – the British and French both had groups which they sponsored, including Semenov, – but neither supported their protégés to the degree that Japan supported Semenov. It seemed logical therefore that Kolchak should meet Semenov sooner rather than later. At the time, the Ataman was not in Harbin but fighting the Bolsheviks on the Siberian border 600 miles away. Prior to departing from Harbin, the Admiral sent the Cossack a signal advising that he, the Commander-in-Chief, was *en route* to their first formal meeting.

After a long, taxing, and boring railway journey northward, Kolchak arrived at the small, drab railway station of Manchuli. The station was little more than a halt serving the ramshackle settlement tucked just inside the Manchurian frontier. Kolchak and his entourage detrained and assembled expectantly on the low platform. There was no one there to meet them. The Admiral demanded of the Manchurian station master whether his message had been received and relayed to Semenov's headquarters situated in a sumptuously appointed railway train in the adjoining siding. The reply was to the affirmative but it was regretted that Semenov was not aboard. Here amid this stark contrast of abject and rich surroundings, the Ataman lived with his mistress Masha Sharaban, the beautiful Jewish widow of a Russian merchant. Madame Semenov, herself a noted athlete and beauty, was at the time in Japan being fêted by her husband's major sponsors. Kolchak seemingly had no alternative but to seek out the station waiting room where he could quietly fume. When the ingratiating station master confided in him that Semenov was indeed in his railway carriage but did not wish to see him, the Admiral exploded in a rage and stormed off to confront what was, after all, one of his subordinates. The reality was, however, that in that part of the world, Semenov was all-powerful. The following account is taken from Captain (later Lieutenant-General) Sir Brian Horrocks's *A Full Life*. It tells of an occasion when he was in what passed for a Manchuli night club and what came to pass when Semenov's personal anthem was played. Bloodshed was averted by the timely appearance of the military police.

Then suddenly, after several loud chords, the band broke into some special tune and everyone jumped to his feet. We of course followed suit, but our host begged us to be seated as we were his guests. So down we sat; the only people in the whole place sitting down, two gypsy girls and three British officers. We all felt rather embarrassed, but what could we do?

Our embarrassment increased when a swarthy Cossack colonel approached our table. He was a magnificent figure in a wonderful furry cap, long coat and flared skirt girdled with a belt complete with revolver and small knives, while on his legs were the most beautiful long, black riding boots I have ever seen – with enormous spurs which jangled at each step.

"Get up", he shouted. But as his manner was extremely insolent we had no intention of doing so. Our host, the cavalry colonel, leant forward and slapped him smartly across the face saying, "These are my guests and will remain seated, you Cossack dog."

Then the fun really started and the whole place collected around our table. Our host turned to me, bowed and said, "Will you honour me by acting as my second in a duel which I now propose to fight with this Cossack?"

Semenov was a conundrum. He saw himself as, and modelled himself on, Napoleon, whose distinguished lock of hair he slavishly copied. His own men were devotedly loyal, being in direct contrast to those of Russian origin living to the south who added nothing to Semenov's order of battle. To the bevy of diplomats he appeared plausible and would invariably leave an extremely favourable impression. Not so easily convinced were regimental officers such as Major Phelps Hodges of the British Mission who arrived later on the scene at Chita:

The Japanese garrison prevented any serious attack from the local Red bands, and Semenov was able to live under their protecting wing, and send forth his Cossacks to murder and pillage, without fear of reprisals, while his control of the frontier served as an excuse to relieve both speculator and refugee of a great part of their worldly goods. He had unearthed an old Russian law that forbade anyone to cross the frontier with more than 250 roubles, and this he enforced with considerable profit to himself.

It was therefore into this self-important presence that Kolchak, the visitor from the south, was grudgingly and unceremoniously ushered. The meeting of the two leaders was decidedly frigid. Semenov was unimpressed by Kolchak's efforts to develop a co-ordinated military policy and even spurned the 300,000 roubles brought from the Chinese Eastern Railway. 'He replied to me rather evasively that he was not in need of anything at present, that he received funds from Japan.' The visitor recognized that further dialogue was pointless, and with his ego severely bruised he returned to Harbin to tackle his problem at its source – the head of the Japanese Military Mission.

The Japanese general was rude, off-hand and obstructive, indicating that their relationship with Semenov would not be changed by Kolchak or anyone else. The Admiral succumbed to that same feeling of impotent exasperation which had overwhelmed him in the Black Sea. Horvath was weak, inept, and unsupportive. Life in Harbin was characterized by raucous, ill-disciplined licentiousness. The town fully lived up to its unsavoury reputation and Kolchak, unable to tolerate the place any longer, resigned and set out on a crusade to Tokyo to confront the Japanese Chief-of-Staff. If there were any remaining doubts as to the man's political innocence, they were dispelled by this visit to Japan. To his simple, honest, and uncomplicated mind, Japan was an ally of Russia and it appeared reasonable that problems could be amicably resolved between officers who had grown up under a similar code of honour. It would have been as well had Kolchak had his attention drawn to an illuminating article in the Japanese newspaper *Kokumin* written by a former Premier, Marquis Okuma:

> International relations are quite unlike relations subsisting between individuals. Morality and sincerity do not govern a country's diplomacy which is guided by selfishness, pure and simple. It is considered the secret of diplomacy to forestall rivals by every crafty means available.

Before meeting the Japanese Chief-of-Staff in July 1918, Kolchak was briefed by the Russian Ambassador in Tokyo. He was told very clearly that the Japanese considered him a threat to the progress of their own regional aspirations. 'They have come to regard you as an enemy of theirs, who is going to oppose anything they initiate, the whole work; therefore, naturally, they not only will not help you but will oppose your work.' Kolchak came away from his meeting with the Japanese Chief-of-Staff with no guarantees but an offer to restore his health in a Japanese cure resort. Kolchak gratefully and innocently accepted, thereby removing himself for two months from the centre of the fast-developing activities in the Far East.

The extent to which Kolchak had played into Japanese hands despite British advice is not clear. Major-General Knox, the British Military Attaché, met the Russian Admiral in Tokyo and was immediately impressed by him. 'He possesses two characteristics uncommon in a Russian – a quick temper which inspires a useful awe among his subordinates, and a disinclination to talk merely for talking.' Knox sent a favourable signal to the War Office claiming that there was no doubt 'he is the best Russian for our purpose'. However, in Knox's view the time was not yet ripe for Kolchak to travel to Vladivostok where he still had enemies. Kolchak's leadership potential had already been noted by right-wing parties but, perhaps more ominously, it had also been noted by the forces of the left. Trotsky wrote in *The History of the Russian Revolution*:

> One of the offshoots of the family of the newspaper magnate Suvorin undertook the publication in those days of a Little Newspaper, which as an organ of 'independent socialism' advocated an iron dictatorship, advancing Admiral Kolchak as its candidate. The more solid press, without as yet quite dotting its "i"s, tried in every way to create a popularity for Kolchak. The further career of the admiral testifies that already in the summer of 1917 there was a broad plan connected with his name, and that there were influential circles behind Suvorin's back.

During Kolchak's absence from Russia, the allied interest in that country had moved on apace after the landing of 130 Royal Marines at Murmansk on 6 March 1918 with the local Soviet's agreement. The Western allies were less inhibited intervening in the west than they were in the east which was subject to its own pervasive political chemistry. Even the Americans could see military advantage in intervening in the west but not in the east. France was the moving force in recommending intervention in Siberia but little that was tangible had come of this proposal other

52

than the customary display of gunboat diplomacy. The boats had grown somewhat, now being cruisers and a battleship, but the principle of protecting national interests remained much the same. The first ship to arrive at Vladivostok was the six-inch-gunned cruiser HMS *Suffolk* from Hong Kong; she was joined by the Japanese cruiser *Iwami* and the battleship *Asahi* which in turn were joined on 13 February 1918 by USS *Brooklyn* from Yokohama. There they sat with their embarked marines and waited among the large, broken ice floes.

Again, it was to be the spectre of the Russo-Japanese War which injected its own sensitivity into the Far East. The presence of the Japanese battleship *Asahi* conveyed her own silent message, for she had played a leading part in the destruction of Rozhdestvenski's Baltic Fleet at Tsushima. The British and Americans were well aware of Russian paranoia towards the Japanese. The existence of what US Secretary of State Robert Lansing described as 'racial difficulty' spawned among the allies the fear that any overt Japanese activity would lead to the Bolsheviks inviting Germany to come to their aid. So concerned was Robert Bruce Lockhart by this prospect that on 5 March 1918 he sent a cable from the British Embassy in Moscow to the Foreign Office. 'If, however, the Allies are to allow Japan to enter Siberia, the whole position is hopeless. Every class of Russian will prefer the Germans to the Japanese.'

The prevailing concept of British, French, and American intervention in Russia, although tempered to varying degrees by a desire to support anti-Bolshevik forces, was still seen principally as part of the war effort against Germany. The allies dwelt on the perceived threat that the 250,000 German and Austro-Hungarian prisoners of war posed to the railway, the Siberian war resources, and the strategic port of Vladivostok. Within and around that city were the scattered allied supply depots containing an estimated 600,000 tons of valuable war *matériel*. If somehow the highly improbable became possible, by an unlikely logistic miracle that could transport these stores and supplies to Germany, they would be admittedly beneficial in topping up Germany's own diminished stocks. President Wilson remained understandably unswayed by such logic as suitable justification for sending US troops to intervene. However, he was beginning to show concern at the expressed Japanese Government view that if intervention was to occur in Siberia it should be by Japan and Japan alone.

The allied warships at anchor in the Golden Horn provided a

stabilizing, even dulling influence on events in Vladivostok although a state of complete mayhem lay uneasily just below the surface. However, it had remained the only Siberian city of significance not to have come under Bolshevik control. Banditry and political murder were commonplace as Bolsheviks strove surreptitiously to strengthen their position without triggering the intervention of the naval force sitting in the bay. It had been unwise for a group of uniformed Bolsheviks, out on the unending search for political funds, to visit a Japanese shop on 4 April and demand money. It was disastrous that the Japanese reluctance to contribute to the revolutionary cause should lead to the shooting to death of three of the Japanese storekeepers. The Japanese marines responded next morning by going ashore to protect national interests. In addition, a party of Royal Marines was despatched to guard the British Consulate. The Americans did nothing, for they saw no threat to American lives or property. Their caution paid off, for this apparent lack of allied solidarity exposed the British and Japanese to the strongest possible Bolshevik opprobrium. Both nations responded to the Moscow-inspired protest by withdrawing their marines back to their ships. The local Bolsheviks thought that this political retreat indicated that they were no longer encumbered by the threat of allied military intervention. On 2 May they took over Vladivostok.

In allowing themselves to be mesmerized by the naval presence, the Bolsheviks had failed to take account of their enemy within, namely the Czechs of whom a large advance party had taken quarters in the city. It will be remembered that Czech progress eastward along the Trans-Siberian Railway was suffering from the widespread obstruction of the Bolsheviks. The news that their goal, Vladivostok, was in the hands of those regarded as their enemy required direct action. On 29 June, the supposedly apolitical Czechs seized Vladivostok's Bolshevik leadership, hauled down their red flag, and replaced it with the old blue and white flag of Tsarist Russia. There was widespread rejoicing in the city. The marines were to be encouraged once more from their ships in the harbour and this time they included the Americans. An international declaration advised that Vladivostok had been placed under the temporary protection of the allied powers. With their bolt-hole now secure, those Czechs who had reached Vladivostok turned back along the route on which they had come, with the aim of securing the city of Irkutsk some 2,570 miles to the west in order to facilitate the further evacuation of their brothers in arms.

Whereas President Wilson could reject as reasons for intervention the presence in Siberia of enemy prisoners and the potential war booty, he found it less easy to set aside the question of the plight of the Czechs which was now striking a moral chord. Demands that he should do something to save the Czechs came thick and fast from diverse sources. On 19 June he had received and been impressed by Thomas Masaryk. Four days later, the Secretary of State sent him a copy of a cable written by Bruce Lockhart in Moscow. 'If we leave the Czechs to their fate and if we fail to intervene now, we shall suffer a blow to our prestige in Russia from which it will take us years to recover.' On his accompanying memorandum. Lansing had penned: 'As these troops are most loyal to our cause, and have been unjustly treated by the various Soviets, ought we not consider whether something can be done to support them?' All of Wilson's political intuition told him to keep out of the Far East; not to become involved. It was a matter over which he had long agonized. Now, on 3 July, he had before him a further appeal to intervene but signed this time by all his allies of the Supreme War Council. This was followed by news of Czech developments in Siberia and Vladivostok which Wilson admitted had introduced 'a sentimental element into the question of our duty'. On 6 July he convened a meeting at the White House attended by Secretary of State Lansing and the political and military heads of both services. Here Wilson announced his capitulation to the many pressures to intervene in Siberia which was conditional upon receiving Japanese co-operation. The outline plan involved both America and Japan landing 7,000 troops at Vladivostok to protect the Czech lines of communication. A joint announcement would give as justification the need to protect the Czechs from German and Austrian prisoners of war. Reassurances would be given to the effect that there would be no interference in Russian domestic affairs or their political and territorial sovereignty.

The British and French allies had not been privy to this plan and were not to be informed until after Japan had been consulted. An *aide mémoire* which followed the verbal briefings of the Ambassadors at the State Department was sent to London, Paris, and Rome. Here the leadership, still aggrieved at the lack of consultation, despaired as much at what the document said as what it did not. The British, for example, held the view that the purpose of intervention was to reconstitute the fighting front against Germany in the east and saw the Czechs as the tools by which that aim would be achieved. The American attitude to the second front was never elucidated, although the *aide mémoire* did provide for the landing of American troops at Murmansk to guard military stores. Lloyd George was furious. He believed the planned token American and Japanese presence to be totally inadequate to fulfil their purpose and he told Wilson as much. In his response, Wilson stood firm. Intervention, he insisted, would 'add to the present sad confusion in Russia rather than cure it, injure her rather than help her'. In reality, the size of the commitment was academic. The presence of but one battalion in Russia involved the sending country in the political ramifications attendant upon that act. Now, the green light had been given for the allies to enter Siberia.

While American diplomacy was intent on maintaining a bilateral stance with Japan over Siberia the Japanese were equally intent on following a unilateral line due to their 'special position'. Japan would not restrict her force to 7,000 men, and determined to despatch a division – 12,000 men – with the proviso that even more men would be sent if the need arose. The need did arise and a division was deployed in the sensitive Chinese Eastern Railway zone, gradually gaining complete control. In Siberia proper, the strength of the Japanese force grew to 72,000 providing the United States with real cause for concern.

Siberia includes all the Russian territory lying between the Urals and the Pacific, an area one-third again the size of Europe which, at that time, had a population of 450,000,000. In 1917, Siberia's population had grown to over 9,000,000 largely due to the expansionist influence of the Trans-Siberian Railway. Major development occurred on either side of the track along a strip 100 miles wide. This belt contained the majority of the important towns, the industry and the most arable and fertile land. To the north of this dark, highly productive soil lay deep forests the size of entire nations, before they too thinned to give way to the inhospitable frozen tundra which seems to represent a common view of Siberia. The topography from west to east also has three distinct divisions. The plains of western Siberia lie between the Urals and Obi Basin, from where central Siberia squeezed by lofty mountains reaches out for the Yeneisei River, from which the mountains and plateaux of eastern Siberia run through into the Pacific Ocean. The temperature is extreme. Winter begins in October, from which point the temperature falls to $-20°C$. Daylight gives way to darkness at 3 p.m. Over the period of the Intervention very little snow fell in Vladivostok and unlike the interior there was little wind, which gave the impression it was less cold than it actually was. To the west, southerly winter gales accompanied by blinding powdery snow were common. When the fine ice dust struck the eyeballs it froze in cakes, blinding individuals in minutes. Winter therefore was a major inhibitor of military operations and although the weather improved in April, mobility was severely affected by the sodden ground. Summer is hot, very hot, with temperatures reaching $35°C$. The heat brings with it swarms of ferocious mosquitoes. When the Middlesex Regiment was preparing to depart Hong Kong for Vladivostok, their quartermaster bid for mosquito nets. He was laughed at. 'There are no mosquitoes in Siberia.' When these insects bit into wrists they swelled to the size of the hand, and bites near the eyes would render the individual blind for the days it took for the swelling to subside. Summer was the time men and horses worked the land. Consequently, absenteeism from the ranks of the indigenous military was rife, whereas in winter when military operations were limited the ranks were full.

The manpower and resources of Siberia were important to both Reds and Whites. The economic possibilities of the region, both minerals and agriculture, had not escaped the attention of the allies. Politically, Siberia was the most conservative and least revolutionary of the Russian regions. Its people were a mirror image of the early settlers who had populated America's west. They were not an oppressed people. Indeed, many owned their own farms which averaged over 100 acres. Compared with their fellow farmers in the European west they were well off. Siberian independence groups flourished in the major population centres. The potential of Siberia to become an autonomous anti-Bolshevik nation looked most promising. Britain favoured a policy of separate development for Siberia and in April 1918 sent in an exploratory economic mission led by a businessman named H.E. Metcalf.

The efficiency of Siberian agriculture needs to be set against the crumbling inefficiency of the Trans-Siberian Railway, now unable to move grain and other produce to the export markets. Almost 17 per cent of the entire Russian grain production had nowhere to go and, in consequence, had accumulated at such centres as Omsk and Novonikolaievsk. These reserves were to become a key Bolshevik goal. A major reason for the upsurge in agricultural development was mechanization introduced by such private North American companies as Massey Ferguson and International Harvester. The latter company is reputed to have had 200 sales outlets in Siberia. The American State Department was fully conscious of the commercial benefits to be derived from Siberia. This, in part, would be the source of an unfortunate conflict between them and the United States' Department of War.

5

EGGS LOADED WITH DYNAMITE

The effects of the fickleness of fate can rarely have been better demonstrated than in the examination of two quite diverse careers of two quite different Lieutenant-Colonels, one British, the other American. Both would play crucial roles in the unfolding Kolchak story.

John Ward grew up in humble conditions in the Hampshire village of Appleshaw. He had already spent a number of years working the fields as a ploughboy when, at the age of 12, he went to work as a navvy on the Andover–Marlborough–Swindon Railway. He was tempted into the services while still in his teens and went off to the Sudan and adventure. On returning to England at the age of 19 he joined the forerunner of today's Labour Party – the Social Democratic Federation. His political affiliations ranged across the left-of-centre spectrum although in some political aspects he would prove himself to be ultra-conservative. At the age of 24 he formed the Navvies' Union. In 1906 he fought and won Stoke-on-Trent for the Labour Party, remaining the town's MP in various political guises until 1929. At the outbreak of the First World War he returned to the colours when many of his political colleagues, such as Bertrand Russell and Fenner Brockway, were active pacifists. Fighting initially on the Western Front, he was posted to what might have appeared to be the safe and enviable duty of commanding the Twenty-Fifth Battalion the Middlesex Regiment, a garrison battalion in Hong Kong.

One morning in November 1917, Lieutenant-Colonel John Ward was summoned to headquarters and placed under orders to hold himself and battalion in readiness to proceed to an unknown destination. The only hint he was given was that the battalion would operate in a very cold climate. More than somewhat intrigued, Ward stopped off to take tiffin in the ante-room of the Hong Kong Club. While still deep in thought as to what it all meant and where his ultimate destination might be, a voice arose from the depths of a cosy leather armchair: 'Well, Colonel, what date do you expect to leave for Vladivostok?' No sooner had the battalion been prepared for its unknown adventure than it was stood down. In June 1918, it was on again and the battalion's Singapore detachment was ordered to return to Hong Kong in the first available ship. Once reunited, the whole battalion left on 27 July 1918 aboard the *Ping Suey* bound for Vladivostok.

Lieutenant-Colonel William S. Graves was at this time Secretary of the General Staff in the War Department, Washington. He had been in post for a number of years so, when the United States entered the First World War on 6 April 1917, he had high expectations of being relieved of staff duties to go on active service in France. His Chief-of-Staff, General Peyton C. March, had other ideas, seemingly being content for the time being to leave Graves where he was. While in the course of a normal discussion, Graves was stunned by a one-liner from March: 'If anyone has to go to Russia, you're it'. Graves knew his Chief was aware of his keenness to serve in France and, since he regarded the prospect of intervention in Russia as highly improbable, he thought no more of March's aside.

Graves's proposed part in any Siberian adventure was seemingly killed in June 1918 when March informed his Secretary that he was to be promoted to Major-General. Furthermore, he could have command of any division that did not have a permanent commander. Graves asked for, and was assigned to, the Eighth Division scheduled to leave for France in October 1918. On 18 July, Graves assumed command of the Eighth Division located near Palo Alto, California. On the afternoon of 2 August 1918, the new Divisional Commander's Chief-of-Staff advised Graves that they had just received a coded message for Graves's eyes only. The General chose to ignore the privacy markings and ordered the immediate decoding of the signal. When the message came back to Graves's desk he confessed that it was 'one of the most remarkable communications I ever saw come out of the War Department'. The General was to 'take the first and fastest train out of San Francisco and proceed to Kansas City, go to the Baltimore Hotel and ask for the Secretary of War, and if he is not there, wait until he arrives'.

Graves set out immediately for Kansas City wondering what the mysterious meeting could be about, but he guessed, correctly, that the spectre of Russia had again raised its head. The train arrived later than scheduled at Kansas City, at 10 p.m., and the General was guided by a porter into the station waiting room. He had but a very short moment's interview with Secretary Baker before the latter left by train. Baker expressed his sadness at having to send Graves to Siberia. There was barely time to hand over a sealed envelope which Baker thrust into Graves' hand. 'This contains the policy of the United States in Russia which you are to follow. Watch your step; you will be walking on eggs loaded with dynamite. God bless you and goodbye.' At his hotel that evening, Graves opened the envelope and withdrew the seven-page document. It was headed *Aide-Mémoire*,[6] was unsigned, but at the bottom appeared 'Department of State, Washington, July 17, 1918'. Graves did not know at the time that the document had been personally prepared by the President and was identical to the documents released the next day to the allied political leaders. The General admitted:

> I have often thought it was unfortunate that I did not know more of the conditions in Siberia than I did when I was pitchforked into the mêlée at Vladivostok. At other times I have thought that ignorance was not only bliss in such a situation, but was advisable.

In *The Siberian Fiasco*, Clarence A. Manning described the *aide-mémoire* in the following terms:

> It breathes President Wilson's well known spirit of disinterestedness and idealism. It is in every sense of the word for most part a sermon embodying the President's views on the duty of one nation to another in the time of misfortune and chaos.

Its fundamental shortcoming was that it attempted to be all things to all men; a single document ranging from, at the very highest level, a brief for the world leadership, down to being the working manuscript for the guidance of United States' diplomats and soldiers out on the ground. Having read the *aide-mémoire* several times, Graves felt no need to question its suitability as a guide to his actions in Siberia, its relevance or its adequacy: 'I felt there could be no misunderstanding the policy of the United States and I did not feel it necessary for me to ask for elucidation of any point.'

The Army Department had made a wise choice to suit their purpose. Accepting that the underlying, yet undeclared, reason for United States intervention in Siberia was to monitor and limit Japanese expansionism, their need was well provided for in the form of this inflexible and dogmatic military bureaucrat. His function was not the winning of military victory but to assume a role in support of diplomatic goals. As to what those diplomatic goals should be, there was division not only among the political executive but also among the military. Secretary of State Lansing was on leave at the time Graves's appointment was announced. When he heard the news he sent an immediate telegram of protest insisting that Graves had neither the tact nor diplomacy for the job. Since the appointment had the approval of the President, Lansing's objections were ignored. Lansing had been well advised, for Graves's time in Russia would be characterized by a blind obedience to orders and complete inactivity where there was any hint of the need for initiative or there involved any element of risk. He immersed himself completely in what he believed the *aide-mémoire* to mean. According to Captain Robert L. Eichelberger, one of Graves' Staff Officers, this outward impression of complete confidence in the *aide-mémoire* reflected more than an element of doubt and uncertainty in the General's mind.

> One would think that General Graves would have discussed the *Aide Mémoire* with his principal Staff Officers. At times General Graves would read to me a paragraph and ask my opinion about what it meant but I never saw the *Aide Mémoire* in complete form until just before I left Siberia.

President Wilson said he 'sweated blood' over the preparation of the *aide mémoire* which he typed out on his own typewriter. It has never been satisfactorily explained why such a vague and unreliable document was spawned or why no effort was made to update it in the light of the changes to the Russian scene. The *aide-mémoire* failed to acknowledge that at the time it was written Russia was in the throes of bloody revolution. Further, there is no attempt to divide the generic term 'Russian' into either Red or White. The State Department had been less coy in refusing to recognize the Soviets as the bona fide government of the Russian people. It became clear that some elements within the State Department believed that Graves should be supporting the forces of the old regime but no instructions to that effect were ever given. The course that Graves chose to steer would leave him open to accusations of being pro-Bolshevik and anti-Kolchak.

Wilson's publicly declared justification for intervening had been to protect the Czechs operating out of Vladivostok. By the time United States land forces arrived at Vladivostok, there were no significant numbers of Czechs within 3,500 miles. Graves would shrug off this difficulty and characteristically choose to do very little other than post guards on ordnance stores and police those small areas of the Trans-Siberian Railway for which he was held responsible. George Kennan, a former United States Ambassador to Russia related Graves' attitude to the *aide-mémoire*.

> That it was, even at the time it was presented to him, utterly inadequate to its purpose, that it was still further out of date by the time he arrived in Siberia, and that within two months after his arrival it had lost all conceivable relevance, seems never to have occurred to him. He accepted it with that unquestioning and religious reverence which sterling soldiers normally bear for directives from supreme authority. For one and a half years he would cling to the letter of it with a stubbornness that would drive his Allied colleagues and associates to despair; and he would never cease to regard with baleful suspicion and hostility anyone who professed to have other orders or anyone who had the temerity to question the relevance and wisdom of his own.

To return to Russia, the problem of what to do with the Tsar and his family was one of those matters never far removed from the thoughts of Lenin and Trotsky. Trotsky had formed the idea of a public trial with himself as prosecutor, but Lenin took a more pragmatic view, recognizing the inherent political dangers in putting the Tsarina and her children on trial. He preferred to sit and await an appropriate opportunity. In April the family was moved from Tobolsk to a two-storey house belonging to a trader named Ipatiev in the industrial city of Ekaterinburg. Here the family suffered great privation, being denied the right to worship and access to the little luxuries which would have helped to make life bearable in the deteriorating conditions in which they found themselves. The guards, often drunk, behaved like savages; brutal, insulting, and being particularly cruel in the most lewd manner to the teenage Grand Duchesses. The position of the Tsar's family was unenviable. Admittedly there were a very few who wanted to see a restoration of the monarchy, among them Colonel Kappel, destined to become one of Kolchak's staunchest Lieutenants. There were some too who wished to see a restoration of the monarchy, but specifically excluding the Tsar and his immediate family. The critical view on which both Reds and Whites did find almost complete unanimity was that there was no place in the new Russia for Nicholas and his family. An emigrant had said to John Ward, 'it is all right so long as they (Kolchak) do not want to bring back the old régime, but if that is their object I can tell them that Russia will never submit to live under the old régime again.' 'I thought', wrote Ward, 'and think now, that in that workman's words I heard the voice of Russia.'

Unfortunately for the Tsar and his family, Lenin could not take the risk of leaving the Tsar as a rallying point for the monarchists. A policy of complete extermination of the Romanovs had the political advantage of signalling to Russia the undeniable end of the old régime. One implication of such a policy, however, was the creation of the headroom to present to a people conditioned to authoritarianism the possibility of Dictator in lieu of Tsar. Unwanted at home or abroad, taunted, bullied, and utterly isolated, the family clung desperately to one another and awaited a fate that must have been apparent at least to both the Tsar and Tsarina. The Tsar's brother, the Grand Duke Mikhail, had been shot dead the previous month. There had been a local attempt at a coup to release the Tsar and his family from their torment but it was unrepresentative and easily suppressed. The reason seized upon by the Bolsheviks as an excuse to deal with the royal family was the move of the Czechs from Chelyabinsk towards Ekaterinburg. Naturally, it was well within the gift of the Bolsheviks to move the Tsar away from the line of advance of the Czechs, but they preferred instead to accept this move as the excuse they had awaited. Two days after the event, the following announcement was released in Moscow:

> Lately the approach of the Czecho-Slovak bands seriously threatened the capital of the Red Urals, Ekaterinburg. At the same time, a new plot of counter revolutionaries, which had as its objective the taking of the royal hangman out of the hands of the Soviet Government, was disclosed. In view of this the presidium of the Ural Territorial Soviet decided to shoot Nicholas Romanov, which was done on July 16.[7]

The Ural Territorial Soviet had discussed their proposed policy of extermination with Sverdlov, the President of the Soviet Executive

Committee. In fact, the city of Ekaterinburg was renamed Sverdlovsk in 1924. It is difficult to imagine what degree of civic pride is engendered by honouring in perpetuity the perpetrator of such a barbaric crime.

One conundrum of the Revolution was the part played by the Jews. It is generally true that as a group they were despised by the ruling classes. It is also generally true that many featured prominently on the revolutionary side. Given this positive contribution, therefore, their subsequent treatment within Russia has been distinctly inequitable. Kolchak was among those who were anti-Semitic, claiming as one of the reasons for his low regard of the American forces, the high proportion of Jews within their ranks. This claim may be largely attributed to pique and a sense of exasperation arising from the independent line that would be taken by General Graves.

Yakov Mikhailovich Yurovski was a 40-year-old Jewish clock repairer. He was also a hard-line Bolshevik only recently arrived at Dom Ipatiev as the replacement for the former sadistic warden of the Tsar and family. During the course of the evening of 16 July, the fateful telegram arrived from Perm ordering Yurovski to execute the Tsar, Tsarina, Tsarevitch, and the Grand Duchesses Olga, Tatiana, Maria, and Anastasia. Yurovski arranged for a lorry to arrive at midnight to take away the bodies and spent the rest of the evening in planning and briefing his team of assassins. There were eleven in the group, which included two secret police and seven Latvians. Each man was issued with a revolver and then given each his own individual target. Two of the Latvians reacted strongly when nominated to kill a girl and, as a result, the victims were reallocated. 'Aim for the heart', they were ordered, 'then there will be less blood.'

Midnight came, but the lorry had not. The unsuspecting Romanovs were asleep in the upper rooms. Below, the group of assassins was agitated and extremely nervous. The Latvians in particular were drinking heavily. When at 1.30 a.m. the lorry did arrive, Yurovski went to the room of Botkin, the Tsar's doctor, and told him to rouse the royal family. On being asked why, Yurovski responded to the effect that there was unrest in Ekaterinburg and the Tsar and his family were being moved to a lower room for their own safety. Thirty minutes after being awoken, the Romanovs and servants, dressed in their day clothes were led downstairs into the cellar by Yurovski. In his arms the Tsar carried his 14-year-old haemophiliac son Alexei. The room in the cellar was large and papered with a regency wall paper over a plaster wall. One of the reasons for the selection of this room for the executions was the fond but groundless hope that the bullets would not ricochet off the plaster. The Tsarina surveyed the empty room and asked whether they might be permitted to sit down. Yurovski accordingly had two chairs brought down, one of which was taken by the weak Tsarevitch. The remainder of the family and staff stood in a row with their backs to the wall awaiting further instructions. At their feet were a number of cushions brought down from their rooms. It was at this stage that the killers descended the cellar steps.

When all had assembled, Yurovski confronted the Tsar. In view of the continuing attacks by Nicholas' relatives on Soviet Russia, he was told, the Tsar and his family were to be executed. That fatal message did not dawn immediately upon Nicholas, who had turned to face his worried, wide-eyed family, but when the partly deaf Tsar turned back to face Yurovski, the realization of what had been said was perfectly clear. 'What? What?', said the Tsar. Yurovski repeated his message, at the same time signalling his men to position themselves to carry out the sentence. Words failed Nicholas, but the consternation was apparent from those behind him. In fact, Nicholas said nothing more. Yurovski raised his Colt .45 revolver and killed him. That was the signal for the remainder of the killings to begin. In an orgy of inaccurate and frenzied firing the family and servants were mown down. When the shooting ceased, the bodies on the floor were examined. The Tsarevitch, three of the Grand Duchesses, and Dr Botkin had only been wounded. A further outbreak of firing and bayonetting then took place until all bodies registered no pulses. When Yurovski was convinced his victims were all dead, he had them wrapped in cloth to avoid the spillage of blood. One by one they were taken upstairs and outside onto the waiting lorry. Unsupervised individuals who had remained in the cellar began to loot the bodies. The Tsarina's ring finger was cut off and the rings disappeared. When an angry Yurovski returned he quickly restored order and recovered gold watches and a diamond-studded cigarette case. At 3 a.m. the lorry drove away from Dom Ipatiev with its grisly cargo to make rendezvous with the members of the Ural Executive Committee who had ordered the executions.

The organization had been haphazard and amateurish. When the two groups met, the Committee members were incensed to discover that the executions had already been effected. They had thought that to be their privilege. Then the lorry broke down. It was unloaded, and the corpses transferred onto ramshackle carts while outriders went in search of the mine where the bodies were to be buried. In the early morning, the reconnaissance party returned, having found a disused mine near to the village of Koptyaka. In the meantime the bodies had been stripped, revealing in the corsets a hidden fortune in pearls and diamonds. The latter weighed a total of 8 kilogrammes. This was a complication Yurovski had not anticipated and, with some difficulty, he managed to disperse the majority of his helpers. Once the royal clothing had been burned, the Bolsheviks set off in the direction of the mine, pulling the carts over the uneven ground. Yurovski was again disappointed, for the mine proved to be a deep excavation rather than a shaft. The bodies were tipped in, followed by hand grenades to tear asunder flesh and bone. But Yurovski was not happy. The remains were too close to the surface and if the secret were to be compromised, this place could become both shrine and focal point for resistance. The leaders of the Ural Executive Committee agreed. The solution was to dispose of the butchered remains down a disused well some 9 miles along the Moscow road. The pieces were recovered and put back in the carts. After just a short distance had been covered, the carts fell to pieces and a lorry and two cars had to be requisitioned. All the while, the Bolsheviks feared detection. Czech and White forces were not far distant and the loyalty of the peasantry could not be relied upon. It was now thirty-six hours after the murders, and the shattered bodies of their victims were still not disposed of. To add further to the problem, their lorry bogged down and could not be budged. There was no possibility of the group reaching the well. Yurovski had brought with him a quantity of sulphuric acid and kerosene. He decided to bury or burn the bodies but, due to their condition it was now difficult to determine who was who. A bonfire was lit, upon which some of the bodies were burned while the remainder, doused in sulphuric acid, were buried in a common grave close to the abandoned lorry. There had been one survivor of the massacre. However, it was not Anastasia but rather Joy, Alexei's blind spaniel. The disorientated and bewildered little dog was found blundering around Ekaterinburg by a Russian liaison officer to the British Military Mission. Eventually the dog was shipped to England, spending its last days on a farm in Windsor. Anastasia's Pekinese was less fortunate, having been shot with her family.

The Bolsheviks had observed in the ordinary people a macabre habit of collecting human remains as souvenirs of bomb outrages or other similar bloody atrocities on the nobility. So determined were they that there should be no possibility of any such necrophilia arising from the murder of the Romanovs that they took extremely stringent precautions. Despite their supposedly efficient system of disposing of the royal remains it was not equal to the resourcefulness of the people who had been associated with the murders and the aftermath. Some of the 311 relics salvaged from Ekaterinburg and which were to surface at the end of the Intervention were collections of royal bone, human fat which had seeped from the burning bodies, the Empress's ring finger, strands of hair, and the Tsarevich's belt buckle. Twenty-four hours after the murder of the Tsar's family, in the Urals mining town of Alapayevsk, the Tsarina's sister Elizabeth, her husband Sergei, and their children were also murdered. The sisters were the daughters of the Prince of Hesse and granddaughters of Queen Victoria. The Soviets therefore had ample reason to remain coy as to what they had done; confirmation of the atrocities was not released to the stunned West until December 1918.

On 3 August when the *Ping Suey* arrived off Vladivostok's Golden Horn with the embarked Twenty-Fifth Middlesex, the first of the allied troops to deploy in the east, she failed to make rendezvous with her Japanese escort of two destroyers. They had been delayed while on coastal mapping duties to the north of the city. Ward gave the reason for the British Expeditionary Force being ordered to Siberia as 'to assist the orderly elements of Russian society to reorganise themselves under a national Government and to resurrect and reconstruct the Russian front'. The Middlesex did not bear close examination. The Middlesex Regiment enjoyed the nickname of the Die Hards, but their Twenty-Fifth Battalion was unkindly called the 'Hernia Battalion'. The men were old or unsuited to arduous employment, having done their duty for their country in earlier campaigns. 'I had', said Ward ruefully, 'to carry out the services of a first line service battalion with the personnel and equipment of second grade garrison troops.' The doubts concerned equally the question of quantity as well as quality, but in the new world of modern diplomacy, although there were insufficient men of Middlesex to gain military victory there were sufficient to make a political point. The sole purpose of sending this aged battalion to Siberia was to goad the United States into action. The real flag bearers of British interests in Siberia were not these veterans but the British Military Mission – Britmis – installed in Vladivostok under Major-General Alfred Knox. Britmis's *raison d'être* was to distribute British equipment to the Whites and then train them to use it.

Knox had been the former Military Attaché at the British Embassy in St Petersburg. He followed and documented the military disasters of the sad and tortured Russian Army. Never slow to leap into political arenas, he seized and held a high profile. It was he who negotiated the release of the women's battalion after the attack on the Winter Palace. 'This quiet, energetic and exceptionally well informed officer commanded the esteem and admiration of the best elements of the Russian Army.' Such a recognition by a Russian diplomat is reflected also in this fawning profile penned by a British officer.

> This is a type of British officer one meets occasionally. They make one proud to belong to the same race and eager to spare no effort to work for the patriotic and unselfish ideals which evidently form the mainspring of their lives.

Knox was a charismatic and natural leader ideally suited to harmonize a joint allied approach in Siberia. Japan wanted no such harmonization. France's attitude to the Siberian adventure, although more closely akin to the British, nevertheless insisted upon France having a dominant position. She had a colonial battalion in Siberia as well as a Military Mission under the leadership of the thus far absent General Maurice Janin. The French General regarded himself as a political general, having enjoyed twenty-three years' experience in Russia which he would emphasize was fourteen years more than the favoured General Knox. This did not mean that Knox's enemies resided only in suspicious French or warring Red camps. His relations with the American General Graves were decidedly frigid, as can be judged from Graves' description of Knox:

> He spoke Russian and was personally known to many of the Tsarist officials, he was naturally autocratic and could not, if he had desired to do so, give sympathetic consideration to the aspirations of the peasant class in Russia, whom he character-ized as swine.

This was no rogue antipathy; it found general support across the American political and military spectra.

Thus the allies divided into two camps, the British and French enjoying an uneasy coalition arising from the need to resurrect the

Eastern Front, and the Japanese and their American chaperons. By 8 August, 1,000 British and 500 French had gone ashore at Vladivostok. On that day the Japanese landings began with their Twelfth Division[8] and in less than three weeks 18,000 men were put ashore. A further 6,000 Japanese troops were deployed to Manchuli to reinforce their mutual interest with their puppet, Ataman Semenov. In invoking her military agreement with China, Japan occupied the length of the Chinese Eastern Railway. Despite political differences at home, the Japanese military in Siberia were determined to seize and retain possession of the driving seat.

America was powerless to intervene. The allies had vaguely agreed to the Japanese commanding the allied force in Siberia – a point not conceded by Graves. He arrived on 2 September to join the 7,500-strong American contingent comprising the Twenty-Seventh and Thirty-First Infantry Regiment from the Philippines. These regiments were in fact peace-time cadres requiring an additional 5,000 men from the Eighth Division to bring them to their wartime establishment. Selection of these reinforcements was to be guided by the following criteria: 'The men should be strong, hardy, fit for service intended, and should represent all parts of the United States; it being desired that they should not contain a large proportion of men from the Pacific Coast States.' When to this Siberian force with such divergent interests and motives are added among others a smattering of Canadians, Italians, Poles, Serbs, and Romanians, the stage is set for a tragi-farce of monumental proportions. The only key absentee was the man to play the leading role.

Kolchak was still in Tokyo awaiting the all-clear signal that would permit him to cross the Sea of Japan to Vladivostok. He was a man without political mission and money, but with a simple desire to seek out his wife and child, believed to be living under an assumed name near Odessa. On 21 September, shortly after his return to Russia, his train left the grand Vladivostok station heading westward along the Trans-Siberian Railway. It is not known whether it was contrived, or simply fate, that placed in the Admiral's coach for this long and tedious journey the Czech military firebrand, 26-year-old Rudolf Gajda. General Gajda had more than a passing interest in securing the undivided attention of what promised to be the new Russian Messiah, not least because he had grown heartily tired and disillusioned with Kolchak's predecessors. This ambitious Czech general also nurtured an aspiration that one day he might be found a senior position in a reconstituted White Russian hierarchy. Whilst *en route* to Omsk, Gajda briefed Kolchak on the Legion's early successes in clearing the Red forces along the line of the railway from the River Volga to the Pacific. It was no mean achievement for a small foreign army to hand over on a plate to the Whites two-thirds of Siberia almost equivalent to the size of the African Continent. 'What', asked Kolchak, 'is the progress towards a unified command?' 'There is none,' replied Gajda. 'Until now, the Russian and Czech detachments have fought side by side. When the Czech troops were more numerous, the Russians were subordinated and vice versa.' Kolchak expressed his view that the lack of unity in an armed force was a great drawback and then asked Gajda what kind of power he considered appropriate to the present conditions. 'It can only be a military dictatorship,' was the blunt response. 'But dictatorship', added Kolchak, 'is military government and, in the final count, is based upon armed force; and since there is at present no armed force, how will you create this dictatorship?'

In their localized battles against the Reds, no quarter was offered or given by the Czechs. Their achievement is nevertheless a reflection rather of the lack of coordination, command, control, and communication among the Red forces than of the undoubted superior military prowess of the Czechs. In the Baikal region, for example, the railway is squeezed along the lake's precipitous southern shore passing through no less than forty tunnels driven through the rock of sheer cliffs. The Reds blew but one of these tunnels in an attempt to stem the eastward movement of a Czech army that even overran their enemy's rail-mounted ammunition supply. When the train exploded, it also removed Baikal station from the face of the earth.

That was all history as the train carrying the two leaders made its slow progress westward towards the moribund concentration of demoralized Czechs now based in the general region of Omsk and Ekaterinburg. Fleming gives four reasons for the crucial reappraisal which had seen the Czechs not only actively intervene in Russian domestic affairs but also recall Gajda's Second Division from the Far East back to the Urals. The first and most significant factor was the perceived promise of aid from the allies. It had been suggested that the Czechs were ideally situated to launch an offensive westward from the territory they had secured. Such encouragement came from the American Consul in Moscow and also the French

Ambassador, but the most plausible and consistent stimulus came from the French Liaison Officer with the First Czech Division. Major Guinet was an optimistic, self-important officer who had over-exercised his authority. When General Knox wrote in November of the state of the exhausted, dispirited, and disillusioned Czech Army he records that 'Gajda, like everyone else, blamed Major Guinet of the French Mission, who for the past four months had constantly promised immediate and ample help from the Allies.' The second reason lay in the identification of the Germans as the Czech *bête noire*, attributing to them all of the blame for the difficulties and delays. The Czechs thought 'that by striking back at the Soviets they were saving Siberia, not for the Whites from the Reds, but for the Allies from the Central Powers'. Both the two foregoing factors were based on little of significant substance, but it was the second pair which underlines the depth of the Czech miscalculation. They had assessed that the Whites would prove the best and most proficient of allies while the Red Army would prove to be of little consequence. The Germans, of course, never arrived, but of more profound importance, neither did the allies. Instead, the Czech rank and file, who cherished nothing more than to go home, were embroiled in their fledgling generals' private war against the Reds while the Whites acted for the most part as disinterested and unhelpful spectators.

So far in the fighting neither the Reds nor Whites had distinguished themselves. As so often happens, success favoured those who took the offensive – the Whites, or, more accurately, the Czechs. The Reds found themselves in a parlous situation, bogged down as they were by appalling domestic conditions. Their hastily thrown together groupings of workers and peasants were militarily unequal to the task, as was the fragile leadership which needed something rather more to win their battles than grandiose political idealism. The task of building the new Red Army fell logically to Trotsky, leaving Lenin free to establish the Soviets' vital, unified political base. Few had any illusions that feats of arms could achieve anything but a temporary state in Russia for, without a solid political foundation they would be building their new Empires on sand. The Whites were unable to capitalize on the unexpected success of the Czech forces and the defeat and disarray of the Soviets. The political vacuum throughout much of the nation's periphery continued to be dominated by autocratic tribal leaders while in the centre, at Samara and Omsk, there were separate and competing anti-Soviet Governments, both incapable of mobilizing significant popular support.

When on 8 June the Czechs entered the town of Samara, the Social Revolutionary Party that had been in hiding assumed the power base vacated by the Bolsheviks. These were men whose idealism and moral concepts were perhaps too unrealistic for the time. Some were members of the old Constituent Assembly, but most had been involuntary emigrants sent to Siberia where their radical views would not sully the equilibrium of European Russia. It was opportune that the Social Revolutionaries should strike a chord of empathy with what was an essentially Socialist Czech army. The civilians were not natural fighters, particularly against other left-wing interests, but accepting the need to fight to maintain their position they embraced the convenience of a 'shotgun wedding' with a willing, in-place surrogate Czech army.

Colonel Vladimir Kappel, a Russian officer, had been a former leader of the Czech Legion but had fallen victim to the Czech perception of the need to nationalize their leadership. Kappel departed with good grace and was now in Samara organizing a People's Army with the full support of his Czech friends. Both People's Revolutionaries and the Czechs were guilty of the same misappreciation that the allies would link up with them from Archangel and Vladivostok. This joint effort was fundamental to their plan. Had they known the real truth, that for example only 1,200 men had landed at Archangel and that the prospect of support from Vladivostok was remote, they would not have stepped out on to a fragile limb with such enthusiasm. Kappel's mixed force enjoyed some initial success. They were not to receive any co-operation from the Omsk Government who had gone so far as to attempt to poach officers from the People's Army. Kappel did gain some support from local Cossack groups and on 6 August was able to seize the old Tartar capital of Kazan. The door to Moscow, only 500 miles distant, now appeared open. An unexpected bonus was the capture from the Bolsheviks of the old imperial bullion reserves thought to be worth £100 million. Concurrently, the Social Revolutionaries pursued their political aim of reconstituting the Constituent Assembly.

The Omsk Government also began life in Social Revolutionary colours, but its liberal and appeasing attitude towards the Soviets prompted its replacement by a right-wing government. Gradually, that government fell under the control of the officer corps, thereby becoming ultra-right wing. The aims and interests of the Samara and Omsk governments therefore seemed incapable of reconciliation. When a further competing government emerged in Ekaterinburg, the Czechs encouraged the holders of these divergent interests to come together to attempt to form one united anti-Soviet government.

On 8 September a meeting of the disparate groups was convened in the neutral town of Ufa which lies between Samara and Omsk. The groups discovered that their common desire to defeat Bolshevism was insufficiently strong to form a consensus on the way forward. The arguments and disagreements were to be stemmed temporarily by the movement of Trotsky's new vitalized Red Army on its first victorious campaign. Trotsky's remedial measures were utterly ruthless yet effective. The commander and political commissar of any unit which left its position without orders were shot. On one occasion, every tenth soldier in a regiment that deserted in the face of the enemy was put before a firing squad. Such measures concentrated the minds of the Bolshevik soldiers. Kazan fell to them on 10 September, followed two days later by Simbirsk (Ulyanovsk), Lenin's birthplace. Samara would fall on 8 October. The effect of this new Soviet offensive was to strengthen the hand of right-wing interests. When a coalition, or rather a Directorate of five persons was formed claiming to be the natural successor of the former Provisional Government, it comprised two Socialists, two Conservatives and a 'liberal' general, General Boldyrev.

This all-Russian Provisional Government was a doomed, unworkable alliance, failing to be sufficiently reactionary for the officer corps or radical enough for the republicans. It lacked popular support, had no army and no machinery with which to exercise its assumed power throughout Russia. The collapse of the Samara front left the weak Directorate little option but to establish itself in Omsk, the one remaining political centre not in Bolshevik hands. By this move the Directorate became beholden to the whim and administrative support of the reactionaries. Rarely has the threat of a *coup d'état* appeared so obvious.

6

TOWARDS THE PEAK

The city of Vladivostok had undergone a complete transformation during Kolchak's year of absence from Russia. It had never been a highly populous city, having perhaps 100,000 inhabitants prior to the Revolution. Now, that population had doubled, having within these ranks an extremely diverse range of people. The saddest grouping among this cocktail of humanity; cutthroats, robbers, speculators and refugees, were the remnants of the old nobility.

They had travelled from the west in search of the security they believed existed in this the remaining bastion of the old order. What they found, however, was an evil, lawless, and squalid port city. Their luxuries and rich trappings were gone and now they subsisted among the rest of the half-starved population living in condemned railway carriages or festering hovels. It was the men who most felt the wretchedness and degradation of their new circumstances. A number of contemporary observers noted how much more resilient the womenfolk appeared. They always seemed capable of rising to the occasion, to put on a brave, but invariably painted face. Ever fashion conscious, they sought out or hand made bright clothes using whatever material was available. Colourful curtains were much in demand. Many were the Louis XV heels that skirted the ruts, mud, and puddles in narrow streets flanked by tumbledown timber dwellings running off the two main thoroughfares. These two cobbled avenues were lined with buildings of quality and substance. They ran at right angles to each other along the Golden Horn's western and northern sides. Elsewhere, the wooden one-storey buildings which comprised the other accommodation in the city rose in tiers from the water's edge. They climbed the steep slopes but demand failed to carry them to the northern and western peaks whose crests were still crowned with pines.

The harbour was groaning with ships of every type. They were not bringing to the city the benefit of trade but the one-way traffic of men and *matériel* assembling for battle. The wharfs were crammed with supplies. Those used by the Japanese to receive their provisions were chaotic and remained that way until withdrawal. Close by was the flourishing brothel area. This particular quarter was so murderously dangerous that it had been dubbed by the allies 'The Bucket of Blood'. All along the waterfront there were patches of dynamic mobility as *droshki* (a type of hansom cab) dodged around the wheezing and complaining shunting engines, and sailors and soldiers in national uniforms mingled with the mix of gaily and drably attired civilians; some working, many watching.

For most of those in this by now notorious city, the strain and uncertainty attendant upon the Revolution, shortages of supplies, money, and lack of accommodation, had all conspired to bring about a return to primeval behaviour. Speculation and plotting were rife and humanity had become debased. Men continued to be exterminated for their political beliefs and others were simply killed for the price of a cup of tea. In fact murders had become so prevalent that no one now dared to leave home unarmed. Civilized law and order had broken down giving way to the law of the jungle. A visiting British army officer wrote of the situation: 'The bold and the unscrupulous overawed the better element. Everywhere was the uneasy current of fear, suspicion and evil. It was to me a new and somewhat terrifying experience.'

This, therefore, was the allied port of entry into Siberia. From this base the separate national aims branched out into quite separate national directions. It had become apparent to the non-Japanese at a very early stage that the brave nobility of the Japanese soldier as evidenced in 1904–5 was a thing of the past. The son had not emulated the conduct of the father. They found this new generation of Japanese soldiery high-handed, possessive, arbitrary, aloof, contemptuous, and supremely over-confident.

Japan was harbouring the not unreasonable doubts that those allies who had joined her in Siberia would in fact win the war in the west. Their description as the 'Germans of Asia' was common and was one of which they were proud and sought to emulate.[9] One aspect of Japanese behaviour which infuriated Lieutenant-Colonel John Ward before the Armistice was their refusal to salute allied officers. This little rankle paled into insignificance when the meticulous civil–military relations programme as seen in Manchuria in 1904–5 was compared with Siberia in 1918. 'The presence of the soldiers of the Rising Sun', wrote Ward, 'and the manners and general attitude of her officers towards the Siberian population, will, if persisted in, certainly result in changing fear to universal hate.' Ostensibly allied, albeit loosely, to the White cause, by their conduct, they were to help engender the polarization of local sympathies around the banner of the Reds. Despite his undisguised distrust, Ward was content to be placed under Japanese orders to get into action. The War Office approved the despatch of half his battalion to the Ussuri front. On 5 August when the troops took leave of their dirty, insanitary camp on the outskirts of the city they marched to the railway station of this place the Cockney soldiers had nicknamed 'Vladdy'. For some of the veterans it was all too much and their state on arrival in the city must have raised the quizzical eyebrows of civilians and allies alike. 'The four miles, over heavy, dirty roads, were covered in fair time, though many of the men became exhausted, and at the end of the march', records the 52-year-old Ward, 'I found myself carrying four rifles, while other officers carried packs in addition to their own kit.' Safely and thankfully entrained, the Middlesex departed for the Ussuri front in a dilapidated train of cattle trucks and one second-class carriage (for the officers) above which flew the Union Jack.

As ever, the Americans were able to display that knack of finding for themselves the very best in comfort, a trait which for many years has annoyed and frustrated her jealous and disadvantaged allies. The American headquarters was established in a large, roomy and elegant building that had once belonged to Kunst & Albers, a German mercantile company. This building served as both office and officers' mess. The Russians were no less generous in providing good accommodation for the GIs. 'Fortunately, for the comfort of the troops', wrote Graves, 'we were comfortably settled before the Russian and Allied representatives in Vladivostok knew what my attitude would be towards "combating bolshevism".' Even when the pressure on accommodation grew, the Americans were obdurate in their refusal to share their comforts. Graves continued:

> We would not give up the barracks we obtained when we first arrived and, in this way, we were able to comply with War Department orders as to the required air space for soldiers, although at times it became embarrassing to justify the need of twice the air space considered necessary for a Japanese or Russian soldier.

The Twenty-Fifth Middlesex passed through their Ussuri experience totally unscathed. Ward ignored his Mission's orders to remain on the defensive and side-stepped the intention of Lieutenant-General Oi, commanding the Twelfth Japanese Division, that the British should play only a minor supporting role. The British CO wanted action and cobbled together an *ad hoc* force with Cossacks and the remnants of a Czech battalion that had been fighting in the region. The main shortcoming of this rag-bag little army was the absence of direct support artillery. A signal for assistance was transmitted to Commodore Payne RN at Vladivostok. Immediately the artificers of HMS *Suffolk* were put to work. In a matter of days the *Suffolk*'s own armoured train under command of Captain Bath, Royal Marines, set off for the front. Its armaments included two 12-pounder naval guns and two machine guns.

The jousting of armoured trains along the confines of the Trans-Siberian Railway was a bizarre though frequent feature of the campaign. The Bolsheviks had used the rail workshops under their control to custom build substantial rail-borne armoured 'battleships'. What these machines of war lacked initially was the professional skill of the gunner, so that when they duelled with the British sailors they were invariably defeated. On the other side of Siberia, near to Omsk, the Czechs were using to good effect an alternative to the 'battleship', the more discreet but no less effective 'Q ship'. These were trains comprising protected and disguised common rail trucks bristling with machine-guns. When these ostensibly harmless trains pulled into the stations *en route* to the east, the resident Bolsheviks were overwhelmed and overthrown.

The British were appalled at the display of brutality inflicted by the Bolsheviks on their Czech prisoners. Horrific photographs of the remains of disfigured, dismembered and tortured Czech soldiers circulated among the allies. The anti-Bolshevik resolve of the Czechs hardened, while to simple Cockney minds the unmistakable message as to the desirability of not getting caught needed no further emphasis. Throughout the short Ussuri campaign, however, they lived a charmed life, well exemplifying their nickname of 'Die Hards'. On one occasion the Bolsheviks prepared a massive ambush based on a stabled passenger train. The British soldiers were uncharacteristically leading the advance with the Japanese main body following on. The Tommies were allowed to pass through the ambush, fire being held until the main group of the despised Japanese was well within the killing zone. The Japanese suffered 600 casualties on the Ussuri. The joint allied action, however, was a complete success. Due also to the prodigious efforts of the Czechs, the Bolshevik threat east of the Baikal had been totally nipped in the bud. Well satisfied with their achievements, the British settled down to guard the railway and take to their quarters for the winter.

Kolchak arrived in Omsk on 13 October, four days after the Directorate had settled themselves uneasily into the city. Like all other railway travellers of that time, the Admiral reached his destination along the branch line running off the main Trans-Siberian track. When the engineers responsible for the construction of the railway had arrived at the outskirts of Omsk, the town elders refused to pay the dues that would bring the rails into town. In consequence it passed by. At this time Omsk was a large, undistinguished steppe town. Before the Revolution the population numbered 100,000 but now it had swollen to half a million. Many of these additional inhabitants were soldiers occupying requisitioned quarters, but the unending stream of refugees existed in squalor. There was a haphazard mix of buildings with but few of any great substance. The notable exception created its own irony, for it was the grandest building in all of Siberia built by prisoners of war for the Trans-Siberian Railway administration. Now it was home to the *Stavka*. Between the buildings threaded unsealed roads, the dust from which would be whipped up into pedestrians' eyes by the wind. The city lay astride the little River Om at its confluence with the Irtysh, yet there were only buildings situated on the right bank. Not a structure existed across the river, just open steppe on which were pitched the circular felt tents of a Kirghiz village seemingly afloat in a sea of cotton wool. The absence of a bridge and total dependence on a ramshackle ferry meant that the left bank was completely undeveloped. The contrast of this pedestrian way of biblical life surrounded by sheep, horses, and camels could not have been more stark in comparison with the bustle, conspiracy, tension, greed, and industry on the other side of the narrow river.

The stage had now been reached in Omsk where the redemption of the Czech forces and the future of the Directorate lay in allied hands. Something had to be done. The British Government agreed to the *de facto* recognition of the new Russian Government and even drafted the enabling telegram. It was never transmitted, being overtaken by future events. Allied scope for positive intervention was limited. The Americans had always been lukewarm to the Anglo-French Eastern Front philosophy. Their landing in

Vladivostok gave great encouragement to the Czechs but soon it would be revealed that the Americans intended to help only those Czechs deployed in the Maritime Provinces. Since there were no Czechs on the Pacific coast, Graves's forces waited passively until a revised *aide-mémoire* guided them into the desired course of action. No such new directive came but the War Department did confirm that the Americans were not to operate west of Lake Baikal. In consequence the American army satisfied itself in minor duties and in monitoring Japanese activities in and around Vladivostok. They were to be politically preoccupied with Japanese intentions in Eastern Siberia and in keeping open their own quite substantial economic options and aspirations.

As late as August 1918 the Japanese had not been averse to helping save the Czechs before the onset of winter. At an allied conference the Japanese Military Commander, Otani, asked of his military colleagues: 'What would be said of the Allies in future history if, owing to Allied failure to relieve them, the Czechs were crushed?' In the event, joint action to save the Czechs was to be frustrated by the one nation everyone believed had entered the foray for that specific purpose. America knew that the Japanese would match whatever Ural initiative she took. It seemed a reasonable assumption to the United States, therefore, that she could protect the Trans-Siberian Railway and the regional economy from the Japanese if America remained east of Baikal. This logic was flawed, for among the first visitors to call on the Directorate were the Japanese offering to take over the Trans-Siberian Railway. By October, 40,000 Japanese troops were deployed along the railway as far as Chita, half of which were stationed in the town. All along a Chinese Eastern Railway that American Commissioner Stevens claims to have denied to the Japanese were stations under Japanese command and control. What the American political decision did achieve was the similar decision that no operational Japanese troops would move westward beyond Baikal.

The British and French prompted speculative allied forays from the north and south but the incontrovertible fact remained that any positive assistance would have to originate from the east. Both countries held the quite genuine but arrogant belief that they needed only to send token forces into Russia to reinvigorate the flagging Czechs and Russians. This was a serious misappreciation. The Czechs in particular resented the presence of these well-fed, well-dressed soldiers, finding their determination not to become involved in the fighting a contradiction in accepted military philosophy. An allied division at Omsk to bolster the devastated Czechs and encourage the lackadaisical Whites would have had far-reaching results. The Japanese had the capability, and it fell to the British on 16 October 1918 to discover whether they had such an intention. Tokyo was strongly encouraged to state its aims for Siberia but for the time being to push on to relieve Omsk. A week later the response came: an emphatic no. It was not a goal of Japanese foreign policy to assist in the rebuilding of a strong Russia and they had their own monopolistic economic and strategic aims to pursue in eastern Siberia. In the absence of support from Japan and America, a number of insignificant European contingents did head towards the Urals. The French found themselves included in that number, providing only a handful of soldiers as part of their Military Mission. Their French Tonkin battalion was deployed to the borders of north-western Manchuria. As early as 24 August 1918 the French Government had somewhat confusingly appointed General Janin Commander-in-Chief of all allied forces in Russia. Not only was the General without a national army but he was not to arrive in Siberia until his ship docked at Vladivostock on 16 November 1918. As for the British, the only bayonets they had on call were those of the Middlesex. The War Office's warning order stirred the men from their anticipated hibernation, ordering them into western Siberia.

On receipt of his deployment orders Ward first reported to the British Military Mission Headquarters at Vladivostok. He was informed that the manner of his movement, or, 'to worm his way to the Urals', was one of those matters to be left to him and his regimental staff. The CO needed no reminding of his regiment's move to the Ussuri where his arthritic force had been transported in cattle trucks, *teplushki*, with only tiers of planks for resting and sleeping upon. This had proved particularly galling when, on arrival at his destination he found 'a first class car retained by every little officer who commanded a dozen Cossacks'. Ward, the ultimate jingoist, had no intention of selling his country short by accepting anything but the best that was available for what in any event would be an exhausting 5,000-mile journey through a semi-hostile land. 'Your means of locomotion fixes your place in the estimation of the East, because it is visible to them while your credentials are not.'

The magnitude of the Russian disaster soon became apparent from the windows of the British carriages. For hundreds of miles these representatives of a nation undergoing the most stringent food rationing passed through millions of acres of unharvested, rotting corn. Travelling in the opposite direction came an endless stream of starving refugees stumbling along the *trakt* running parallel to the railway, their few roubles devaluing with every step they took. The labourers had left the farms, machinery was in disrepair, and the fabric of local administration had collapsed. Half-hearted local initiatives to prise the squirrelled-away surpluses from the peasants only fostered disorder which the Bolsheviks were quick to inflame. To see such pitiful hunger when all around there were plentiful foodstuffs merely in need of processing, was more than the British soldiers could bear. Individual breakfast rations were passed over to starving Siberian children whose parents recounted stories of atrocities and barbarism in the areas where they had once lived.

The train with its three massive engines steamed on, barely able to cope with the forty coaches carrying the Middlesex. The neglected machinery complained loudest as it crossed the mountain range which separates Siberia from China, but then settled gratefully into the long wide plains of Manchuria. It was planned that the regiment should stop every four days to exercise their horses, but the number of unscheduled halts became progressively more frequent as they moved deeper into Manchuria. There was evidence of some hidden hand at work out there, endeavouring to prevent the British troops from reaching their destination. When an engine's boiler burst there promised to be an indefinite delay. Ward took positive action, commandeered a replacement engine, put a soldier with a fixed bayonet on the footplate, and threatened with military arrest any station master who did not clear the regiment's way through to Harbin.

On their arrival at Harbin the British enjoyed a rapturous reception attended by the Chinese Governor, Mayor, British Consul, and the local Commander, General Pleshkov. All along the line there was a similar misconception as to the role and function of this battalion. They were not, as was widely believed, the advance guard of some wider military commitment; nor was it ever intended by their government that the soldiers should become involved in fighting. For the time being, tea and pleasantries were exchanged while competing bands played on. The rendition of the National Anthem by the Cossack band was so appalling that it caused a tittering in the ranks which threatened to give way to an all-out display of merriment. The opportune intervention of the stern regimental Sergeant Major prevented what might have been an embarrassing political *faux pas*.

Seen off on their way with a sumptuous Chinese banquet, the British entrained to continue their journey, which for days would take them through the northern Manchurian plains into a continuation of the flat lands of Mongolia. The onset of winter had become more pronounced and it had been Ward's hope while at Harbin to improve his rail accommodation. Even with the assistance of the British Consul they had been unable to find suitable and available carriages. The station master did however advise him that large stocks were held by the Japanese and Semenov at Manchuli. Manchuli was the centre of Semenov's expanding empire in Transbaikalia. The Ataman's authority had been further enhanced by a decision of General Otani to appoint Semenov as Commander-in-Chief of the Transbaikal region. Unable personally to dominate the total area, Semenov divided up his massive parish into 'killing areas' overseen by favoured, rapacious, and bloodthirsty lieutenants. None was more brutally sadistic than the pale-faced, watery-blue-eyed, red-haired Baron von Ungern-Sternberg. The Baron fed selected victims to his wolf pack, others were torn apart by horses, and to ring the change to satisfy his sadistic pleasures, some were burned alive at the stake. Such atrocities surpassed even those of Semenov, who boasted that his sleep would be impaired if he had not killed someone during the day. He too was a mass killer, having people extracted from transiting trains for execution, robbing, extorting, and demanding taxes from villagers on pain of their homes being put to the torch. Control of his stretch of the railway was exercised through his two personal armoured trains, 'The Terrible' and 'The Ataman'. The undeniable implications of such extreme measures were to drive the persecuted peasants into the ranks of the Bolshevik partisans. Later, Semenov sought to excuse such conduct when he wrote: 'It must be remembered that the abnormal circumstances in which we were working necessitated, in certain cases, the employment of measures that would not be possible under normal conditions.'

Lieutenant-Colonel John Ward MP detrained at Manchuli. He sought to purchase fresh bread, to exercise his horses and to take from Semenov, by force if necessary, more comfortable carriages in which to complete his battalion's journey. Two suitable and available carriages were found in the yard and Ward ordered their connection to his train. In the event the Japanese intervened, instructing the station authorities that such a demand was not to be complied with. The provision of 'class' carriages might indicate to the people along the way that the British were representatives of a first-class power. Ward's response was to cordon the station, refusing any movement in or out until the two earmarked carriages were coupled to his train. For a time the supposed allies, British and Japanese, faced each other on-guard staring over fixed bayonets. In another part of the station, Japanese officers ordered the Russian liaison officer attached to the British to haul down the Union Jack flying above the HQ carriage. To them, the flying of any flag in Siberia or Manchuria, other than the Rising Sun, was an insult to Japan. The Russian stood his ground until the officers, like their soldiers involved in the confrontation, eventually disappeared one at a time until the way was clear for the British to resume their journey.

At Chita the trains stopped again so that fresh bread might be procured and horses exercised. Chita was also a Semenov stronghold from which he maintained an alternate headquarters. He was thus able to stop through traffic between Omsk and Vladivostok. Such abuse brought chaos upon what was already a dilapidated railway whose workers were often on strike for higher wages to compensate for the rampant inflation that had forced up their cost of living. The cosy relationship between Semenov and his Japanese allies flourished so successfully that by October Manchuria and much of Siberia was under effective Japanese control. Chita had developed into a major trade centre of Nippon. Civil–military collusion saw to it that American goods travelled no further west while the through-running of inflated Japanese products avoided customs dues, frequently being consigned as Red Cross stores. The effect of all these unwelcome controls forced up prices everywhere, adding to the difficulty of the embryo government at Omsk. Japan's determination to destabilize Siberia was eventually achieved but those who would reap the dividend were not they but the Bolsheviks.

All this was of course of no great interest to Ward whose need at that time was simply for new engines. Faced with predictable obstruction Ward stormed off into the engine shed, ordered out engine and driver and then rode shotgun on the tender as the train took leave of the unsavoury town – Chita by name, Cheater by nature. The British arrived at Lake Baikal on a Sunday. The lake, the size of Switzerland, a country which the surrounding area closely resembled, was being lashed by a westward snow-bearing wind causing great waves to be hurled against the rocky shore. The train stopped ostensibly to take on the renowned fresh water for engine boilers and breakfast. The lake contains one-fifth of the world's supply of fresh water. Ward's intention was to spend the night alongside the lake so that in the morning he might witness the dawn.

When the train's passengers stirred it was still dark outside as they stumbled from the carriages into what was a chill morning. The storm had blown itself out. Ward was captivated by what he saw:

We could not see that welcome giver of warmth and life, but the beautiful orange and purple lake embraced half the world. From its centre shot upward huge, long yellow streamers which penetrated the darkness surrounding the stars and passed beyond into never-ending space. Gradually these streamers took a more slanting angle until they touched the highest peaks and drove the cloud lower and lower down the side of the mountains. Some of the men were as entranced as myself, while others (including officers) saw nothing but plenty of clean fresh water for the morning ablutions. We all have our several tastes even in His Majesty's Army.

After breakfast the train moved off for Irkutsk, the ancient commercial and cultural capital of Siberia, via Baikal. The evidence of surrounding destruction and the blasted station reminded those on the trains that they were passing through what had recently been a bitterly contested war zone. After leaving Baikal, the soldiers soon arrived at Irkutsk having travelled along the left bank of the Angara. Their arrival coincided with that of a detachment of Japanese soldiers escorting a group of their traders intent on establishing a major trading post in the city.

The evidence of months of Bolshevik anarchy and murder was still apparent in the lines of blackened and ruined houses, while in the market a cautious resumption of trade had begun. Since time immemorial the city had been a military town whose cadet school competed with the Greek cathedral for architectural supremacy. Ward inspected the remnants of those cadets who had been spared the massacres. Looking at their faces only, he had upset their officers by assuming they were girls. Alongside he saw soldiers of good physique but who were 'slow and stilted in movement'. But, for the civilians their love affair with the army – any army – was waning. They had been ravaged by the Reds and now found themselves suffering the insidious attention of the Whites.

Their new occupying force had broken that fundamental rule of civil–military relations during an insurgency – that of operating within the law. They committed their crimes in the name of high patriotic idealism. Those civilians found to be in possession of money or goods were labelled Bolsheviks and their assets forfeited for the common military good. Elsewhere was seen the unacceptable face of unrestrained capitalism. Military entrepreneurs aligned themselves with the army of traders spurred on by the sheer greed that would feather their nests. Freight cars exchanged hands between the military and speculator for $40,000 thereby contributing to what was now a well-defined and uncontrollable inflationary trend. A Russian officer passing through Irkutsk *en route* for Omsk recalled his feeling of the city.

> I felt that something was wrong with Irkutsk. The population was wholly lacking in loyalty or any expression of enthusiasm for the White regime. The civilians seemed to do their best to stay away from the military and, although they showed no great antagonism, their whole attitude was one of distrust.

It was therefore little wonder that in yet another effusive welcome the British troops should be so warmly greeted as 'saviours'. The Commandant asked the populace to raise their cheers for 'the only country which came to our help without conditions'. 'I wonder', thought Ward, 'how that will pan out.'

Soon after departing Irkutsk the British found that they had unmistakably entered bandit country. Small stations were protected, bridges guarded, undergrowth cleared from vulnerable points with coils of barbed wire closing off or limiting the choice of approach. At one station the forward progress of the British was obstructed by a group of armed workers under Bolshevik orders to halt the movement of the allies until their own Baikal survivors arrived to deal with the situation. Ward would have none of this nonsense, threw a cordon around the station, confiscated all the arms in the village and put the workers' leaders before a General Field Court-Martial. The locals were stunned by this rare display of positive action but equally surprised by the man's capacity to 'do good'. He ordered all the workers to assemble so that he could hear their grievances. Ward's unrestrained behaviour throughout his journey to the west was one of total involvement unlike that of Graves languishing uninvolved in the east. In quite unprecedented behaviour for a Socialist, Ward tore down the Bolshevik flag wherever it was found, insisting that the inhabitants of the towns through which he passed should fly the old Russian flag – without the crown.

While in the process of resolving the foregoing problem the special train bringing General Knox, who had grievances of his own, stopped at the station. Despite having Union Jacks painted on his train, a squad of Japanese placed General and staff under arrest. They had some notion that these were not men of the British Military Mission but German emissaries in disguise. 'I did not for a moment know whether I should die with rage or laughter', wrote Ward.

For a fortnight the Middlesex train passed through the hundreds of miles of a virgin forest broken only by occasional settlements of *izbas*, low peasant log cabins. Krasnoyarsk was an important, sprawling town on the River Yeneisei. As the train steamed slowly through the town's outskirts, huge stocks of abandoned war *matériel* in need of both major and minor repair lay abandoned, useless and rusting where it had been dumped. The journey thus far was as good a preparation as the British could have had for their arrival in western Siberia. According to Ward the state of that equipment was 'a monument to the entire absence of organisation in everything Russian'.

Developments in Omsk had already seen the British High Commissioner, Sir Charles Eliot, and General Knox arrive there on a damage control mission. Since they would need a guard, Ward was ordered to detach a company at Krasnoyarsk and proceed with the rest of his battalion to Omsk. On the last evening before their departure, the usual farewell banquet was held. What happened that night was to leave a deep impression on Ward and accounts in some respect for his future behaviour in Omsk. Assembled for dinner were all those representing the town's anti-Bolshevik interests; splendidly attired Cossack Atamen, gaudily dressed Russian generals, civilians representing town and district councils as well as those from the public organizations. The usual round of speeches were under way when Ward's eyes fell upon a dark, sombre group sitting opposite. They seemed out of place at the banquet. He discovered that they represented Social Revolutionary interests. Meanwhile, those with the desire for a party were making the most of the opportunity, voices steadily rising in competition with the best efforts of an orchestra consisting of Austrian and German prisoners of war. Suddenly, a Cossack officer stood up. He gave an order to the band. They had played but three notes in response to this direction when the banquet broke up in disorder. Cossacks and Tartars shouted their enthusiastic encouragement, the generals ordered the band to be silent and the black, sombre group stormed out of the hall in a loud and wild commotion. Ward was unable to take in the full significance of what had just happened until someone explained that the three notes he had heard formed the first bar of 'God Save the Tsar'. Such differing actions of admittedly different groups yet supposedly sharing a common cause could not have more clearly underlined the difficulties which lay ahead in uniting the disparate White groups. On 18 October 1918, the Twenty-Fifth Battalion the Middlesex Regiment arrived in Omsk.

7

COUP

By October 1918 the allied national interests had polarized into two rough groupings, with mutually exclusive aims. The activity in the east saw Americans and Japanese indulging in a battle of wits for control of the railway and the attendant economic benefits to be derived therefrom. The American motives remained essentially honourable; the same could not be said of the Japanese. The situation was summarized in a brief written by General Knox to the Canadian General Elmsley:

> In relation to the policy of Great Britain, France and Italy, America may be said to be neutral while Japan is actively hostile. The Japanese do all in their power to weaken Russia by subsidising every freebooter in the Far East and so enable them to defy the central government which the other Allies wish to strengthen. They irritate the local population beyond endurance and among the Allies they make nothing but enemies. Their opposition to the American Railway Scheme has indefinitely postponed the provision of economic assistance and so immeasurably increased the difficulties of the much tried Russian Government; Russia and the Allied cause would benefit if every Japanese were withdrawn and the Americans only were left in garrison along the railway from Vladivostok to Baikal.

The Bolsheviks derived much comfort from the division and disarray among the allies. Trotsky admitted that: 'when the Allies manage to act unanimously and to undertake a campaign against us, we shall be lost'. The Bolshevik leaders were convinced that a singleness of purpose would not occur and set about organizing and funding revolutionary cells to further destabilize those areas technically under allied control. The British and French who had originally intervened to save the Czechs and keep open the Eastern Front were therefore left to paper over the cracks in western Siberia.

The Czech army, which had been on continuous operations since May, was now a shadow of its former self. It had grown heartily tired of the Russians, who had left to the Czechs a lion's share of the fighting while many of their number were cosseted in the rear, living in rich surroundings, impeccably attired, well fed, and pampered by available and amenable ladies of their own nationality. The fact that Czech morale had evaporated appeared common knowledge although it seems not to have registered in Paris. As if to emphasize the severity of the Czech decline a regiment in Gajda's former division refused to comply with an order to entrain for the front. General Švec, the new divisional commander, committed suicide.

It was in the political arena however that the pointlessness of further Czech involvement in Siberia was unveiled. The tottering Austro-Hungarian Empire succumbed to its own decrepit weakness, opening the way for the bloodless Prague revolution of 28 October to usher in Masaryk's Czechoslovak Republic. This is what their army in Siberia had been striving all along to achieve. Now, the soldiers found themselves in the wrong place at the wrong time, unable to capitalize on the employment and land acquisition opportunities open to those living in Bohemia. The sooner they could uncouple from Siberia the better: no longer did they see anything further in Russia for which Czech lives should be put at risk.

The entire French plan for the restoration of an acceptable order in Russia hinged on the performance of the Czechs assisted by the allies. The White Russians, written off in despair, had no part to play in the French grand design. Paris played their Czech card close to their chest, claiming it to be their undiluted right to oversee and direct Czech military interests. This French myopia was fortuitous for London. The Foreign Office's Hobson's Choice of directing their interest through the White Russians left them in a strong position when the Czech fortunes evaporated, leaving Paris politically exposed. Subsequent British moves and their continuing strong support for Kolchak gave rise to increasing French suspicion and jealousy. On 12 October the French Consul in Omsk sent a signal to Janin urging him to hurry. The message had no obvious impact on speeding up the self-important General's progress which included official calls on the President of the United States and the Emperor of Japan.

Sir Charles Eliot's appearance in Omsk was at the personal direction of the Foreign Secretary, Lord Balfour. The Foreign Office's approach to the Russian situation contained more than a touch of flexibility and pragmatism. London was concerned by the disunity shown among the Whites and was inclined towards a short-term dictatorship which they believed could be led by General Alexeiev, then fighting in the south. The Directorate's emergence relegated this course of action first as a reserve then as a discarded option.

General Knox's train arrived on 21 October, three days after those of the Twenty-Fifth Middlesex. With him he brought a bilateral Anglo-French military plan which he put before the large-framed General Vassily Boldyrev, Directorate President and Supreme Commander of a month's standing. The plan had a distinctly French flavour, stating that General Janin should be appointed Commander-in-Chief of all allied and Russian forces. The combined British and French view that the Russian army was quite hopeless was reflected in the untimely requirement that the way forward was behind the Czech army. As a quid pro quo the Whites were promised arms, *matériel*, and the necessary training support. Boldyrev had little option but to agree, although neither he nor his successor paid anything other than lip-service to the Accord signed on 24 October. Under this same agreement General Knox became the Commander of the Rear Area – not an entirely satisfactory role for an arms officer whose superior would not arrive at the crumbling front for a further two months.

The theoretical handover of command of the Russian forces provided Boldyrev with a free hand with which to wrestle with the Directorate's severe political problems. The group of five arrived in Omsk to a cold and hostile welcome. No accommodation had been provided. To the Government of Russia fell the indignity of existing among a large number of assorted railway carriages drawn up in front of the *Stavka* on the Vedka siding off the branch line. Eventually, an old school house was found from which to conduct the affairs of state. Nothing was learnt in the new venue. In fact, in overmobilizing, the Directorate slavishly pursued earlier Tsarist mistakes. Knox pleaded with Boldyrev that he should reduce by up to half the 200,000 men thus far mobilized. They could then be conscripted once the equipment and instructors were in place. As a sign of good faith, the British undertook the training and equipping of 100,000 men. Boldyrev was moreover encouraged to take a firm line; to send equipment as a priority to the front line and order out of uniform officers who could not pass their medical. Boldyrev agreed, as Kerensky had done, that all this would of course be achieved in time. Knox persisted. There should be a firm policy of disarming the armed civilians along the length of the railway and any disorders should be dealt with positively. Finally, Knox stressed that wide powers should be given to the newly appointed Minister of War, Admiral Alexander Vasilevich Kolchak.

Kolchak's intention was to remain but a few days in Omsk before proceeding south to join General Alexeiev's army. At the same time he hoped the opportunity would present itself to enjoy a reunion with his wife and son. (This was not to be. Never again would he see his family. They were later moved into exile in Paris under British auspices.) Those who greeted him at the station told him of Alexeiev's death. They implored him to remain in Omsk because there was little he could now achieve in southern Russia where the army was under the capable command of General Denikin. The Admiral's rest in his carriage was interrupted by an officer representing General Boldyrev. Boldyrev was keen to enlist Kolchak's support. The recent arrival knew none of the Directorate and was known by the key groups in Omsk only by reputation. Thus far he had no alignment with any particular interest but he did bring with him the full support of the British and the grudging endorsement of the French. At this first meeting, Kolchak restated his intention of going south. He was an officer of the old school, not politically aware, even politically naïve, but he stood by his original mission of rejoining the colours. The General intervened. 'You are more needed here. I beg you to stay.' By way of tacit agreement, Kolchak had the railway car he had brought from Vladivostok put into the dormitory sidings in front of the *Stavka*.

Two days later, Kolchak was again summoned by Boldyrev and offered the posts of Naval and War Minister in the Siberian Government. In the absence of a navy, the naval portfolio was more to do with the administration of the many naval personnel scattered throughout White Russia. It was a job which appealed to the Admiral but he declined the post of War Minister. 'I beg you to accept,' pleaded Boldyrev, 'as there is no one else who enjoys a real measure of reputation and confidence.' With reluctance Kolchak agreed, expecting more power than Boldyrev at first appeared prepared to concede.

The reason the British were so fulsome in their support of Kolchak was because they saw in him a reflection of themselves – a man with British values, standards, and west European looks. *The Times*'s correspondent penned this impression: 'His swarthy, smooth shaven, aquiline features, his black hair and piercing eyes, and a long head like a Norman, make up a portrait that recalls the British quarter deck rather than his native Cossack steppe.' To the British guru of things Russian, Professor Sir Bernard Pares, there was 'something kingly' about the man. It was these very qualities in John Ward's mind which spelt hope for Russia's salvation, and is why he took upon himself the protection of the Admiral from what would be a growing band of detractors. After the banquet described in Chapter Four Ward was convinced he had set eyes upon the one man who was able to save Russia from anarchy.

Kolchak described the situation in Omsk as 'extremely tense', a condition to which his arrival had unintentionally contributed. Talk of coups and dictatorship prevailed as the only acceptable solution to replace the weak and divided Directorate. On 15 October, Boldyrev wrote in his diary: 'There is definite agitation against the government, in which detachments of the type of Krassilnikov's and other representatives of monarchy indirectly participate.' Krassilnikov was an Ataman of the lesser nobility who modelled himself on Semenov. His Cossack unit was quartered in the Agricultural Institute on the outskirts of the town. At that time the unit was in limbo, for their leader was in a form of open arrest. On the first count, he had done that which was guaranteed to excite and antagonize the heterogeneous Omsk population by singing 'God Save the Tsar' at a public banquet. More seriously, he had refused to entrain his detachment for the front. It could be said that under normal circumstances he was a man in serious trouble. But normal circumstances did not prevail in Omsk and it would fall to interests within the *Stavka* to ensure that Krassilnikov repaid his debt to their society.

The two Social Revolutionary members of the Directorate, Avxentiev and Zenzinov endeavoured to ride out the storm of animosity. They felt uncomfortable, ostracized, and isolated. Even Knox treated them as though they had come from another planet. 'He admits', wrote Boldyrev, 'of no point of contact between a general and a socialist.' Such comment would seem to support what

Graves had been saying of Knox's aloofness, but balance can be found in an assessment of the Social Revolutionaries by the nominally Socialist Colonel Ward. 'They were members of the same futile crowd of useless charlatans who by their pusillanimity had made their country a byword and the Treaty of Brest Litovsk possible.' The Social Revolutionaries wrote to their friends of the deteriorating condition. 'Monarchical circles are allowing themselves to behave in a manner which could not be tolerated in a State where all citizens should be able freely to enjoy their rights,' and, later: 'Every evening we sit and expect that they will come and arrest us. We desire one thing: that what must happen should happen quickly.' The Social Revolutionaries were not without their own political allies in Omsk. The 3,000 Czechs in the town were represented by a pair of political activists who offered to act on behalf of the Social Revolutionaries to clear Omsk in two days of 'all reactionary scoundrels'. Avxentiev and Zenzinov kept the moral high ground by declining the Czech offer of assistance because the Directorate could not 'consolidate its power with foreign bayonets'.

The crisis point over which the Directorate argued in the last week of October was that of proposed new ministerial appointments which, if endorsed, would swing the government even further to the right. On 25 October Knox took tea with Boldyrev. 'He threatened to gather a gang and overthrow us if we did not come to terms with the Siberians. "I am getting to be a Siberian myself", he joked.' The Czechs took a strong line, and through the Social Revolutionaries voiced their opposition to the inclusion of the right-wing candidates in the Siberian Government. They threatened that 'the Czech troops would leave the front' if the measures went ahead. Kolchak regarded the transparent Czech threat as an idle boast since the Czechs were known to be leaving the front of their own accord. On 29 October he personally proposed that the Directorate should be reduced to one person. Patiently, Boldyrev explained the consequences of a left-wing resignation and the 'complication with the Czechs'. The clumsy Czech attempt to interfere in Russian domestic affairs caused deep resentment among the reactionaries. The right-wing appointments went ahead and on 30 October Boldyrev recorded for the first time in his diary the observation that Kolchak had been nominated by influential military circles for the position of dictator. It is true that Kolchak was convinced of the need for a Directorate of one, but he saw that person not himself, but Boldyrev.

Kolchak soon discovered that as Minister for War he had little real power. When he remonstrated with Boldyrev against units in the rear being equipped before those at the front, he was rebuffed. It was made clear to the Admiral that he owed his position as a member of the government to one of the allies and the continuance of this situation was conditional upon his non-interference in government affairs. Kolchak resigned, but in the interests of displaying harmony to the all-important allies, was persuaded to withdraw his resignation. Both parties agreed that a cooling-off period was required and a personal visit to the front by the Minister for War would seem to satisfy that purpose.

On 4 November, Colonel Ward received a request from Preston, the British Consul at Ekaterinburg, to despatch a detachment to take part in a planned ceremonial presentation of colours to four Czech Battalions on 9 November. General Knox authorized the move and Ward prepared to depart for the Ural front with 100 men and the regimental band. Kolchak had by chance been invited to the same ceremony and, since the supply of engines was scarce, he requested that he might attach his carriage to the British train. Ward readily agreed and the train set off flying the Russian flag flanked by two Union Jacks – an event that did not pass unnoticed. Together, War Minister and British CO attended the parade and the 'usual banquet at which Admiral Kolchak delivered the first important speech since his appointment as Minister for War'. Those who might have expected him to be lavish in his praise for the achievements of the Czechs and for their great contribution to the White cause would be disappointed. It was strange that he should have allowed his vision to become clouded by the unreasonable criticism of the Czechs by Russian officers. The resentment would prove fatal. Sir Charles Eliot noted this surprising blind spot: 'I was struck by the harsh and ungrateful manner in which Kolchak spoke of the Czechoslovaks. He said they were no good and the sooner they cleared out the better.'

Kolchak and his British escort pressed on over the Urals into Europe and the Kunghur front. The positions here were held by both Czechs and Russians. 'Huge forests, all loaded with snow, covered the mountain sides, and there was a temperature quite impossible for British military operations,' reported Ward. The arrival of his battalion gave rise to much hope and optimism among the defending troops. The Czechs had waited six long months for such a promised manifestation of allied support. To the ill-fed, poorly clad Russian soldiers whose boots had long since gone and whose feet were bound in bags to protect them from the snow, the arrival of the Twenty-Fifth Middlesex was particularly cruel. They could not understand that these plump, prosperous, well-accoutred soldiers had come so far not to fight.

What happened next was inane, insensitive and inexcusable. The Middlesex band detrained in the protection of a cutting and played a medley of First World War music, including 'Colonel Bogey', to the assembled, unbelieving soldiery. The Bolsheviks responded by shelling their enemy's positions. Displaying a curious blind spot, Ward wrote with misguided humour: 'It shows an utter lack of culture among the Bolshevik officers that they could not appreciate good music after we had taken so much trouble to bring it within their reach.' The Czechs were also numbered among those whose humour had failed. After so much had been promised, they watched the Middlesex entrain, resuming their tour by withdrawing from the danger zone. Of this 'toot and scoot display', a Czech officer wrote bitterly: 'The demonstration was over, and all it had done was to supply our pessimists with ample matter for their many and none too complimentary remarks.'

It was at lunchtime at Chelyabinsk that Colonel Pichon, an officer who had been with Ward on the Ussuri, burst into the dining car carrying a bottle of champagne. With him he brought news of the Armistice. It is to be wondered whether anyone present at the time, amidst all the excited chatter and mutual congratulations, actually reflected upon the implications the Armistice held for Russia. The Czechs had by now saved themselves, and the argument for the allies to remain to form the Eastern Front had evaporated. Any further activity could only be an undisguised exercise in 'Bolshevik-bashing'. But that, of course, would only remain good so long as the three essential prerequisites for a successful Intervention remained in place. The enterprise needed to retain popular support within the sending state, within the target country and, not least, among the Interventionist forces. Democratic government was to fall under siege to the promises enshrined in the new social order of Communism in 1919. It proved to be a simple matter for agitators and propagandists within the international Socialist movement to sow the question, 'What are our boys doing in Siberia?'

According to Ward the tour of the front was unexpectedly cut short due to 'there being urgent reasons for an immediate return to Omsk'. At Petropavlovsk the returning train was halted by the station master who advised Kolchak of Boldyrev's intention to hold a conference there. Whilst waiting, Kolchak told Ward of the deteriorating situation in Omsk. Fearing that the Admiral's life might be in danger, Ward picketed the station and assigned two personal guards to protect Kolchak. At 12 noon on 16 November, Boldyrev's train pulled into the station and the Admiral went aboard. Five hours later, Kolchak called into Ward's carriage for a bite to eat. After the meal the two talked. 'In England does your Minister for War have any responsibility placed on him for the supply of clothing, equipment and for the general condition of the British Army?' Ward replied in the affirmative. 'What would you think in England if the Commander-in-Chief told the Minister for War that these matters had nothing to do with him, that he would be allowed to keep a small office with two clerks but no staff, as it was the Minister for War's name only that was of any use to the Directorate and the less he interfered with the affairs of his department the better for all concerned?' 'If I were Minister,' volunteered Ward, 'I should claim to have absolute control of my department, or resign.' 'That is what I have done,' said Kolchak bluntly. When asked what Boldyrev's response had been, he said: 'General Boldyrev is a very good man, and although he does not see everything as I wish, I think he understands the situation, and will himself ask that greater power should be given to enable me to save the new Russian army, that it may be able to resurrect the Russian State.'

At 5.30 p.m. on 17 November the Middlesex train pulled in to Omsk town station. The Admiral was quite fulsome in his thanks to his escort, to which Ward promised his 'continued help and sympathy in his patriotic attempt to revive the spirit of his people'. Two *Stavka* officers called on Kolchak while he was in his lodgings. They told him of the Directorate's declining fortunes. What was needed now, they opined, was a united power. When cross-examined as to the suggested form of this new united power and who the single head should be to lead it they said, 'You must do it.' Kolchak backed away; he was no political animal and had no general support either civil or military. In a letter to his wife he explained his reluctance to accept 'the terrifying burden of supreme power', reminding her that he was 'a fighting man, reluctant to face the burden of Statecraft'. He told his callers and the Council of Ministers of his intention to resign the War Ministry on Boldyrev's return. He still hoped to retain the Ministry that still held interest for him – the Ministry of Marine.

During the night of 17/18 November the anticipated coup came about. Krassilnikov and a group of his Cossacks swept aside the government-controlled troops supposedly guarding the Social Revolutionary group engaged in a political meeting. Avxentiev, Zenzinov and two other officers were kidnapped and taken back to the Cossacks' quarters. The news of the kidnapping spread quickly through the town. An emergency meeting of generals and politicians was convened to be held at 6 a.m. in what was the former Governor's residence. By chance, the Middlesex Regiment was accommodated in an adjoining building close to the cathedral. What must have surprised right-minded neutral observers was the calm, unquestioning acceptance of what had happened. No one was punished and in fact after a mock enquiry Krassilnikov was promoted to Colonel. It all seemed most reasonable to Kolchak: 'Since members of the Government had been subjected to some sort of arrest, and had proved unable to resist or avert it, they were consequently bound to resign their powers.'

Being acquainted with the Government's destruction, it was clear to those assembled that morning that there was a need to produce a substitute to prevent a perceived power struggle between reactionaries and the republican interests represented by the Czechs. Vinogradov, a Directorate member, resigned and, with Boldyrev still at the front, the initiative lay in the hands of the one remaining right-wing member, a lawyer named Vologodsky. The military restated their proposal that power should be held by one man. Kolchak agreed to the concept of a military dictatorship, recommending that Boldyrev was the person most suited to be dictator. Others present were not so certain and Vologodsky asked Kolchak to leave the meeting 'since we shall have to speak of you'.

Out in the streets the light of dawn revealed a picture of outward calm. Colonel Frank, Ward's Russian liaison officer, relayed the news of the coup and said, 'Russia is doomed never to rise out of her troubles.' Ward's reaction to this news was predictably positive. British machine-guns covered all the approaches to the former Governor's building while inside Ministers continued to talk and Kolchak sat alone in Vologodsky's office. Ward recalled:

> Things were now in such a state of tension that for the safety of my command I informed both the Russian and Czech authorities that I should not allow bodies of troops or citizens either to approach or collect near my cantonment; that such approach or collection would be treated as hostile and dealt

with accordingly. ... That these arrangements gave the Ministers greater confidence to proceed with their policy I have no doubt. That was one of the inevitable consequences of the preparations for our own defence, but not the inspiration of their policy, which was entirely their own, but it did steady the situation.

After a few hours had elapsed, the door to Vologodsky's office opened and Kolchak was invited to rejoin the Council of Ministers. Vologodsky informed the Admiral that it was the Council's unanimous decision to hand him all power as Supreme Ruler. 'I saw there was nothing more to say and gave my consent.' He then went to a quiet corner to draft his proclamation to the people:

> I shall not go either on the road of reaction or on the fatal road of Party partisanship. I set as my main objectives the creation of an efficient army, victory over Bolshevism and the establishment of law and order, so that the people may choose the form of government which it desires without obstruction and realise the great ideas of liberty which are now proclaimed in the whole world.

The responsible Russian desks in various Foreign Ministries had barely assessed the implications of the formation of the Czechoslovak Republic and the Armistice when news of the coup was heard. In the by now politically constipated British Foreign Office, the mood was one of seething anger and exasperation. The carefully worded telegram recognizing the Directorate was filed away, never to be transmitted. The coup had been orchestrated by members of the *Stavka* and certain right-wing ministers although Kolchak admits, 'I do not know what members of the Council of Ministers it was.' There can be no doubt, however, that Kolchak's schedule and genuinely expressed reticence to assume personally the post of dictator indicate that he had no part in the coup. In 1920, General Maurice Janin, with good reason to deflect attention away from his own role in Siberia, blamed the British for organizing the coup 'whose consequences were the ruin of Siberia'.

Janin's view was shared in other French quarters. What Britain dismissed as the coincidence of British soldiers escorting Kolchak to the front and then seemingly guarding the Council of Ministers was all beyond French belief. Janin maintained that Knox had set up the coup through two of his military agents prior to departing from Omsk to meet Janin at Vladivostok. A review of the available evidence suggests this to be unlikely. On the day Knox left Omsk, ten days before the coup took place, he telegraphed the War Office: 'Kolchak is being urged by right elements to effect a *coup d'état*. I told him that any attempt of this sort would at present be fatal.' Besides, Knox would have been aware of his political masters' intention to recognize the Directorate. This does not mean that after the coup had occurred Knox was filled with remorse.

This bloodless revolution was necessary because the Socialist Revolutionaries were intriguing to undermine the discipline of the Army, he wrote to a friend. . . . From the Allied point of view it is a matter of indifference of what complexion the Government may be, so long as it is strong and just and willing and able to defend the new Russian army from internationalists and other harmful propaganda. Kolchak is honest, patriotic and capable. He is the best man for the post in Siberia.

There were two members of Knox's Mission in Omsk when the coup took place; Colonel Nielson and Captain Steveni. It seems highly improbable that the plotters would have involved foreign representatives in an event so singularly Russian. It was not the Russian way. It was, however, a further coincidental act involving Colonel Nielson which would again cause French hackles to be raised and cause Nielson to be reprimanded. (He was subsequently exonerated.)

As chance would have it he met Kolchak leaving the *Stavka* building. The Admiral was well protected from the cold of the early evening by a heavy woollen British greatcoat on which he wore the epaulettes of a Russian admiral. Would Nielson like a lift, he asked? Believing he was off to a celebratory party, Nielson accepted the invitation, not knowing that Kolchak was on his way to make his first official call – on the French political representative in Omsk, M. Regnault. The Supreme Ruler's appearance at the French train accompanied by a British officer could have no interpretation other than collusion. The telegraph lines between Omsk and Paris, and Paris and London were busy. As a result, the British War Office warned its representatives in Russia to keep out of 'operations or movements of a political character'.

At 9 p.m. on 18 November, having taken his leave of the suspicious Regnault, Kolchak made his call on the senior British officer in Omsk, Colonel Ward. Kolchak explained what had

1 Dom Ipatiev – The Ekaterinburg house where the Tsar and his family were imprisoned and murdered. The house was dynamited in 1977. (*K Vítězné Svobodě*)

2 The Dom Ipatiev cellar room where the murder of the Tsar and his family was alleged to have taken place. (National Archives)

3 Admiral Kolchak's Imperial Russian Navy mission to the United States.
(National Archives)

4 A reason for the Intervention was to save the Czech Army.
(*K Vítězné Svobodě*)

5 Another reason for the Intervention was to keep allied stores such as these at Vladivostok from the clutches of central powers. (National Archives)

6 USS *Brooklyn* arriving in Golden Horn Bay, Vladivostok, with HMS *Suffolk* in the foreground. (*K Vítězné Svobodě*)

7 Allied commanders at Vladivostok drawn up to greet the arrival of the Twenty-Fifth Middlesex. From left to right, Commodore Payne RN, a Japanese Admiral, Admiral Knight USN, and the Commander-in-Chief Allied Forces Siberia, General Otani. (Ward)

8 General Janin.
(*K Vítězné Svobodě*)

9 Major-General Knox. (National Archives)

10 General Gajda. (*K Vítězné Svobodě*)

11 Major-General Graves
(National Archives)

12 General Otani.
(National Archives)

13 Lieutenant-Colonel John Ward (Ward)

14 General Syrovy (centre) (*K Vítězné Svobodě*)

15 Ataman Semenov
(*K Vítězné Svobodě*)

16 Admiral Kolchak at a banquet in Erkaterinburg 19 February 1919. On his left, General Janim, on his right General Gajda. Also in the picture, bottom left, General Syrovy.

17 The Bolsheviks offered little resistance to the concentrated Czech firepower.
(*K. Vítězné Svobodě*)

18 The level of sophistication varied among the Czech trains.
(*K Vítězné Svobodě*)

19 But none was more utilitarian than that representing HMS *Suffolk* mounting a naval gun, which fought from Vladivostok into European Russia ... (Baerlein)

20 ... with devastating effect (National Archives)

21 The approach to one of the strategic tunnels on the Trans-Siberian Railway along Lake Baikal. (*K Vítězné Svovodě*)

22 Baikal station after the explosion of a Bolshevik ammunition train. (Baerlein)

23 Omsk. The most substantial building in Siberia: the administrative offices of the Trans-Siberian Railway built by prisoners-of-war but later requisitioned by the Whites as the *Stavka* building. (Montandon)

24 Omsk. Admiral Kolchak outside the *Stavka* building just after being appointed Supreme Ruler. (National Archives)

25 Less grand was the busy mortuary. (Montandon)

26 Vladivostok. The 1st/9th Hampshires *en route* to joining the Middlesex at Omsk.

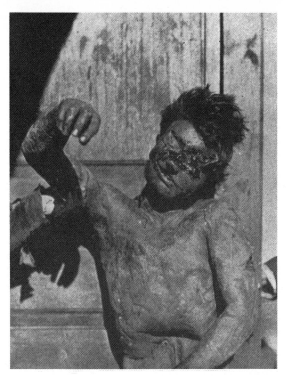

27 No quarter was offered or given in a bloody civil war. Part of this Gdansk officer's torture was to be kicked in the face with hob-nailed boots. (Grondijs)

28 The Trans-Siberian railway was the key to strategic victory. Action did not stray far from this 6,000-mile-long metal ribbon. *Little Orlik* – a Czech armoured train captured from the Bolsheviks. (*K Vítězné Svobodě*)

29 The Red Army entering Irkutsk. (Montandon)

30 The Prison at Irkutsk, with the river Ushakovka in the foreground
(*The Fate of Admiral Kolchak* by Peter Fleming, Rupert Hart Davis, 1963)

happened and why the coup had been necessary. Ward agreed that the reasons 'appeared to justify the action' but came directly to the point concerning the fate of the Social Revolutionaries because:

> if I did not press my point vigorously Avxentiev and Co. were as dead as mutton. I also knew that my countrymen have a dread of dictatorships, and that if Admiral Kolchak's assumption of power was either connected with or prompted by the execution of his opponents without trial, assistance or eventual recognition by the British Government would be made almost impossible.

The word was out that the Social Revolutionaries 'were to be quietly bayonetted in the night, as shooting would attract attention'. A solution was to be found, in sending the Social Revolutionaries into exile. To the Vladivostok-bound supply guard of the Twenty-Fifth Middlesex under command of Second-Lieutenant Cornish-Bowden were entrusted the four Social Revolutionaries. Whether the intention of the British escort was to prevent their escape or capture is not entirely clear, but according to the subaltern's report, he had heard 'all traffic between Irkutsk and Chita was stopped by order of General Semenov, and that trains were searched for the exiles after we passed, but I have no evidence to support this'. Suffice it to say that the former government men reached Manchuria safely, from whence they travelled on to Paris. For this act of clemency, the allies voiced their approval. The truth is, had it not been for Ward's intervention they would all have been killed, probably with the concurrence of Kolchak who harboured no sympathy for men whom he described as 'traitors'.

8

QUO VADIS?

The news of the Armistice was greeted by the recently liberated Czechs fighting in western Siberia with great euphoria. Pressure increased to disengage from a commitment for which they no longer cared. The coup occurred at the same time the realization dawned on these weary soldiers that their new government was content for them to remain in Siberia in order to gain favour and concessions from the allies. The allies, however, enjoyed little esteem in the eyes of a Czech army disappointed but unsurprised that a clear statement of allied policy towards Russia had not followed on from the Armistice.

The coup was in effect the straw that broke the camel's back. That it had brought to power as the Autocrat of All the Russias the distrusted and recently promoted full Admiral Kolchak appeared to be the ultimate damnation. A spontaneous assault by the Omsk Czechs on the meeting of ministers proved an impossibility, protected as they were by the machine-guns of Ward's battalion. On 21 November, the Czech National Council meeting in Ekaterinburg had to satisfy itself with a strong protest that the coup

> violated the principle of legality, which must be placed at the foundation of every state, including the Russian. We, as the representatives of the Czechoslovak troops, on whom falls the main burden of struggle with the Bolsheviks at the present time, regret that violent coups are carried out in the rear of the operating army by forces that are needed at the front.

The Czechs viewed the replacement of democracy by an autocracy as being but one step away from re-establishing the discredited monarchy. Czech negotiators made immediate contact with the surviving Social Revolutionaries but the prospect of a counter-coup was nipped in the bud by the intervention of two personalities, Generals Gajda and Janin.

A counter-coup could in all probability only have been orchestrated by the capable General Gajda. Whilst he was still a friend of Kolchak, such a possibility was remote and this may have contributed towards the former pharmacist's appointment as commander of the Siberian army. The other calming influence came from a man described by a Czech officer as 'a fat general without an army'. Nevertheless, the French General Janin was the *de facto* commander of the Czech armed forces; a fact underlined by the presence of his travelling companion, Major Štefánik, the newly appointed Czech Minister of War. On 19 November, still in Vladivostok, Janin ordered the young, one-eyed General Syrový not to intervene. 'The Czechs', cabled the Frenchman, 'were in Russia to fight the Bolsheviks and not to meddle in Russian internal affairs.' Syrový stated the Czech military case most clearly: 'The change of government has killed our soldiers. They say for four years they have been fighting for democracy and now that a dictatorship rules at Omsk they are no longer fighting for democracy.'

General Janin's credentials were impeccable. The problem was that he had arrived too late to restore either France's waning influence and prestige or to be taken seriously as Commander-in-Chief of all allied and Russian forces west of Lake Baikal. An Anglo-French declaration of 26 November 1918 sought to confirm the myth mooted some weeks previously. The original White Russian decree however, which announced Kolchak's appointment, placed the Admiral as Commander-in-Chief of 'all the Forces of the land and sea of Russia'. Herein lay a source of immediate conflict. There was no such similar sensitivity in confirming Knox as commander of the rear areas, responsible for training and supplies. Kolchak and Knox were *d'accord* as to the priority of establishing a new Russian army capable of standing on its own feet with allied support. It was for this very purpose that Knox had been sent into Siberia. He tackled the project with enthusiasm, selecting staff and preselecting centres for training. It was while in this planning stage that France, fearing a new Russia reliant upon British support, successfully interceded. Revised orders were passed to Knox from the Allied Council in Paris directing him to do nothing further until a thus far unnamed French general arrived to take command. Ward wrote:

By this uninformed Allied interference a well-thought-out scheme of army reorganization was hung up for four of the most precious months to Russia. By the time General Ganin [sic] arrived the time for the project had passed and the whole business had been taken out of Allied hands.

On 16 December 1918 Janin reported to Kolchak with his orders from the Allied Council to assume the command of allied and Russian forces in Siberia. Kolchak was furious. He was also suffering from pneumonia, and what Janin described as a 'tempestuous' interview ensued. The Frenchman had not seen the Admiral since 1916 and was amazed to see the change in him: 'there is a hollowness about his cheeks, his complexion and his eyes are feverish'. After Janin had attempted to proffer advice, an angry Kolchak brought the interview to an end with these words: 'I have no need of anything but material assistance, of boots, which I will get from the enemy if necessary.' As he took his leave, Janin was left in no doubt about Kolchak's point of view.

Had General Knox or any other Allied commander organized, paid and equipped the new Russian army he would have naturally controlled it until such time as a Russian Government could have been established strong enough to have taken over the responsibility. The French would not allow this to be done, and we ourselves undertook the duty. Having formed our own army in our own country, it is an unheard of proposal that we should be forced to place it under command of a non Russian officer. It would be derogatory to the influence and dignity of the Russian Government and lower the Government in the estimation of the people.

It was, therefore, a chastened and deflated General Janin who, thus far having enjoyed a triumphant path to Kolchak's door, now closed it, having secured very much less than he had anticipated. Janin had no option but to comply with the Admiral's wish that he replace Syrový as Kolchak's plenipotentiary. Offended and hurt, the French General took leave of Omsk on 20 December to carry out Kolchak's wishes. Little was required to convince Janin that the Czechs were a spent force. They maintained that if they were required to remain in Siberia to achieve purely political goals then their presence should be under the same conditions as those enjoyed by the Americans and Japanese. The Czechs demanded that they should be withdrawn from the front line to enjoy what they perceived to be the relative safety of rear area security duties guarding a section of the Trans-Siberian Railway. In January 1919 their wish was granted and they were withdrawn from the front and replaced by Russian troops. France's hopes of maintaining a high profile and influence evaporated with the absconding Czechs. Janin had lost his credibility, and his discomfiture and pessimism were exacerbated by the refusal of many Russians to have anything to do with him. The small staff surrounding him became progressively smaller as they responded to individual calls to demobilize. Numerical reliefs were slow in coming forward.

The newly arrived Commanding Officer of 1st/9th Hampshires was shown Janin's quarters as they passed among the dormitory collection of railway carriages drawn up in front of the *Stavka* building. He saw the General sitting inside, 'a solitary though dignified figure'. There was no capacity for sympathy, however: 'He gives no orders and takes no responsibility, is thoroughly sick of the whole business and is pining to be back in France. Also there is French jealousy of the British so he cannot even be taken into confidence as he is all for withdrawal.' The sad General attributed his failure to the existence of a British plot and became convinced that Kolchak was a British puppet and drug addict. Paris conjured up a new plan to circumvent their representative's lack of power by endeavouring to make an indirect approach to Kolchak through the means of francophile Russians. History would repeat itself for one such protégé, a General Lokhvitsky, whose troops in France had mutinied, as did the Whites entrusted to his command. Another French initiative thereby came to nought. In putting down General Janin, Kolchak unwittingly helped create some of the circumstances which would combine and lead towards his own execution.

Britain, France, and Canada unlike America, had been engaged in battle for the duration of the First World War. What is more, and unlike the Japanese, they had been involved in continuous conflict draining both their manpower and money. The implication to the fortunate survivors at the time of an Armistice ending 'the war to end all wars' was that they could return home to peace and security. It was the attendant world-wide washing hands of war which was to be a key factor in the undermining of Kolchak's position. In Churchill's opinion 'The Armistice proved to be the death-warrant of the Russian national cause.'

By comparison with the deployments in north and south Russia the commitment of British troops to Siberia was small. In Murmansk for example, the 150 marines who landed in 1918 had grown to a force of over 18,000 British soldiers. Disenchantment was evident even before the Armistice. According to General Ironside the worst unit under his command was the American 339th Regiment which hailed from Michigan. 'We have had numerous cases amongst the American officers from living with women to selling the men's rations and embezzlement of funds. There have been cases of cowardice also.' Displays of cowardice were not confined to the Americans. After what had been an encouraging start to their tour of duty the 1,650-strong French colonial contingent had, according to the British Brigadier Finlayson degenerated into a 'sullen band of strikers and shirkers, who increase the difficulties of the commander enormously.' Much worse would be seen in Odessa, where a general mutiny affected four French and Greek divisions.

The normally stolid British Tommies were not to be spared the ignominy and shame of cowardice. As rumours of peace in the west circulated the billets, fewer and fewer were prepared to risk their lives in a war for which they had neither stomach nor interest. A low category company of the Royal Scots, the British First of Foot, panicked when attacked by Bolsheviks and bolted, discarding the personal weapons impeding their escape. 'British prestige is suffering very greatly,' Finlayson wrote to Ironside, 'not only in the eyes of our friends the Poles, the Americans and the few Russians who help us, but we are descending without a doubt in the eyes of even the Bolsheviks.' A number of famous but diluted British regiments lost their names in this campaign for cowardice, including a battalion of the Royal Marines Light Infantry.

The Commanding Officer of a battalion of the Hampshire regiment was relieved of his command for refusing to take his unit on operations. This in itself would not have been so significant had he not won the Victoria Cross at Cambrai in 1917 and then permitted himself to become embroiled in a hot political debate in the *Daily Express*. The popular newspapers across the whole political spectrum were well nigh universally opposed to a continuance of the intervention in Russia. The position of the Socialist *London Daily Herald* was understandable, particularly since it became a beneficiary of Bolshevik financial support, but the militant line taken by the conservative *Daily Express* ran less to form.

Ostensibly, the British continued their presence in Russia after the Armistice only for defensive purposes. In commenting on the changed circumstances Lord Balfour, the Foreign Secretary, said:

Recent events have created obligations which last beyond the occasions which give them birth. The Czechoslovaks are our allies and we must do what we can to help them. In the south east corner of Russia in Europe, in territories adjacent to the White Sea and the Arctic Ocean, in Siberia, in Trans-Caucasia and in Trans-Caspia, new anti-Bolshevik administrations have grown up under the shelter of Allied forces for whose existence His Majesty's Government are responsible and whom they must endeavour to support.

That such support frequently involved offensive action merely served to disillusion and heighten the desire to return – to use soldier slang – to Blighty (a name derived from corrupting the Hindi word for England, *belayat*).

The 1st/9th Hampshires was an A1 category Territorial Army cyclist battalion which had been posted in 1915 to the eastern Punjab. By First World War standards the 32 officers and 945 soldiers had enjoyed a quiet, easy war. Now, in mid–1918 they eagerly anticipated an end to the European war which would trigger their return to home and demobilization. Such are the vagaries of military service that the unexpected is one of those factors which separate soldiering from more routine and mundane pursuits. The 1st/9th Hampshires were told that it was not yet their lot to return to the rolling countryside of their beloved county. Instead they were posted to Siberia. That day their humour was sorely tested. The battalion sailed from hot, humid Bombay to frozen Vladivostok. Whilst their ship was *en route*, the Armistice was declared. Some of the supremely optimistic nurtured the hope that they might be diverted homeward. On 15 December 1918, Colonel Robert Johnson entrained his battalion's main body at Vladivostok's railway station for the month-long journey to Omsk. A signal was sent from General Otani's headquarters to Omsk to enquire whether the mission of the Hampshires was in any way concerned with the removal of Semenov. Although Kolchak would dearly have loved that to have been the case, it was not. Instead of easing the Japanese mind with a straightforward denial, a non-committal answer was relayed instead.

Johnson, a former civil servant and President of the Oxford Union, broke his journey at Chita to celebrate Christmas with his battalion. His presence gave rise to intense local speculation. Following church parade, and while his regimental cooks prepared the pheasant Christmas dinner, he fell in the battalion behind the regimental band and marched on the freebooter Semenov's house. Johnson knew little of Semenov's reputation as murderer, or the real extent of the wholesale theft of Kolchak's war supplies and general intimidation of the local inhabitants. An assassination attempt on 22 December had slightly injured Semenov who was resting in bed when the sound of approaching music could be discerned. A short while after it had stopped, Semenov's Chief of Staff entered his leader's bedroom to inform the bandit that a British Commanding Officer had arrived to see him. Robert Johnson's visiting card was handed over. Perplexed, Semenov invited Johnson to join him. At the very least he may have thought he might be arrested, but instead he received an unwarrantedly civil lecture on the need to buck up and work with Kolchak for the common good of Russia. Semenov responded with reassuring platitudes, joining Johnson in a glass of champagne while the Chief of Staff gave a long-winded address to the frozen Hampshire soldiers standing at ease outside in the street.

The 1st/9th Hampshires arrived in Omsk on 5 January 1919. It had been the intention that they would replace the Middlesex. The impact of the Armistice meant, however, that no further formed bodies of British troops could be deployed to the Siberian theatre. Instead, the British looked to their Canadian, Japanese, and American allies for manpower support. A plan to put the two British battalions under the command of the Canadian Elmsley caused Ward to demand that his battalion be returned to Vladivostok. He need not have been alarmed, for circumstances intervened to make that plan academic. In the meantime, Ward grew acquainted with Johnson, 'a great accession of strength to those who held the purely English point of view, and his battalion, recruited as it was from my home county, helped to make all our relations wonderfully cordial.'

Both battalions obeyed the letter of the law relating to defensive duties. The only British offensive action being exercised from this quarter consisted of the armoured trains of HMS *Suffolk* operating well into January 1919 along the Ufa front, 6,000 miles from base. A rueful Ward added his comment: 'The British navy fighting on the Urals was the only reminder the Russian soldier had that the Allies of his country had not entirely deserted her.'

The principal British contribution in Omsk now became the training commitment for the new Russian army. Cadres of British officers and NCOs were deployed forward for this purpose. Few of those selected spoke Russian although there was a wealth of talent available to choose from. One exception was the linguistically adept Captain Brian Horrocks. Despite this change of emphasis, the British Government still persisted in its belief that the presence of British troops was essential to bolster Russian morale when in reality their inactivity produced the opposite effect. The culprit who helped foster this erroneous impression was Robert Wilton, *The Times'* Omsk correspondent. Wilton took upon himself a fawning, personal crusade in support of Kolchak, a man he much admired. What flowed from his pen was not always the truth but pro-Interventionist propaganda aimed at redressing the antipathy seen elsewhere in Fleet Street. He reported that the key personalities were still to be found to the west of the Urals and recorded accurately that Omsk is:

only a huge overgrown village, and the Russian Government perforce is composed of local celebrities who are doing their best to grapple with a colossal task. It seems a thousand pities that the most competent brains of Russia should not be available at Omsk.... These are undoubted handicaps to Admiral Kolchak, and the wonder is that he manages so well.... Also it has been borne in upon me that Admiral Kolchak was the centre of things and that people look to him alone.

Under the heading 'Popular British Soldiers' Wilton exercised his bias by means of some economy with the truth:

The Ural front is held exclusively by Russians. The new regiments forming are required to break the Bolshevist line and sweep into Russia. Admiral Kolchak cannot do without the support of the Allies on the lines of communications. He owes much to the presence of Allied troops in the cities of Siberia. The men of the Hampshire and Middlesex battalions gaily promenade the streets of Omsk in the fiercest frost without overcoats. This does much to strengthen the confidence so essential to the success of the new Government. All Omsk is flocking to its Cathedral for the Sunday service, with Anglican rites, to the accompaniment of the Hampshires' band. The Hampshires and Middlesex men also are in great demand for the exchange of Russian and English lessons.

The same may be said of other cities where the British soldiers have taken up their abode. Tommy has made himself immensely popular. The 'sing-songs' and weekly dances

109

given by the British battalions are in great request. The conduct of our men reflects the highest credit upon them and their commanding officers. They are doing a great work for their country and Russia. I say it without reservation, could the hasty critics of intervention judge for themselves on the spot, as I have been able to do so, they would encourage a substantial increase of our contingents.

To withdraw them at the present juncture would be tantamount to a direct incitement to Bolshevism. The nascent confidence in the wise and prudent role of Admiral Kolchak would be seriously, perhaps irrevocably, compromised.

That Wilton could be party to the misleading of soldiers and politicians thousands of miles from the seat of action is understandable but a key question still remains. How did the respected High Commissioner Sir Charles Eliot and the Military Mission's General Knox permit themselves to be similarly misled? The answer is that they did not. They had another reason why the two non-combatant British battalions should remain in Omsk and it was a reason which touched upon all the other major allies – economics.

H.E. Metcalf, the man sent into Siberia in April 1918 at the head of a British economic mission, made his report to the Government in September 1918. Concurrently, a government-sponsored trading company, The Siberian Supply Company, was formed by the Board of Trade to ease the way of British consumer goods into Siberia. One of Commissioner Sir Charles Eliot's primary functions was to unravel Siberia's economic chaos. It was he who supervised the Siberian Supply Company through an expatriate entrepreneur named Leslie Urquhart. The relationship between loyalties and the economic facts of life was neatly encapsulated by the British Director of Military Operations in a letter to the Foreign Office on 13 November 1918.

Leaving aside the fact that we shall be deserting those whom we have encouraged to expect assistance against the excesses of Bolshevism, we should be in danger of losing for an unknown period the resources of Siberia, which are indispensable for reconstruction after the war. It is necessary to emphasise the importance of maintaining our hold on the resources, both from the point of view of denying them to the Bolsheviks and as a guarantee for the acknowledgment of

their financial obligations to us by whatever Russian
government ultimately assumes control.

Metcalf suggested that since such an aim was shared by all the
major allies, there was merit in co-ordinating their competing
expectations.

Britain hoped to be able to derive benefit from the undeniably
good relations which had developed with Kolchak. It was known
that he held both Eliot and Knox in high esteem. Fedoseyev, his
financial adviser, was also of indirect benefit for he was one of
Urquhart's directors. Knox saw no contradiction in supporting
friends on one hand and feathering the nest with the other. There
was, he wrote to the War Office, 'greater ultimate gain in trade and
prestige', and the presence of the Omsk troops were 'as much a
factor of trade and empire as Clive's men'. The British War Office
shared the Knox view, as did the Board of Trade and Treasury. The
Foreign Office was divided. The main stream did not have the same
opinion as the Russia Committee who saw intervention as entirely
'political and not, for our purposes, commercial. Our views and
those of the Board of Trade are fundamentally opposed on the
matter of principle, and there will be a deadlock until there is an
authoritative decision on the character and aims of our Siberian
economic policy.' Fortunately the discussion was largely irrelevant
for although aims differed, the course adopted was the same.

It had seemed quite natural that Canada, which freely joined the
mother country in the First World War, should also follow that lead
by putting a small force into Russia. The Armistice provided the
opportunity to review the Russian commitment. The Prime
Minister, Sir Robert Borden, was not only for continuance, but keen
also to reinforce. In his opinion, the troops stood-by on the west
coast should now be despatched 'to Siberia for the purposes
indicated, as well as for economic considerations which are
manifest'. After some protracted discussion his cabinet agreed.

Problems arose from two quite separate sources. A proportion of
the Siberian force comprised conscripts raised for the defence of
Canada under the Military Service Act. Now that the First World
War had ended, there was no further legality in their employment
elsewhere. The second problem was caused by a ground swell of
largely uninformed public opinion to the effect that the Russian
working classes were attempting to secure their own democracy.
They believed it to be immoral to divert the masses from their
destiny, particularly for veiled economic reasons. Some Canadian

troops were already in Murmansk and Siberia, an advance party even reaching Omsk, but their employment fell progressively under such severe restrictions that they served no useful purpose. Morale deteriorated and, bowing to public opinion, the Government withdrew the Canadian troops. The Dominion of Canada demonstrated that she had come of age. In another future war, Australian Premier Curtin would also display his nation's growing independence from empire in an argument with Churchill over a similar matter of troop deployments.

The ally most affected by the defeat of the central powers was Japan. She was forced to modify both her attitude and excesses in Russia. The immediate manifestation of this change of course was that her soldiers began saluting the officers of her victorious allies and there was a noticeable improvement in the treatment of Russians. At the outset of the First World War, Japan moved into the global markets which the warring Europeans were no longer able to service. Japanese manufacturing industry boomed. Her inability to buy from former suppliers what had now become strategic raw materials encouraged her to find and develop these resources in eastern Siberia. War's end now meant that her competitors were free to reclaim their previously established markets. Visionaries insisted Japan must be permitted the room she needed for expansion and what better place, they argued, than the frozen, sparsely populated wastes of eastern Siberia. The State Department was unconvinced. Immediately following the Armistice, Secretary Lansing presented Japan with Four Points aimed at reducing her expansionism in Manchuria and Siberia. The first point questioned the need for the large numbers of troops deployed in northern Manchuria and eastern Siberia. The second drew Japanese attention to the United States' dissatisfaction with what had developed to become a monopoly of control. The State Department also wanted its say. The third point dwelt on the need for the settlement of the vexed question of control of the railways. Finally, the Americans insisted that troops should be used to assist the Czechs and for no other purpose.

The British, who had been informed of the delivery of the Four Points, held a less ambivalent and more tolerant attitude towards their historic ally. Both the United States and Japan had the reserves of troops envied by Britain. It remained British policy to try to encourage her allies into the west Siberian vacuum. The Foreign Office grew increasingly agitated by the relative inactivity of Japan and the United States in the far east of Siberia. Every opportunity would be seized to encourage both countries to cross the artificial boundary to the west of Baikal, into the west proper, towards the Urals.

Japan's acknowledgement that the Armistice had brought new pressures to bear on her Siberian adventure saw her withdraw 50,000 men from Siberia and Manchuria. In addition, she entered with her allies into the long-awaited Railway Agreement to introduce order and efficiency to the decrepit railway system. These moves to co-ordinate allied activity, to bring order and co-ordination to military operations, ran entirely contrary to the previous Japanese aim of destabilizing the Russian regime. The desire for global control, consultation and peace were all embodied in President Wilson's Fourteen Points, the blueprint of the League of Nations. Given the unmistakable fact of this new converging trend in international relations, Japan decided that it would be politic to work with rather than against the Omsk Government.

The proposal presented to Kolchak by the two Japanese emissary generals sought to achieve for Japan what had eluded her in 1905. The Admiral was promised that Japan would deploy 'an army to Western Siberia which would crush the Bolsheviks in two months'. The price was the northern half of Sakhalin, part of Kamchatka, and control of the Chinese Eastern Railway. Kolchak, a veteran of the Russo-Japanese War and one-time prisoner of the Japanese, indignantly declined. This was not a political judgement, but Kolchak was no Lenin prepared to trade face for time as happened after Brest-Litovsk. The Admiral was a simple patriot, unable to forfeit Russian sovereign territory no matter how compelling the reason.

At eleven o'clock on the morning of 15 November 1918, the American General William S. Graves stood alongside the Canadian General Elmsley on the Vladivostok saluting dais. In front of them, smartly exchanging salutes with the marching representatives of the city's allied contingent, was the senior Interventionist officer in Vladivostok, the Japanese General Otani. Uncomfortable as he was, the American could reflect that the departure of these and the other allied forces in Russia would be imminent. 'I expected Allied troops, as well as United States troops, to be withdrawn from Siberia soon after the signing of the Armistice,' wrote Graves. Instead, 'The Armistice had absolutely no effect in Siberia.'

The Armistice effectively destroyed any lingering value that may have existed within Wilson's *aide-mémoire*. Yet the President did not act immediately to recall his troops. He found himself embroiled in an unfortunate diplomatic conundrum which served to create tensions in Washington and contribute towards the ruination of the President's health. Wilson agonized over the situation in which he found himself. His position as custodian of the moral high ground and credibility as the architect of world peace were undermined by the continuing blockade and occupation of Russia. It was unavoidable that sporadic fighting would break out between Russians and Americans[10] yet there had been no declaration of war. The United States stayed on in Russia not so much to indulge in an anti-Bolshevik crusade or even to maintain solidarity with pushy allies, but rather to frustrate Japan's territorial and economic ambitions. The time was ripe to take advantage of the loosening Japanese grip brought about by the Armistice. Economic possibilities were pursued by the War Trade Board operating under the State Department's umbrella.[11] The political importance of the continuation of the Intervention, therefore, was not lost on the Washington diplomatic corps. This significance, however, was not recognized by the War Department, operating as often as not in the opposite direction. That such a situation should come about was due largely to the United States' self-righteous military commander in Siberia, described by Acting Secretary of State Polk as 'a useless old woman'.

General William S. Graves held his country's political representatives in Siberia in almost complete contempt:

> These men had contacts with and formed friendships among the class with whom they associated, and if Russians, they were universally pro Tsarist. It is possible the men I have in mind belonged to the class of Americans who have no sympathy with the aspirations and desires of the so called submerged class, whether in Russia or in the United States.

Graves's intelligence officer, Robert L. Eichelberger, held the view that 'generally speaking our consular representatives were pro-White, anti-Red and, in most cases anti-Graves'. Graves did nothing to endear himself to the State Department's representatives in Russia. He had already demonstrated that he was not reticent in issuing threats to newspaper editors. A major *faux pas* arose soon after the overdue Railway Agreement had been promulgated and areas of responsibility confirmed.[12] Graves made a proclamation relating to the track under US control.

> Our aim is to be of real assistance to all Russians in protecting necessary traffic movements within the sectors on the railroad assigned to us to safeguard. All will be equally benefited, and all shall be treated alike by our forces irrespective of persons, nationality, religion or politics.

The State Department's policy was to deny to the Bolsheviks the railway and its immediate area. Graves believed such a policy ran contrary to his own orders to remain even handed. Such displays of military evangelism were misunderstood and soon claims were abroad that the American forces in Siberia favoured the Bolsheviks. Pro-Kolchak Russians were not slow to encourage anti-Graves propaganda upon which the American press proved eager to feed. Graves's humour was further tested by an approach from a number of Russian generals close to but not representing Kolchak, who offered to end the smear campaign for some substantial financial consideration.

These overt displays of corruption did nothing to dissuade Graves from believing that all the pro-Kolchak forces were tarred with the same brush. Knox's persistent requests that Graves should give the White forces constructive support were all firmly rejected. 'I believe it is well known,' replied the American, 'in fact it has been published, that the United States does not intend to interfere in the internal affairs of the Russians. I have consistently followed this policy.' The last direct appeal from Knox to Graves arrived in Vladivostok on 2 March 1919. From that point Knox strove actively through diplomatic channels to have his fellow general removed. He wrote:

> I wish we could see more eye to eye in matters here. The objects we wish are undoubtedly very similar but we are falling into different ruts. The policy of our Government is to support Kolchak, and I believe in that policy, for if he goes there will be chaos. I don't for a moment pretend that Kolchak is the angel Gabriel, but he has energy, patriotism and honesty and my eight years in Russia has taught me that when you get these qualities combined in one man he is a man to keep. There is widespread propaganda to the effect that your countrymen are pro-Bolshevik. I think in the interest of Allied solidarity, and of the safety of Allied detachments you should try to contradict this.

Collocated with Graves in Vladivostok were the stores and supplies – mainly of British origin – intended to be used during the war years by Imperial Russia. It was the presence of the stores here and in north Russia and the risk of their falling into the central powers' hands which had been one of the original reasons for Intervention. Graves took upon himself the task of ensuring that the Vladivostok war supplies and *matériel*, valued at a thousand million dollars (including a submarine), should go to neither party. In that manner, by denying Kolchak munitions with which to fight his war, Graves built up a lasting enmity. Kolchak wrote:

> The American troops consisting of the off-scourings of the American Army, Jewish emigrants, with a corresponding commanding staff, are only a factor of disintegration and disorders. I consider their removal from Russian territory necessary because their further presence will lead only to a final discrediting of America and to extremely serious consequences.

Harris, the rotund, bespectacled American Consul in Omsk, who had offered Kolchak his support the day following the coup, engaged himself in damage limitation. He was among many who argued that Graves wrongly assumed all the Russian leaders to be as evil as Semenov and an equally villainous character operating within the American sphere of interest named Kalmykov. The State Department believed that a journey by Graves to Omsk would be beneficially enlightening.

The opportunity presented itself when a visit to Omsk was planned for the American Ambassador to Japan, Roland S. Morris. The purpose of Morris's visit was to assess the possibility of giving American recognition to the Kolchak government. A warning order was conveyed to Graves that he should be prepared to accompany the Ambassador. The General's objection was immediate. He insisted that such a visit would 'give the impression that I had something to do with establishing the policy of the United States in Siberia.' Washington remained adamant: 'If Morris goes to Omsk, it is desired that you accompany him.' As the train neared Omsk, Morris was handed a message which he read and turned to Graves. 'Now General, you will have to support Kolchak.' Graves replied to the effect that he had been given no such instruction from the War Department. The Ambassador responded with what Graves described as 'some asperity': 'The State Department is running this, not the War Department.' 'The State Department is not running me,' retorted the indignant Graves. Harris met Morris at the railway station. The men walked up and down the platform in deep conversation. When Morris returned to the train he said to Graves: 'Harris says no one can get along with you.' In the event, Graves was not to meet Kolchak. After a cool reception he toured the environs of Omsk before returning to Vladivostok having seen nothing to change his firmly established first impressions.

As conflicting situation reports arrived in Washington, the planners found they had to choose between the State Department's optimism and Graves's pessimism. They preferred to accept the State Department's reassuring messages. This was unfortunate for despite his uncooperative attitude, Graves's reports contained elements of the truth. As allied demands for his removal escalated to presidential level, Wilson and Secretary of War Baker refused to be swayed. Among the enemies in Graves's camp was the uniquely named Director of Military Intelligence, Brigadier-General Marlborough Churchill. Fortunately, the distinguished Chief of Staff, General Peyton C. March remained Graves's loyal patron. It was he who maintained that 'the sending of a little handful of our men like our expedition was a military crime'. He further surmised with some relevance to activities in Vietnam two score years later that if Graves had succumbed to Knox's pressures to become involved, it would have taken '100,000 men to get them out alive'. The most damaging claim to come out of Russia was that the American military were pro-Bolshevik. As if to lend credence to this fear, the GIs did not return home at Intervention's end as they might have hoped. Instead, they were dispersed to Manila and Hawaii. Congresswoman Jeanette Rankin went so far as to propose that the United States should purchase land in Siberia on which to settle the discharged soldiers.

At a Siberian veterans' dinner held in November 1921, in the Commodore Hotel, New York City, an early germ of McCarthyism was seen. Both Graves and Admiral Knight were present along with sixty others. They discovered seated among themselves an unknown person. On being questioned, the interloper displayed his Justice Department badge. 'I have been ordered to be present by Washington and it is my intention to remain. I hope no one will cause any trouble.'

9

THE ISLE OF DOGS

At the time, there existed within the interested Western nations an image of the Russian situation which held all the similarities of a contemporary morality play, albeit one of considerable proportions. There was a cosy reassurance that given time, the good (the Whites) must ultimately overcome evil (the Reds). While allied means and ends consistently failed to meet, the optimists argued that in the final event right would prevail. Such imaginative yet hollow arguments sought to go some way towards excusing an allied predicament which had come to a head in January 1919. With the notable exception of the Japanese, the weary allied governments accepted the fact that they could no longer send into Siberia a fresh transfusion of reliable troops either for offensive or defensive purposes. Some would argue that perhaps this was unimportant for in this heady age of new horizons in international relations, a peace conference might be able to bring to a close Russia's long, cruel conflict. A political consensus did agree to take such a course of action which was the least unpalatable of three options introduced by Lloyd George. The allies rejected as militarily impossible a proposal to destroy the Bolsheviks by force and, as politically impractical, the imposition of a stricter blockade. Initially, France dismissed any possibility of entering into a dialogue with the Bolsheviks. There was therefore, in the planning stage, no prospect of being able to convene in Paris a separate Russian peace conference as an extension of the larger in-being Peace Conference. It seemed appropriate that the invitations to the Russian Peace Conference should be drafted by President Wilson on behalf of the 'Great Friendly Powers' who called 'upon all the Governments, parties and peoples in States and territories in question to abstain from further aggressions, hostilities and reprisals and require them to keep peace both at home and with their neighbours'. The invitation beamed out in morse code from the Eiffel Tower on 22 January 1919, setting 15 February as the time and Prinkipo Island as the place.

Prinkipo is a small island set within a group of islands in the Sea of Marmora 13 miles south of Constantinople. Its position and several hotels located in picture postcard settings could offer both accommodation and security to the delegates attending what proposed to be an early example of summitry. On 4 February, the Soviet Government signified their agreement to participate. Their acquiescence, tempting economic offers, and promises of concessions were all reminiscent of the opportunist compromise of Brest-Litovsk which had lasted all of eight months. The ill-advised invitation was destined to come to nought because the indignant White leaders, notably Kolchak and Denikin, rejected almost immediately what has sometimes been inaccurately described as the Isle of Dogs Proposal. The actual Isle of Dogs is the name given to a small island lying within the Prinkipo group. Before the First World War, thousands of pariah dogs were rounded up off the streets of Constantinople and abandoned on the barren island. It was therefore a simple choice of dog eat dog or starvation. 'To Bolshevik sympathisers the place seemed oddly chosen for a peace conference,' wrote Churchill. 'To their opponents, it seemed not altogether unsuitable.'

Ward met the convalescing Kolchak along the riverbank near to his unpretentious home. The usual bevy of close protectors was absent, although the Admiral remained under the watchful eye of the sentries posted to the rear of his house. The purpose of the meeting was to introduce Colonel Johnson, but it was not long before the question of Prinkipo arose as a point of discussion. 'We can talk and make compact with every party and Government in the different districts of Russia,' said the Admiral, 'but to compromise with Bolshevism, or shake the hand, or sit down and treat as equals the men who are outraging and murdering the Russian people – never! No decent Allied Government acquainted with the facts would ever expect it.' The truth of the matter is that the allied governments were not acquainted with the facts. They needed to be in Russia to feel and understand the depth of the hatred that existed between Whites and Reds. Kolchak's outrage and bewilderment was felt equally by the allied representatives in Russia who responded by sending signals of protest to their capital cities. 'Suddenly,' penned Knox in his telegram, 'the whole of Russia is informed by wireless that her Allies regard the brave men who are here fighting for part of civilisation as on a par with the blood-stained, Jew-led Bolsheviks.'

The timing of the allied peace initiative could not have been worse, coming as it did close to the zenith of the Whites' success. Harris informed Washington that a recent White defeat was due to the impact of the Prinkipo proposals upon morale. The impression remained that Kolchak, who allegedly had not 'slept a wink since he heard about Prinkipo', no longer enjoyed the full and unqualified support of the allies. As if to lend credence both to this view and in the implied decline in the Admiral's authority, the Canadians were withdrawn shortly after. Prinkipo had been, declared the increasingly nervous and depressed Kolchak, 'a hostile act'. On 16 February a cable arrived in Omsk from Paris. 'The conception of a meeting on Prinkipo is apparently definitely abandoned.' If Prinkipo was dead, it refused to lie down. One man who had either not heard or rather would not believe, was among the peace principle's staunchest proponents. William C. Bullitt had been one of the most vociferous of the anti-interventionists and, while still only a junior State Department official, played no small part in stalling early initiatives by the President. He was ambitious, clever, confident, and so well and richly connected in Philadelphia society that he had no need to rely upon his political salary. He ran in that mould of wealthy men who might expect the reward of some worthy ambassadorial post for services rendered to a grateful President. Indeed, he did eventually become Ambassador to Moscow although, in his full career, he failed to rise to early expectations.

Two days after Prinkipo had formally been declared to be abandoned, Wilson decided to send the impetuous Bullitt at the head of an exploratory mission to Moscow. In setting out his terms of reference, Secretary Lansing had written that the mission's aim was for 'the purpose of studying conditions, political and economic, therein for the benefit of the American commissioners pleni-potentiary to negotiate peace'. Whereas the value of the allied military commitment may not have been fully recognized at home – as demonstrated by the growth of the 'Troops out of Russia Movement' – their continuing presence in Russia was an unwelcome headache for the Bolsheviks. The undeclared war and blockade were serious and provocative thorns in the paw of their revolution. Messages from agents implored the Bolshevik hierarchy to take

Bullitt's mission seriously. They warned that failure to secure a settlement could only lead to a strengthening of the blockade and the delivery of sophisticated weaponry, such as tanks, to Kolchak and others. On 10 March, the Bullitt mission arrived to a warm welcome in Moscow. After only three days of negotiation, Bullitt had secured unbelievable concessions from Lenin. On the signature of an Armistice Moscow promised: 'All existing *de facto* governments which have been set up on the territory of the former Russian Empire and Finland to remain in full control of the territories which they occupy at the moment.' A satisfied Bullitt returned to Paris but his elders were not to be deceived by promises which appeared too good to be true. It was to be a year later that Lenin discussed his offer to give up his claim to three-quarters of Russian territory. He admitted that the treaty would have been unusually advantageous to the allies, 'and unusually unprofitable for us, which left tremendous amounts of territory to Denikin and Kolchak. We proposed the treaty with the knowledge that if peace were signed, those governments could never hold out.' The failure of the Bullitt mission signalled the end of allied peace initiatives for the time being and concentrated attention upon the arrival of spring and the escalation of military activity.

The milestone of the first 100 days of Kolchak's rule was reached at the end of February 1919. Significantly, it also marked the beginning of the last year of the Admiral's life. An analysis of this short period, claimed by many to have been the good times, merely serves to underline the acute weakness and hopelessness of the White cause. Already there were incontrovertible signs of serious failings in politics, military effort, the economy, and the leadership. Recognition of the new Kolchak regime came from the White northern command and also from Denikin, but unsurprisingly not from Semenov. Steps had also been taken behind the scenes to give Kolchak international recognition. There were among the allies those who recommended caution, for they saw in Kolchak unwelcome similarities with the Tsar. Pragmatists insisted that the Admiral needed their endorsement if he was to have any prospect of overwhelming the Bolsheviks. In London, the newly appointed Secretary of State for War, Winston Churchill, toyed with the idea of recognizing Denikin (who, according to Trotsky, was the Whites' best leader) before being persuaded to support Kolchak. Doubt and indecision prevailed so that finally, only a limited offer of recognition was ever forthcoming.

Omsk had a two-tiered political structure. The unofficial National Centre passed for what could be loosely described as an Upper Chamber or Senate. Its membership comprised right-wing monarchist officers who had the dual aim of re-establishing Russia's 1914 boundaries and destroying the Bolsheviks. The official Council of Ministers had its origins in nineteenth-century Siberia. It sought to achieve a constitutional Siberian federation which would ultimately join a democratic, federated Russia. The weakness of the Council of Ministers was its parochialism. The ministers represented a large parish but they were essentially Siberia-orientated rather than all-Russian and this further complicated the question of international recognition. At an early stage Britain was prepared to offer the Council limited recognition as the government of Siberia but not of Russia. Qualitatively the Council was unimpressive, many of the ministers using their positions to give favour or to line their pockets. Kolchak's own political disinterest allowed this damaging situation to continue unchecked. Blunt as ever, Ward said that there was not one in the government he would 'trust to manage a whelk stall'.

Key features of the Kolchak period were the continuing unsteadiness of the political structure and, more importantly, the absence of any real understanding of political reality and the need to put into practice immediate remedial measures. There are two separate American reports which illustrate this fact. They were admittedly written later in the year, but are equally relevant to Siberia in February 1919. On his first visit to Siberia, Ambassador Morris wrote:

> I had expected to find on approaching Omsk a considerable sentiment in favour of Kolchak, or at least an anti-Bolshevik sentiment. I must report, however, that the Kolchak government has failed to command the confidence of anybody in Siberia except a small discredited group of reactionaries, monarchists and former military officials.

Support for this impression is to be found in Graves's book where he quotes from an official report:

> It is estimated that on July 1 (1919), outside the office-holding and military class, the Omsk Government had less than 1% of followers. It was estimated that the Red followers were about 45%, Social Revolutionaries about 40%, with about 10% divided among other parties, giving 5% to the military, office holders and Kolchak followers.

What separated the Whites principally from the Reds was their slowness in building a firm political base. It was this factor which would largely determine why the Whites were destined to lose and the Reds destined to win. Kolchak concentrated his efforts almost exclusively in pursuit of military success. Political aspects failed to excite him as he continued to nurture a naïve belief that politics could wait. By comparison, the Bolsheviks developed their political and military advance in tandem under the competent leadership, respectively, of Lenin and Trotsky. It was the party foremost which would provide that commonality of approach, whether to workers in the cities or soldiers in the brigades. Political guidance was exercised through commissars who strove in a simple, honest but direct manner to keep their political adherents up to the mark. In assessing the importance of the party, David Footman concluded, 'it was the Party that, in moment of crisis, enabled the Reds to pull out a little more ruthlessness of effort and determination than the Whites could muster.'

The first of the major political upheavals to shake and discredit the fabric of Kolchak's regime occurred in Omsk during the night of 21 December 1918. The secret police had endeavoured to head off the trouble by rounding up the known ringleaders the night before. They compounded the problem, however, by summarily shooting their captives. When news of the deaths of the radical leaders spread a mob marched on the gaol and forcibly released a majority of the prisoners. Among these were the Social Revolutionaries of the former Constituent Assembly. The only group to be left languishing in the emptying gaol were the prisoners suffering from typhus. Those who contracted the disease were treated like lepers by both sides and invariably abandoned to die. One who would not die was a young Bolshevik lawyer, Popov, making a slow recovery in the prison's typhus ward. This young man survived to play a key role at the end of the Kolchak story. Before order could be re-established, 300 people were killed. Of these, 166 were shot following the pretence of a trial before a Field Courts Martial. Included in the death toll were the thirty-five young government soldiers who were guarding the prison when overwhelmed by the insurgents. They were executed by their own side.

What was to cause the greatest outcry of indignation was an act described by Kolchak as being 'directed personally against me in order to discredit me in the eyes of the foreigners'. Once the shooting had died down, the reluctant Social Revolutionary escapees returned to gaol and surrendered themselves to the authorities. During the night, a Captain Bartoshevski from Krassilnikov's Cossacks ordered the Social Revolutionaries to be taken from the prison to the banks of the frozen Irtysh. Fifteen were shot and their bodies dumped in the river. Such examples of high-handedness, indiscipline, and general lack of control were all unfortunate recurring features of Kolchak's 'reign'. An enquiry was convened but discovered nothing. In discussing these murders, Graves wrote: 'I doubt if history will show any country in the world during the last fifty years where murder could be committed so safely, and with less danger of punishment, than in Siberia during the regime of Admiral Kolchak.'

From time immemorial, front-line soldiers have been hard pressed to find words of endearment in favour of the general staff. In Russia, there were at least four major indigenous groups of staff, all non-combatant and all safely ensconced in the rear. None was larger than Kolchak's, which packed the *Stavka* building in Omsk. The 200 or so staff officers who had guided the allied First World War effort from their headquarters at Chantilly, did not even compare with the Admiral's personal military staff of 900 officers of whom 58 were employed on censorship duty. The rump of the general staff consisted of a further 4,000 positions occupied in the main by the corrupt and inefficient. Staff officers clung with limpet-like attachment to their desks, but their less fortunate War Ministry changed hands ten times in 14 months. In part, it had been the avoidance of active service by these officers as well as the failure of Semenov and Kalmykov to come forward to fight Russia's war which had turned the Czechs. The Russian officer corps in Siberia was of little substance, as evidenced by the numbers who entrained at Vladivostok for Omsk, yet never arrived. The almost total lack of courage and commitment spilt over into the ranks of leaderless men. In July 1919 a large detachment was deployed to Ischin but only 150 arrived at their destination. By nightfall that number had dwindled to 43. These were locked up by the hard-pressed garrison commander lest they too should feel inclined to abscond.

What focused the attention of the separate battalions of staff officers was the drawing power of Moscow. Denikin's roubles bore the picture of the Great Tsar's Bell of the capital city. It was an unashamed, barely co-ordinated race to relieve the city. Little attempt was made to co-operate between nominal allies, approaching from the north, south and east. Not long after the coup, Kolchak agitated to take some military initiative which would serve both to stamp his authority and to put into effect his anti-Bolshevik policies. Unfortunately, winter was the wrong time of the year for sensible large-scale military operations. Although his army had swelled to 120,000, it comprised in the main untrained and poorly equipped peasants seeking the customary meal ticket while their land was under snow. When Knox heard that Kolchak intended to resurrect the postponed attack on Perm he advised caution, insisting that the cold period would be better spent in training and consolidation. It had been the Czechs who had proposed attacking Perm in the Autumn of 1918 with a view to advancing to Kotlas and Viatka to link up with General Ironside. The plan was shelved when the Reds moved first. Tactically it was the plan of the logistically dyslexic, particularly so in winter. It would have made greater sense to strike in the spring to the south-west where the terrain was more populous, productive and favourable to a link-up with Denikin.

Perm was a strategic industrial town which had suffered severely while under Bolshevik occupation. On one occasion a much respected priest had been taken into the middle of the street where the temperature was 30 degrees below zero. Thereupon he was doused with water until he slowly froze to death in the centre of a block of ice. This was no isolated murder committed by the Bolsheviks, whose cruelty to the inhabitants reached new levels of torture and brutality following the attempt on Lenin's life. For an opposing army with an established civil affairs policy, with but a most elementary grasp of hearts and minds, Perm was ripe for the picking. Kolchak was not to be dissuaded from his winter offensive even though Ironside was in no position to move south to assist. The largest proportion of the available troops was in Gajda's Northern Army quartered at Ekaterinburg. Gajda was by far the best of Kolchak's generals. The staff persuaded the Admiral to allocate the confident Czech the northern sector for they feared that if he were in the south he might make an unauthorized dash to join up with Denikin. The resultant staff redundancies and implied availability for active service could not be countenanced. In the centre was General Khanzhin's Western Army located at Chelyabinsk. In the south, in the Orenburg region were Dutov's Cossacks.

On 18 December, Gajda's army advanced in atrocious weather conditions. This unexpected White initiative caught the Reds by complete surprise. On 24 December, Perm fell and much in the way of booty, weapons, equipment, and supplies were captured from the Bolsheviks who also conceded 30,000 prisoners. A jubilant, irrepressible Gajda moved on, westward out of Perm, but the combined effects of the bitter cold and the snow-blocked passes over the Urals strangled his logistics and he was forced back to winter in the town. In the south, forewarned, the Fifth Red Army occupied Ufa, seeing off Dutov's Cossacks with hardly a contest taking place.

In Perm, the prospect of some form of conflict of interest between the civilians and Whites seemed inevitable, forced as they were by the uncompromising weather to live cheek by jowl, laying claim to the same limited supply of food. The situation should have been containable but robbery, rape and murder became commonplace. Ill-disciplined Whites roamed the town, often as not on their officers' initiative. Gajda did his best to retain control, publicly stripping epaulettes from erring officers. It was not enough, for the officers continued to behave as a clique of low-grade chiefs blissfully ignorant of the importance to their tribe's survival of quantities of dedicated Indians. That this was the time for flexibility, for compromise, for an adjustment of the old social order, had also been lost on Kolchak. Invitations to a number of receptions held in the newly won town were not extended either to workers or their representatives. Perm should have become a new White bastion, but due to ignorance and neglect the town swung firmly behind the Reds.

Governments cannot rule or wage war without capital. Kolchak's short regime was bedevilled by insoluble economic problems. Prices in Omsk moved upward daily, lifted by runaway inflation. There was a flourishing black market and unashamed profiteering by those in authority. Until the Railway Agreement came into being, Semenov continued to interfere with railway traffic. Even then, the new discipline could not prevent selected goods wagons or indeed whole trains from simply disappearing. Among the effects of the hijacking and plunder of the railways was that warm clothing and boots intended for troops at the front failed to materialize. A visitor to the trenches wrote: 'The soldiers were dressed very badly, some were literally in rags. Only a few had boots, the majority were wearing bast shoes or had sacking wrapped around their feet'. The activities of entrepreneurs and the massive profits to be made from organized theft from the railway contrasted sharply with the lot of the railway workers, unpaid, angry, and prone to side with the Bolsheviks.

126

Omsk roubles were in short supply throughout Siberia, never seeming to keep pace with depreciation. There were 500 million roubles in American banks and the authorities were at first not at all keen to accede to a British request for them to be released. America had loaned the Tsarist Government $193 million and was coming increasingly to believe that the loan would fall by default. Humour still rose above this desperate situation. A story had it that the Vladivostok customs had discovered 2 million forged Omsk roubles in the luggage of a Japanese arriving from Nagasaki. Owing to the sensitivity of diplomatic relations with Japan, the Vladivostok authorities wired Omsk to report the incident and seek guidance. The reply read: 'Urgent Stop Deport Japanese subject Stop Put notes in circulation immediately'. One measure introduced to raise revenue was to have lasting social implications for Russia. On 28 September 1914, the production and sale of vodka had been forbidden by Tsar Nicholas II for good. This decree was even maintained and enforced by the Bolsheviks. Unwisely, the Omsk Government reintroduced production; a decision which would have an unwelcome effect on the efficiency of the White forces. Kolchak did still have in his possession £50 million in Imperial gold. He drew upon it rarely and then sparingly. He regarded the gold as his insurance policy to be drawn on if the allies withdrew their support. He estimated that the bullion could keep his regime afloat for three years after the allies had gone.

One day in Omsk, Gajda and Ward were idly observing the distant figure of Kolchak. 'Look at him,' said Ward, 'he is the only man who is fit to be king. Look at my hands,' he said showing them to Gajda, 'they are a workman's hands. And our King has made me a colonel. We love our King and in our country there is law and order. You must have a King or Tsar, and the man for that is Kolchak.' It was Janin who once said, 'I consider Ward to be an unenlightened man, devoid of intelligence and full, with regard to his own merit, of a confidence that is shared by none.' Perhaps Janin was right and Ward's enthusiasm was misplaced. The Frenchman never forgot that he was warned in his initial briefing that Kolchak was too neurotic ever to be a statesman. Certainly, in the Admiral's first 100 days, flaws were appearing both in his character and leadership.

Not once was a voice raised in doubt of Kolchak's honesty, nobility, loyalty, sense of duty and commitment. The subject of frequent discussion, however, is why he never seemed able to cultivate similar qualities among his own nominated subordinates.

127

Some of those were obviously beyond the pale, a law unto themselves and beyond the immediate control of Kolchak. Kalmykov in the Amur region, Semenov and Ungern von Sternberg in Transbaikalia – not to mention the Japanese – were collectively the best recruiting sergeants the Reds could have hoped for. Yet, close at hand, relatively junior officers such as Krassilnikov went their own way unchecked and unpunished. Whenever the conduct of an officer seemed to deserve severe punishment for fraud, desertion, public drunkenness, or something similar, the Admiral would excuse their misconduct saying, 'the Bolsheviks have killed enough in Russia, let us not continue to do the same in Siberia'. Good intentions are not enough for a would-be king and general. Fate had been unkind to lift this noble sailor from his provincial station, elevating him at a time when there was a need for heroes, simply because he had done his duty. Admiral Alexeiev; the Viceroy of the Far East before him, also failed as a land commander. It was Semenov who had remarked, 'we consider sailors to be on a par with civilians.' Yet, despite his narrow experience, Kolchak could have succeeded had he access to sound military advice. That he did not was of his own choosing, for the selection of his subordinates was a matter entirely in his gift. It was as though it was beyond his ability to choose the right man for the right job as surely as he was unable to command his own staff or possess the political enlightenment or mental dexterity to steer Russia into a new, modern age.

The Admiral was impressed by the vitality of youth and, like Montgomery, adopted the habit of surrounding himself with young staff officers. They brought to his headquarters the hopes of restoring a long passed age which they had barely known, whereas maturer officers would have recognized the need to discover for Russia a new formula based on compromise. The impetuosity of the young staff was shared by Kolchak, a trait which, in a head of state, can only be described as a dangerous weakness. He became prisoner to every thought that occurred to him. 'His policy', wrote Grondijs, 'pursued one inspiration after another, often changing between morning and evening of the same day.' The key appointment of Chief of Staff was handed to a young, confident, but incompetent Colonel who had happened to be sent to Omsk to act as Denikin's liaison officer. Not for the first time, a respectful Knox queried Kolchak's decision, pointing out that the newly promoted General Dimitri Lebedev did not have the experience for 'the post that requires more positive qualities'. Among those who had been overlooked was the experienced and dedicated General Mikhail Dieterichs, the former Chief of Staff of the Czech Legion. His continuing pro-Czech attitude effectively debarred him from the post. Another who would have been well suited was the steadfast and loyal 'soldier's soldier', the cavalry commander Vladimir Kappel. Although Lebedev was a virtual unknown, Kolchak told Knox with masterful illogicality that his new Chief of Staff had been appointed because 'I can be sure he will not stab me in the back.' The quality of his advice was therefore not a primary consideration. Baron Budberg, one of the survivors in the turbulent War Ministry, said of the new Chief of Staff: 'Lebedev is incompetent in military affairs and an accidental upstart; in the whole staff there is not one man with the least serious military and staff experience.'

At what stage the realization dawned on Kolchak that he had embarked on an impossible mission, is not known. The burden on this excitable, sad, and lonely man grew to intolerable proportions. In a letter written to his wife on 22 July, he confessed: 'I am surrounded by moral decay, cowardice, greed and treachery.' On hearing that his former interpreter, Fedotov White, was in Omsk after serving in the Royal Navy, he invited him to call.

> The Supreme Ruler made a strange impression on me during that hour. He seemed less highly strung than when I had seen him on the train from Sebastopol and in England on his way to America. There was, however, some sort of listlessness in his demeanour. He looked aged and different from the active, energetic man he was when I knew him in the navy in the old days. There was something fatalistic about him which I had never noticed before. He did not look to me a 'man of destiny', but rather one thoroughly tired of groping and struggling in an unfamiliar environment.

Kolchak had never been an orator, nor did he enjoy public speaking, principally because it was a skill he had never mastered. As the weeks passed he appeared less and less in public. On those occasions when he did venture out he was so engulfed in heavy security that he was unable to make that so vital contact between the leader and the led. John Silverlight suggests that the real tragedy of Kolchak's career and 'the worst disservice he ever did his countrymen was to become their ruler'. But among the most comprehensive summaries of Kolchak and his failings was one which appeared in a 1920 pamphlet *La Vérité sur Kolchak* by Albert Nachbaur.

Kolchak is spoken of as a great man who was ruined by his subordinates. But one has the subordinates that one deserves, and a chief is not a chief when he possesses a staff round which 6000 officers group themselves and vigorously decline to go to the front, since they prefer to live peaceably at Omsk. A chief is not a chief when he constitutes this pitiable Government at Omsk where one searched in vain for an honest man. A chief is not a chief when he surrounds himself with people who hide under the seats of railway carriages fleeing like M. Soukin, the Minister of Foreign Affairs who disguised himself as an American nurse, or Admiral Smirnov, the Minister of the Navy who assumed the garb of a British soldier. A chief is not a chief when he is a man physically and morally ailing, neurasthenic, a mass of nerves, striking the table, of an uncontrollable temper and without will power.

In such circumstances of adversity, isolation and high drama, with his family safely in Paris, Kolchak took a step which would represent a natural ingredient in any work of fiction. He was joined by an old flame, Anna Vasilievna Timireva who became, or perhaps resumed being, his mistress. She arrived from Vladivostok where her husband Rear-Admiral Timirev served as the senior Russian naval officer. He and Kolchak had been together in the Baltic fleet. She came from a well-known musical family, was dark-haired, attractive, and in her early thirties. It was a most discreet affair with the couple living separately. A year later, when Kolchak faced his inquisitors in captivity, they asked him directly whether Anna was his common-law wife. He replied in the negative, describing their relationship in the following terms: 'She is my good acquaintance of long standing. She lived in Omsk where she was active in my workshop for preparing underwear and distributing it to sick or wounded soldiers.'

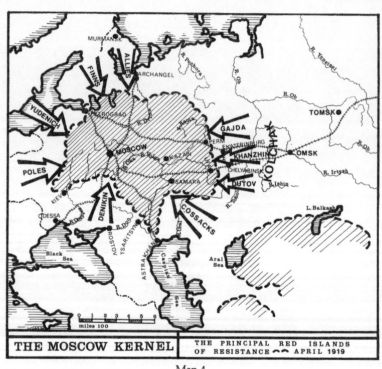

THE MOSCOW KERNEL

THE PRINCIPAL RED ISLANDS
OF RESISTANCE ∿∿ APRIL 1919

Map 4

10

DEATH WISH

The concept of forming an Anglo-Russian Brigade appealed to the moribund British battalions, for here at last was a platform from which they could give constructive support to the Whites. Kolchak's personal commitment to the scheme was met by an almost total lack of enthusiasm among his staff. It had been intended that the Anglo-Russian Brigade would consist of two regiments, each of four battalions, commanded by British officers and NCOs. The Hampshire Regiment was accordingly deployed to Ekaterinburg to provide the nucleus for the brigade. Colonel Johnson's enthusiasm provided an indication of the joy which spread through the unit, having at last secured a proper job to restore both regimental pride and sense of purpose. 'The Hampshire Russian Brigade will be dressed in British uniform, armed with British weapons and drilled in British style with British words of command,' wrote Johnson. 'We hope to march into Moscow as conquerors. Hants and Russian Hants together.'

The appointment of second in command of the Ekaterinburg NCOs' training school went to Captain Horrocks. On hearing the sound of the Hampshires' band leading the first batch of assigned recruits into the camp he went to the main gate to cast his professional eye over the new arrivals. He was appalled at what he saw, being confronted by 'the filthiest and the most unkempt mass of humanity I have ever seen in my life. Many of them were without boots or hats and nearly all were carrying the most dreadful looking bundles which contained their worthy possessions.' Obviously, the Hampshires had been consigned the dregs from the conscription depot, of whom one-third were found to be medically unsuitable.

The haughty arrogance of the Ekaterinburg bourgeoisie riled the British. They lived on an island of make-believe, leading life as it always had been: rich, pleasurable, and punctuated by banquets, visits to the opera and frequent dances. They had been much pleased by the news of the planned move of the Omsk government to Ekaterinburg, for the attendant status was only to be welcomed. Conscience, evidence of human kindness, and compassion were all missing in Ekaterinburg. Not a hand of assistance did they raise for the wounded and dying passing by the trainload through their town or congesting the floor space of their own inadequate hospital. Johnson wrote of them:

> The bourgeoisie are too cowardly to fight even though of course they know that the triumph of the Bolsheviks would mean the torture and murder of every man jack of them and every woman jack too. Really, the bourgeoisie makes one almost a Bolshevik oneself.

Initially the British rather generously attributed the obstruction they faced to the expected Russian incompetence, but soon it became clear that it was deliberate and calculated. 'We had to fight for everything we wanted,' recalls Horrocks, 'water, food, transport. They even declined to remove the refuse from the barracks until they were made to do so by force of arms.' The British infantry rose to what appeared to be an unequal challenge if only to make a point. That they and their recruits came from totally different corners of different cultural worlds very soon became apparent. The peasants just could not believe that after a route march their officers actually wanted to inspect their gnarled, twisted, lumpy feet. Again, at lights out, a perplexed orderly sergeant reported to the orderly officer that the billets were swarming with women and children. Now, such a situation was not provided for in King's Regulations, but the officers felt this Russian custom to be contrary to the spirit of those august regulations. Accordingly, the camp followers were collected together and shepherded out of the main gate, only to re-enter through the wire and barrack block windows. In the end, the British instructors compromised, insisting that all women and children were to be clear of the lines by first parade.

Slowly but surely, the brigade responded to its training, but the more efficient it became, the more it antagonized the plethora of White officers promenading the Ekaterinburg streets. A quite serious point of conflict arose over the trivial matter of paying compliments. The British, rightly or wrongly, taught their 'Russian Hants' to salute in the British manner – longest way up, shortest way down. With an extraordinary sense of timing, the White army introduced a new complicated salute, only serving to accentuate the division between the officer corps and their soldiers. The salute had originated in the Austro-Hungarian army, and was given only to members of the Imperial family. To use Horrocks's words:

> these interlopers who now strutted about in officers' uniforms
> ... used to halt our men in the streets, find fault with them for
> saluting in the British fashion and then upbraid them for
> serving under British officers. They then descended to acts of
> personal violence and hardly a day passed without some
> member of the Anglo-Russian Brigade being beaten up by
> these Russian officers.

The Anglo-Russian Brigade could not last. It could never have functioned within a Russian order of battle dependent upon Russian support. So it was disbanded and a good proportion of the men went over to the Reds, taking their kit with them. This common drift of British-trained soldiers into the ranks of the Bolsheviks left Knox open to Graves's criticism and Trotsky's observation that he had become the Reds' quartermaster. The homegoing British instructors were subjected to taunts, ridicule, and none-too-subtle hints of cowardice. Nevertheless, they had been more fortunate than some of their colleagues in Archangel who were murdered by their charges. Among those taking leave of Ekaterinburg was First World War veteran and Old Shirburnian Major Phelps Hodges.

> We were disgusted with the Russians and they with us. I think
> most of us were secretly in sympathy with the Bolsheviks,
> after our experience with the corruption and cowardice of the
> other side. It was revolting to see wounded men dragging
> their way from the station to hospital over dirty streets for
> perhaps a mile or two, while officers rode scornfully by in
> *droshkies* or motor cars.

The British Siberian honeymoon was over. In London in March 1919, the decision was taken to recall the Hampshires and Middlesex. The sympathy and desire to help a people so obviously unable and unwilling to help themselves was fast evaporating. One commentator[13] was to write of the Whites: 'Most of them, or so it seemed, were still living in the Russia of 1914, and had learned and forgotten nothing.'

March 1919 began as a frustrating month for General Knox. He had everything to do while his French equivalent, Janin, had nothing to do. Knox's supplies and promised reinforcements were simply not getting through the Semenov net; up to half those men recruited locally deserted because they were hungry and because the supply system had failed either to clothe or equip them. He was dependent upon officials and staff who were incompetent and corrupt, lacking in commitment, interest and resourcefulness. Despite these difficulties the word was abroad in Omsk that when spring came, the march on Moscow would be resumed from the positions reached in the winter offensive. Knox sat down at his desk to pen Kolchak a note outlining the logistic facts of life so that this rumoured nonsense might be nipped in the bud. 'We have spoken often of a Spring offensive. We know that there can be no Spring offensive, because we will have nothing ready. If we do not start work at once there will not be a Summer offensive either.' Kolchak's mind was made up. He was not to be swayed. The lure of Moscow proved to be irresistible. He ordered the simultaneous advance of his three armies.

Moscow would now come under severe pressure from all directions. It would not be unreasonable to permit a strategic digression to explain the significance of the Moscow Kernel. Among Clausewitz's strategic concepts was the notion of a centre of gravity. According to that strategy, the centre of gravity is the target or heart of an enemy's power which, if destroyed, will lead to victory. It was, explained Clausewitz, 'the hub of all power and movement, on which everything depends ... the point at which all our energies should be directed.' Its meaning can be extended to destroying alliances or armies but in this case it applied to Moscow, capital of Russia. Moscow is a good example of this strategic principle since she was the focus of the Russian Communication System. The outer perimeter consisted of a hardened shell which also embraced Petrograd. If the shell were to be broken and Moscow siezed, then the war might well have been won by the Whites.

Khanzhin's centre army leapt forward, sweeping aside the Fifth Red Army. So impressive was his victory that two fully equipped Bolshevik battalions, keen to be on the winning side, joined Khanzhin's forces. In the north, still with the bulk of the White forces under his command and facing the weak Red Third Army, Gajda made no move. He had become listless, disenchanted, even war weary, but fundamentally he shared Knox's view; the plan had been bad in winter and was no less bad in the spring. He pleaded for the Whites to fight a defensive war using the great natural barrier of the Urals as a cordon sanitaire to keep the Reds out of Siberia. Was not Siberia capable of feeding itself, he argued? He maintained that a denial programme would ensure that the cities would starve. Insistent messages told him to advance. He thereupon offered a new plan to send a heavily armed force, essentially an operational manoeuvre group, straight through to Moscow once a gap had been opened in the Third Army's forward defences. Patient signals ordered him to conform with Khanzhin. Meanwhile, Khanzhin had pushed on and taken Ufa on 13 March. His Cossacks massacred 670 prisoners. Now, Gajda was obliged to move to protect the exposed flank of the centre army. To him too came success against Red troops, inferior even to the barely adequate Whites deriving unexpected benefit from insurrection breaking out in the Red rear areas. At Glazov Gajda paused; tactically he had become outflanked and logistically hamstrung for all the reasons forecast by Knox. The two armies to the south lost their cohesion as well as command and control as they spread out over the 750-mile front fighting small, uncoordinated formation battles. Dutov's Cossacks attempted to regain Orenburg, both to protect Khanzhin's southern flank and also to act as a springboard to link up with Denikin's force moving northward. The town proved to be too tough a nut to crack and was bypassed, thereby preventing a link-up with Khanzhin's army. Despite this disappointment, by the end of April, Kazan and Samara on the Volga both seemed within easy reach of the Whites.

Trotsky was attending the Eighth Party Congress meeting in Moscow when the news of the serious reverses came through. He rallied the party members in the city to head eastward to plug the gaps in the defence. Insurrections were dealt with severely, feed stock burned, and dilution of the Bolshevik ethic by Social Revolutionaries subjected to intense purging. General Vatzetsis took over command of the eastern front from the dismissed General Frunze. The situation was looking bleak. Lenin told his Revolutionary Military Council, 'if we don't conquer the Urals before Winter, I think the destruction of the Revolution is inevitable.'

Kolchak's forces were now at the peak of their success. The advance in the south had taken in 250 miles, while in the north the 150-mile push was sufficient to permit a tenuous meeting between a sergeant of the Durham Light Infantry from Murmansk and elements of Gajda's forward reconnaissance. The White shop window looked impressive, but the stock room was empty; no reserves and no supplies. On the other hand, the Reds were growing in strength. Beneficial reorganization, as well as influx of dedicated and motivated reserves living off internal lines, had served to compact the Reds as a coiled spring while the Whites now found themselves fatally over-extended.

Khanzhin remained the White general showing the most initiative and promise of reaching the Volga. However, a truculent and immobile Gajda still held under his command a disproportionate number of the available men. Kolchak neglected to redeploy this uncommitted asset to reinforce success, and Khanzhin's prospects, lacking trained reserves and suffering rampant desertion, disintegrated rapidly. Meanwhile, Vatzetsis used the reorganized but unready Third Army to mesmerize Gajda and ensure he did not move any further westward while, on 14 May, he advanced a strong force from the south, along Khanzin's and Dutov's inter-army boundary. The strategy succeeded beyond Vatzetsis' dreams. The result could be compared to a string of elastic, taut to breaking point, being cut, and snapping back out of control. White formations, fearing attacks on exposed flanks, tumbled rearward, tripping over in their haste columns of peasant refugees choking the lines of communication. By early June, the evidence of the total failure of the tactically and logistically flawed spring offensive could be seen winding its way in forlorn withdrawal over the Ural passes, leaving Europe for good. Kolchak's unwise, unrecommended and premature advance on Moscow was a gamble for high stakes. In losing this battle, he would lose the war.

The Whites had failed to take that most elementary of precautions, to build successive lines of defence to contain the Reds, so that those withdrawing and the limited reserves could be reassembled for a counter stroke. The two-pronged Red advance pushed on against the lightest of opposition. As the French predicted, the axes followed the branches of the Trans-Siberian Railway, Perm–Ekaterinburg and from Ufa to Chelyabinsk. On 3 July Perm changed hands again; on 13 July the Reds eased their way through the poorly defended natural barrier of the Urals with, below them, Chelyabinsk, the next domino set to tumble. On 14 July, those of the bourgeoisie who had remained, witnessed the Red entry into Ekaterinburg.

What then of Kolchak? In a civil war which would ultimately be won by the less weak and better organized of two weak armies, Churchill insisted that:

> twenty or thirty thousand resolute, comprehending, well armed Europeans could, without any serious difficulty or loss, have made their way very swiftly along any of the great railways which converged on Moscow; and have brought to the hard ordeal of battle any force that stood against them.

Twice the number of the requisite competent Europeans were in Siberia. No longer were the Czechs in the front line but they still provided a service of sorts, protecting their stretch of the railway line from Omsk to Verkhne Udinsk. The imposition of order by a foreign army where order would otherwise not have existed, riled the more precocious of the White officers. Highly embellished reports of Czech high-handedness ensured that the short-tempered Kolchak was kept in a perpetual spin. Instead, therefore, of seeking *rapprochement*, Kolchak maintained his insensitive, execrable public slander of the only troops capable of saving White Russia. 'I shall have', said Kolchak in April, 'to disarm them forcibly. I shall place myself at the head of my troops and blood will flow.' Janin reported that on 1 May 1919:

> Kolchak embarked on another diatribe against the Czechs. Once more he vows that he will place himself at the head of his troops and that blood will flow. He says that in regard to the railway they are insolently exacting, that they demand powers that are an outrage upon Russia's dignity.

It is safe to suggest that in the absence of the implied support of the allies, notably the British and French, and the willing availability of Gajda, Kolchak would not have agreed to become the Supreme Ruler. At 7 p.m. on 21 May, the Admiral, accompanied by his ADC, called at the railway carriage which for the past 6 months had been both the home and office of John Ward. In the morning the Colonel would begin the long journey homeward. It must have been a sad and poignant meeting, for a real bond of friendship had developed between these two very different men. Ward clearly felt ill at ease for he was to write: 'If I were ruler of a State I should pray the gods to preserve me from half-hearted Allies and over-cautious friends'. A saddened Kolchak thanked Ward for his help and support. 'He said my voice, presence and influence had aroused the better elements to throw off the feeling of despair which had so universally settled upon them.' Finally, before parting, Ward asked Kolchak: 'Admiral, do you think you will carry this through?' Kolchak replied, 'I do not know, but within a year one of two things will have happened: either the Constituent Assembly will have met in Moscow or I shall be dead.'

On 12 July, Kolchak did for Gajda what Truman did for MacArthur, and sacked him. The Admiral had become weary of Gajda's harping but arguably justified criticisms of failures in command and logistics. His unwise decision to dismiss Gajda was an impulsive action, for Gajda was still receiving telegrams from civic organizations and dignitaries congratulating him on his recent appointment as Commander-in-Chief of the Siberian and Western Armies. The final meeting between the two had been a tense, highly charged, angry affair, during the course of which the Admiral broke an inkpot and a number of pencils. 'After all,' said Kolchak sneeringly, 'what else could I expect, for you have not attended the military high school.' 'And you,' replied Gajda standing his ground, 'you have commanded a few ships. Does that qualify you to govern an empire?' Gajda took his leave of Omsk in a train bristling with machine guns. He was unsure of the depths of Kolchak's vindictiveness, nor did he anticipate an uninterrupted passage through Semenov's Transbaikalia. He was a tired and sick man, brimming with hatred and set on taking revenge against his former leader.

The question of recognition of the Kolchak Government had been one of those political footballs kicked around for the first five months of 1919 without having come close to goal. Most of the footwork had been by the British although even within their team there was division. The recent Japanese reassessment of the situation found them amenable towards recognizing Kolchak, as were the French and Italians. It was Wilson who offered the sternest resistance, to such a degree that the best allied consensus that could be achieved was to give the Admiral conditional support rather than unconditional recognition. The preamble of the message sent to Kolchak on 26 May made it clear that the allies wished 'to restore peace within Russia by enabling the Russian people to resume control of their own affairs through the instrumentality of a freely elected Constituent Assembly'. The allies suggested that the Soviet Government's record to date demonstrated that such an objective could not be achieved through Moscow. The allies were therefore disposed to assist the Government of Admiral Kolchak and his associates with munitions, supplies, food and the help of such as may volunteer for their service, to establish themselves as the Government of All Russia, provided they receive from them definite guarantees that their policy has the same object in view as that of the Allied and Associated Powers.

The first condition contained as much optimism as irony for while Kolchak was in the process of reading the translation, situation reports from the front were telling of the initial and crucial White reverses. The allies required Kolchak to summon a Constituent Assembly as soon as he reached Moscow. Second, he was to permit free elections in all those territories under his control. Third, he should not permit the reintroduction of the old order. Fourth, he should recognize the independence of Finland and Poland. Fifth, if his relations with the Baltic, Transcaucasia, and Transcaspia had not been resolved, he should agree to consult with the League of Nations which, sixth, he should join. Lastly, (and for the allies importantly), he should undertake the payment of the Russian national debts repudiated by the Bolsheviks.

On 4 June, Kolchak replied. He agreed to those conditions which had no territorial significance except for that of Polish independence which he accepted. His sense of history ('history will never forgive me if I surrender what Peter the Great won') prevented him from conceding on Finland and the border states. His response in this area remained evasive. It was, however, enough to satisfy a group of allies whose support of Kolchak was now entirely proxy. On 12 June, the allies indicated that: 'They are therefore willing to extend to Admiral Kolchak and his associates the support set forth in their original letter.' The semantic difference between 'support' and 'recognition' was not lost on Kolchak, whom Sir Charles Eliot reported as being 'greatly disappointed'.

General Graves felt most strongly that: 'In my judgement, at no period of Kolchak's regime would recognition have been of service to him.' Notwithstanding Graves's personal foibles, a consignment of weapons procured from America under the terms of the 12 June agreement arrived on US transports at Vladivostok. The negotiated price was $1 million in gold. When Kolchak's agents arrived with the bullion they were informed that there would be no sale. Graves was destined to make the headlines again. As recently as April, his refusal to assist a beleaguered Japanese detachment offended not only a national sense of fair play but also caused a major rift between the United States and Japan. Graves explained his decision not to honour his Government's undertaking with the weapons in a cable to the War Department:

> The one million gold was offered to me this morning and delivery of rifles requested. On account of anti-American activities of Kolchak agents here I have refused to take the gold and have refused to give up the rifles. Mr Morris here and approved.

The allies' belated and arguably academic support was of course a bitter pill for the Omsk Government to swallow but, seen in perspective, it was rather more than they could extract from their own kind. There still remained in Siberia a significant proportion of the population who had not the slightest idea of the aims and goals of those indulging in the bloody civil war. Many, even those close to Omsk, had not heard of Kolchak and many of those who had saw him as an ogre figure, conscripting the young and confiscating stock, food supplies, and savings. Men like Krassilnikov continued unchecked in their evil ways, sending scores of their disillusioned countrymen into the relatively comforting arms of the Reds. Large numbers of troops caught up in the momentum of a haphazard retreat filtered themselves off to the left and right of their withdrawal route and out of the war. Those unwilling to face the uncertainties that lay in the festering *taiga* or swampland persevered in the drift eastward, passing through sieves of Red *agents provocateurs* seeking to divert these martial assets to the Red cause. Emissaries promised to pay 20–30 roubles a day, including food and clothing. Such a prospect proved irresistible to many of the tired, demoralized and maladministered soldiers. Some of their better officers went the same way. By June 1919, there were 27,000 former Imperial Russian officers in the Red army, not necessarily because they had been politically converted, but because the need for the fodder of everyday life became inescapable reality.

Faced with a whittling away of the White army, the ineffective Lebedev pursued a course of action guaranteed to enlarge the gaping social divide. At the end of July, Knox reported that Lebedev still

> has more influence over the Admiral than anyone else. . . . Generally speaking, Lebedev's increased power has brought about rapid turn to the extreme right, which is supported by a

handful of Lebedev's closest associates and a few hangers-on of Cossack officer type, who believe men, provided they are beaten and flogged enough, will fight for present government. Latter have learnt nothing from the revolution and are rottenest, most harmful element in country.

Gone now was Knox's enthusiasm and hope. Reports from the seat of action indicated that as many as 90 per cent of the population 'are growing more and more bitter'. Knox conveyed his conclusion to his Government: 'I am of the opinion it would be useless to send any more military assistance to Siberia.' On 7 August, a telegraphic message from the British Government to Knox signified their concurrence with the implied final washing of hands of the Kolchak initiative. 'It was hoped that some of the other Allies would see their way to give in some tangible form the support which they had promised to Admiral Kolchak in the recent Allied declaration.' With this political buckpassing, British support was transferred forthwith to General Denikin.

Vatzetsis halted his advance at the Urals to await the counter moves of reserves Kolchak did not possess. The effect of this pause was twofold. It provided a short respite for the Whites, and led to the sacking of Vatzetsis. Dieterichs, now commanding Gajda's former army, insisted that a strong defence could be built around any of the three main river lines which lay between the Urals up to and including Omsk. Lebedev counselled Kolchak against such a course of action, proposing instead that a counter stroke would have greater effect. His plan entailed permitting the Reds to take Chelyabinsk unopposed, cutting their line of communication from the west and then destroying those forces caught in the trap. The plan was far beyond the ability of the troops expected to carry it out. When the counter stroke came it was no better organized than that at Telissu.[14] It sucked in all that existed of the reserves and in consequence, when the defeat came, it was that much more emphatic. Over 15,000 men were captured. Convinced at last of Lebedev's dilettantism, Kolchak replaced him with Dieterichs. The new commander ordered all that now remained of the White army in Siberia – estimated at 50,000 – to re-form behind the first of the river obstacles, the Tobol. Their mission was to save Siberia. Dieterichs brought a calming influence to the shocked and barely organized Whites. He took the total available human resource and divided it into what can only politely be described as three armies. An orderly withdrawal was then conducted to the intermediate river line, the Ishin, where they held firm until September.

That the Reds did not advance immediately indicated both the weakness of their force in front of the Ishin and also their preoccupation with Denikin's credible threat from the south. Dieterichs accordingly launched a counter-offensive which drove the Reds more than a hundred miles back and over the Tobol. The fact remained, however, that nothing had been achieved in redressing the Whites' logistic and manning shortfalls. The balance shifted as the Whites ran out of steam and a reinforced Red army marched against them, their advance guard division averaging 26 miles a day. Indeed, so rapid was the Red advance that Kolchak's army suffered fatal disintegration. Omsk lay only 350 miles to the east of the Tobol. Dieterichs informed Kolchak that Omsk, situated as it was on the western side of the Irtysh, could not be defended with the resources at his disposal. Deep winter had not yet arrived in Siberia and the waters of the Irtysh remained unfrozen. Dieterichs argued against fighting in front of a water obstacle for it would prevent the timely evacuation of weapons and equipment if the defence ran to its expected form. The only bridge crossing the Irtysh was a railway bridge – something the artillery's horses could not negotiate. The Chief-of-Staff told Kolchak that the choice of ground was his and the recommendation was that he should put behind him any fond psychological hopes for Omsk and lay down a line of defence on the eastern bank of the river. Dieterichs was not alone in having no love or affinity for this enigmatic town. A Czech officer wrote:

> the thought kept running through my head how lonely and dreary was the stage which Kolchak had selected for his empire-building. In the midst of this treeless steppe, six foot deep with snow in winter, windbound and brown in summer, when the only break in the endless monotony is an occasional horseshoe-shaped cluster of Tartar *yurtas*, Omsk is cut off from all civilisation. This is merely accentuated by the thin steel ribbon of the Trans-Siberian.

It was at this point that General Sakharov, Dieterichs's field commander, contradicted his superior, boasting that Omsk could be defended and he was prepared to prove it. Such promises were irresistible to Kolchak. He had never had any great fondness for Dieterichs whose resignation he readily accepted before appointing

Sakharov Chief of Staff in his place. Sakharov was a man of many words and little action; he was egotistical and militarily inept. The allied High Commissioners demonstrated their confidence in his ability and chances by steaming off eastward in their well-appointed trains. Only a token allied military staff now remained in Omsk. During his final interview with Kolchak prior to moving on to Novonikolaevsk, Janin observed Kolchak's demeanour:

> He is emaciated, worn out, his eyes are haggard and he appears to be in a state of extreme nervous tension. Suddenly, he stops speaking, jerks his neck back while twisting it a little and, as he closes his eyes, becomes rigid.

On 13 November, the Reds prepared to enter the town. Sakharov could not be found and little effort was made thereafter to co-ordinate an effective defence of what had been the symbol of White power and authority in Siberia. The next day, the Red advanced guard entered Omsk relatively unopposed and, soon, after dusk, the town was theirs. The 10,000 prisoners seemingly preferred prison or a simple change of allegiance to the 1,500-mile journey to Baikal in what promised to be a bitter winter, which struck with belated vengeance on 12 November. The White denial plans had been so inadequate that the Reds took possession of forty engines and a thousand assorted railway wagons, all of which would contribute to maintaining the momentum of the advance against their enemy scurrying along rail and *trakt* towards a new haven in Irkutsk. Throughout the rest of Russia, counter-revolutionary forces were also in retreat. General Yudenich's second offensive from the Baltic against Petrograd had been finally stopped in November. His troops proved insufficient for the task. Had it been possible to offer to the Finns and Baltic States some prospect of eventual freedom or similar incentive, something more might have been achieved. Even the neutralist Swedes had found merit in providing Yudenich with troops and military assistance.

The British army withdrew from north Russia in September 1919 having been preceded by the Canadians and Americans. Ironside had never favoured being drawn into the depths of Russia and after the Armistice it became politically expedient that his casualties remained within acceptable proportions. The regular element of a demobilized army was required in Ireland and the only means of securing the additional manpower to achieve a clean break from Archangel was to re-enlist First World War veterans. The press and unions watched the British escalation of intervention in northern and southern Russia with horror as tanks, aircraft, and naval ships engaged the Bolsheviks in bloody conflict. Media and unions played a significant, collective role in forcing disengagement upon a government whose leading protagonist, Churchill, now regarded Russia with fetish-like interest. Britain and Russia were not at war, but the activities of the Royal Navy in the Baltic and Gulf of Finland touched new heights of conflict. The principal ships in a hamstrung Bolshevik fleet were sunk, including the cruiser *Oleg* and the battleships *Petropavlovsk* and *Andrei Pervozvanny*. The damage had not been all one way. The Royal Navy lost seven ships before finally withdrawing on 28 December.

Denikin reached Orel, 200 miles south of Moscow, before the overstretch and attacks in the rear areas forced him to withdraw southward. The British had backed him with the best of modern equipment. The Royal Air Force bombed Tsaritsyn, destined to suffer far greater damage at the hands of Hitler. The city was later to be known as Stalingrad. Wise political intervention stopped the Royal Air Force from going even further and bombing Moscow. The Hampshires sailed from Vladivostok on 7 September and were followed by the Middlesex on 1 November 1919. Kolchak remained in Omsk almost to the end, having sent his Ministers on in advance to re-establish the government in Irkutsk. His sense of isolation and abandonment was almost complete. His own army had all but evaporated. What remained was an increasingly politicized Czech army over which Janin and the allies were unable to exert any real influence.

11

ABANDONED

Something which really bothered the Bolsheviks was why so many of the Siberian peasants fled in terror ahead of their advance. As a measure aimed at combatting what they saw as a credibility problem, they brought into service a number of propaganda trains which arrived at the stations along the Trans-Siberian immediately following the Whites' withdrawal. Emblazoned with stirring slogans and bearing colourful pictures of heroic revolutionaries seeing off the grotesque representatives of the counter-revolutionary movement, the trains often carried a brass quartet to draw the masses to within the hearing of a political commisar.

Omsk had become a great focal point for the thousands of refugees who had abandoned both roots and belongings to escape the Reds. The residents received orders from the housing com-mission to provide shelter for the new arrivals but the town just could not cope with the massive influx. Food became in short supply, the sanitary system broke down and before very long, disease moved among the town's population. 'The dead contaminated the living,' wrote a visitor, 'and Omsk had become a city of living dead.' The most deadly of all the diseases was the lice-borne typhus. To contract the disease invariably meant abandonment, even by kith and kin. That winter, the typhus epidemic in Siberia claimed hundreds of thousands of victims, for example, 70,000 died in Novonikolaievsk and 120,000 in Tomsk. In November 1919, the eastward movement of the peasantry out of Omsk began again in earnest, prompted as much by the spread of this dreadful disease as by the approach of the Bolsheviks. Day and night, the surrounds of the station swarmed with a seething mass of packed humanity scrambling for places in eastbound trains. The majority were to be frustrated in that aim, for the railway's organization remained abysmal and matters were even further complicated by a shortage of coal and boiler timber.

Amidst all this chaos the Czechs stood out as being calm, efficient, and having all their needs provided for. Serious confrontation was only narrowly avoided as the resentment of the would-be refugees boiled over. The Czech *teplushki* were easily identifiable by their distinctive and colourful national pictures painted on the sides. Russian objections to what they saw as the misappropriation of rolling stock regarded as theirs was only part of the problem. Collectively they were angered as much by the Czech air of supreme indifference as by their own sense of utter impotence. All the Czech wagons were comfortable, filled with generous amounts of provisions and booty collected along the way. There was sufficient room to have taken out significant numbers of refugees but the Czechs refused to take Russians aboard their military trains. It was for this reason the Czechs avoided the worst effects of the typhus epidemic.

For the remainder, great lines of *teplushki*, each with a nominal capacity of forty passengers or eight horses, drew away from Omsk hugely overloaded, with people inside, huddled on roofs and even straddling the buffers. In such a manner, they took the disease with them. In more favourable weather these trains would have stopped alongside a river for the daily ablutions. The custom was for passengers to disrobe and take to the water armed with nothing more than a cake of soap. Men bathed upstream, separated from the womenfolk by a few hundred metres. Now, with the onset of deep winter, the layers of warm clothing stayed wrapped firmly around bodies, affording free range to residential lice. Despite the best efforts of ancient engines hauling protesting lines of concertina-ing, snapping, and swaying *teplushki*, little discernible impression was made on the endless queues of refugees. As news and the sound of the approaching Reds spread among the populace, family decisions had to be taken, either to go on or to remain and face the Bolsheviks. The decision to begin the long journey, either on foot or on the local rough-coated ponies was as often as not fatal. Those fortunate enough to secure places in the *teplushki* passed slowly by streams of refugees plodding forlornly along the adjoining *trakt*. There were grim-looking family groups – from grandparents to shoeless toddlers – their rickety carts carrying worldly possessions such as mattresses and kitchen paraphernalia. Occasionally there would be a bony cow or small parties of defeated, dejected soldiers. The sight made a lasting impression on a Czech officer:

> Frightful were the scenes as all those hundreds of thousands of refugees who had put their homes behind them and fled to Omsk for shelter now found that they must flee again, out into the frozen wastes with no destination, no place to lay their heads.

It is estimated that 500,000 perished along the way.

Rioting by soldiers' families in Prague and the threat of general mutiny resulted in the order being given on 29 September 1919 for the Czech army in Siberia to resume its journey to Vladivostok. General Syrový, the Commander-in-Chief, rejected overtures to give military assistance to Kolchak, whom he regarded as a doomed man. The Czechs were even more despised by the Russians than Kolchak, and it was no wish of Syrový to prejudice his own soldiers' prospects of getting out of Siberia alive. Grondijs wrote:

> The relative position of the (White) Russians and the Czechs resembled those of two shipwrecked sailors clinging to a plank which can only support one man. The stronger would survive and the other would be drowned if he stuggled too hard.

Ten thousand Czechs were held back in the west as a Czech rearguard from which, as a concession, one company was nominated as Kolchak's personal bodyguard.

The Admiral's decision to be among the last to take leave of Omsk again demonstrated his political fallibility. He had failed to recognize the differing responsibilities between those of a captain of a sinking ship and a head of government. His ministers, who departed four days ahead of him, made good progress, arriving in Irkutsk nine days after setting off. Now, in front of the Admiral were lines blocked by escapees travelling in decrepit trains prone to breakdown, liable to attack by marauding bandits or to suffer delays imposed by truculent railmen who had not been paid for three months. The only possible hope of achieving the physical and political survival of the Kolchak regime lay in its leader reaching Irkutsk as quickly as possible. In the event, what proved to be a horrendous journey took two months, the Admiral not arriving until 15 January 1920.

The situation which Kolchak's ministers found at Irkutsk could not have been less propitious. Uprisings spread along the length of the railway where a coalition of Social Revolutionaries and Mensheviks held the upper hand. It was this grouping which maintained the close political affinity which existed with the Czechs, who were still under a theoretical remit not to dabble in Russian internal affairs. On 16 November, under the signature of their leader, V. Girsa, the Czech political representatives in Irkutsk sent to the allied representatives an anti-Kolchak memorandum which, in part, declared:

> The burning of villages, the murder of peaceable Russian inhabitants by the hundreds, and the shooting without reason of democratic men solely because they are suspected of holding political views are daily facts; and the responsibility for them, before the Courts of Nations of the entire world, will fall upon us because being an armed force, we have not prevented these injustices. This passiveness is the direct result of our neutrality, our non-intervention in Russian internal affairs, and, thanks to being loyal to this idea, we have become, in spite of ourselves, accomplices to a crime.... As to ourselves, we see no other way out of this situation than to evacuate immediately the sector which was given to us to guard, or else to obtain the right to prevent the injustices and crimes cited above.

The direct result of the circulation of the memorandum was the refusal of the Czech politicians to deal or negotiate with Kolchak. When Kolchak learnt of the contents of the declaration but, more significantly, of its circulation within those areas still under his control, he flew into a rage. He signalled instructions to his ministers to break off relations with the Czechs. Since Kolchak's safety depended upon the Czechs, and since they controlled the communications as well as the stations and railways, this gesture was hardly a wise move. The Czech decision, however, was not unilateral, being adopted also by the Irkutsk *Duma* and *gubernya zemstvo*, both of which declined to recognize the Admiral's leadership.

The popular support of the Social Revolutionaries had placed them in a prominent rather than strong position between Omsk and Irkutsk. Their idealistic and woolly liberal policies lacked the staying power, charisma and robustness required to survive in a revolutionary environment. What they did achieve was to keep the door open for the emerging resolute, ruthless and determined

Bolshevik party. So noble was the Social Revolutionary concept of democracy that they freely admitted onto their own committees Bolshevik members who, in the fullness of time so undermined the political structures on which they served, that they fell, one by one, like ripe fruit in front of the advancing Red Army.

In a politically opportunist move, and in association with Vladivostok's Social Revolutionaries, Rudolf Gajda attempted a *coup d'état* during the night 16–17 November. The European allies remained neutral while General Rozanov, Kolchak's representative in Vladivostok, moved to put down the insurrection. By 18 November, that aim had been achieved. Rumours persisted that selective Japanese obstructionism had been met by those sympathizers wishing to act on Gajda's behalf. After receiving a severe beating, Rudolf Gajda was put on a ship and banished from Russia.

Kolchak's retinue, including Anna Timireva, escaped from Omsk in a convoy of seven trains, each pulled by two engines. One of the seven was armoured but of greatest interest was that hauling the twenty-nine freight wagons carrying 1678 sacks and 5143 cases containing the Imperial Russian bullion. No other measure that could have been adopted could have raised so profoundly the profile of this collection of trains, obliged as it was to negotiate successive stretches of bandit country. At first, the manifestation of an inflexible will and disinterest in Kolchak's plight was assumed to be a matter which could be ironed out by the nominal head of the Czech army. Kolchak remembered Janin's declared intention to go on to Novonikolaievsk and it was here that Janin received a signal requesting that he should wait there until Kolchak arrived. Having no wish to meet Kolchak again, Janin ignored the despatch and left for Irkutsk.

Kolchak's trains lumbered slowly onward until, on 7 December, they reached Taiga where the Pepelyayev brothers were waiting to meet them. Victor was the Prime Minister of a non-existent Government in Irkutsk, while Anatol commanded what little remained of the White Army in eastern Siberia. Anatol had met Janin as the Frenchman passed through Taiga. They had discussed Kolchak's position and had finally agreed that Kolchak should resign. The evening's meeting was therefore understandably heated but frank. The brothers emphasized the importance of compromise and the need for social reform. Furthermore, they recommended the dismissal of General Sakharov, now resurrected as if by magic after his disappearance from Omsk. The Admiral hesitated, offered the job to Dieterichs who declined, then did nothing. The action was left to the Pepelyayevs who arrested Sakharov after Kolchak's departure next morning. Ultimately, the appointment of Commander-in-Chief fell to the only credible and effective White Commander left in Siberia — General Kappel, under whom the remnants of the shattered Siberian armies still remained loyal. Kolchak did offer to resign but a majority present that night dissuaded him, for they could see no acceptable alternative. Thus it was that the ongoing conflict between Kolchak and the Czech politicians was permitted to continue along its terrible path.

Thus far, reasonable progress had been made as the Admiral's trains were switched between the up and down lines. A fuel shortage was now yet another factor which had been introduced to a railway system suffering from the effects of frost, snow, machinery failures, smouldering resentment, and revolutionary zeal among the workforce. Of the 300 civilian trains that had set out from the west of Irkutsk, only 70 arrived. No fuel for the engines also meant no fuel for the iron stoves inside the *teplushki*. Each morning the survivors tossed out into the snow the bodies of those who had not survived the night. Soon, the length of the Magistral, the permanent way, was littered with dead. In some places, grotesquely frozen bodies had been stacked, seemingly in lieu of the absent log piles which, in part, had caused this state of affairs to come about. The bitter cold was now claiming as many lives as typhus.

With effect from 13 December the Czechs imposed rigid movement controls throughout those parts of the Trans-Siberian railway not dominated by the Reds. No train travelling eastward was now permitted on the northbound track, which was reserved for military trains and coal going to the coalless area. Stocks had been so severely reduced in one 300-mile stretch between Taiga and Krasnoyarsk, that there was no coal to move waiting trains whose stokers strove to prevent pipes and boilers cracking in the terrible cold. Above all, Czech trains were given priority over Russian trains and that included the Admiral's, whose own trains had been excluded from official movement orders. Syrový advised Janin that without these measures he could not accept the responsibility for getting the Legion out of Siberia. The move was clearly a politically inspired action effected through the offices of the pliant and unimaginative Syrový. The military excuse, accepted by Janin, was to give reassurance to the edgy and frayed Czech troops that they had absolute priority on the railway. This fact could not have been made clearer than by relegating the Supreme Ruler to taking his turn among the rest of his people.

There was no subtlety or regard for protocol in the manner in which the Czechs promulgated their decision. A movement control subaltern at Marinsk conveyed to Kolchak's staff his orders from Irkutsk that the Admiral was to be denied the use of the uncongested up line. Kolchak flew into an immediate and mighty rage. When his threat to use force was transmitted to the Czechs, they responded by shadowing the Russian entourage with *Praha*, a menacing armoured train. Protests left the Czechs unmoved. They continued to treat the Supreme Ruler in a high-handed and insolent manner. Denying him coal when stocks existed was a blatant display of malice, smacking of the settling of scores. They could have given the Admiral priority on the route had they wished to. Instead, he was subjected to infuriating delay. On one occasion the party travelled only 90 miles in four days, and these were days when a tantalizingly real power vacuum existed in Irkutsk. That is not to say that Kolchak would have succeeded, but he did still possess a presence and reputation at a time when such qualities were at a premium. There is strong, albeit circumstantial, evidence that the Social Revolutionaries and Czech political representatives persuaded Syrový to delay Kolchak's arrival in Irkutsk.

The impact of the imposition of the new Czech priorities reverberated down the line where the White traffic had come to a standstill, falling prey to the advancing Red Fifth Army at the rate of up to twenty trains a day. The kind of treatment captured soldiers and, more importantly, their wives and children, could expect at the hands of the Reds was well enough recognized by those further up the queue. Indeed, rumours of massacres percolated eastward. Kappel felt his sense of complete impotence as keenly as Kolchak. This did not deter him from sending to Syrový an angry telegram of protest in which he challenged the Czech to a duel. Kappel told Syrový to rescind his order and apologize to Kolchak otherwise, 'I, as Commander-in-Chief of the Russian Army whose honour it is my duty to defend shall demand you give me satisfaction on the duelling ground.' The telegram caused a sensation. A broad spectrum of Russians supported the spirit contained in the message, for what the Czechs had achieved was the humiliation not only of Kolchak but also the entire Russian people. Syrový, recognizing the pathos in the crisis, agreed to the duel but only after the Czechs had been evacuated from Siberia. When that had been achieved, brave Kappel was dead.

Meanwhile, in a siding at Krasnoyarsk, Kolchak awaited the remaining four trains in his convoy. Only six trains had passed by all week. Three belonged to the Supreme Ruler and the other three were Czech. The now friendless Kolchak sent his own appeal for assistance to Janin. By this time, General Knox had moved on to Vladivostok, from where he left for England on 26 December believing he had secured a promise from Syrový that Kolchak would be looked after. Sir Charles Eliot had also gone, posted to Tokyo as British Ambassador. When the new British High Commissioner, Miles Lampson, implored Janin to use his authority to rescue Kolchak, he received the bland reply: 'One must understand the feelings of men who think more of their own safety than that of someone who has been publicly talking of them as enemies for the last year.'

On 17 December, Syrový authorized the onward movement of the Admiral's trains. There was nothing humanitarian in a decision which had more to do with safeguarding the Imperial gold. News of unrest and insurrection was common throughout the length of the Trans-Siberian, particularly in the nearby coalmining area of Cheremkhovo where unpaid miners joined in the revolt. The Admiral's agreement that the miners should be paid, fed, and clothed by the State came too late even if it could have been effected. Down the line, trains were under selective attack from partisans, relieving weak defenders of weapons, food supplies, and valuables. On 18 December, the Krasnoyarsk garrison withdrew any further recognition of the Kolchak Government. By this decision the partisans had succeeded in separating Kolchak from Kappel and his few remaining loyal troops.

So acute now was Kolchak's feeling of isolation and need for allies that he did the unthinkable. He sought and reached accommodation with the man who, months previously, had humiliated him at Manchuli. In taking the bandit Semenov as a comrade in arms – he was appointed Supreme Commander of all troops in eastern Siberia – Kolchak convinced those who might earlier have given him the benefit of the doubt that there was validity in accounts of Kolchak-inspired war crimes. The number of those wishing to distance themselves from Kolchak grew accordingly. It was on 20 December that Semenov used his new power to the full by despatching to Syrový a flowery, fulsome but thinly veiled message. When the platitudes and honorifics had been stripped away, Semenov told Syrový that if he did not clear the line for the safe passage of Kolchak, his followers, and the gold: 'I will compel you, with a heavy heart but with all the resources at my disposal, to fulfil your duty to humanity and to your tortured sister Russia.' The Czechs liked Semenov even less than Kolchak, but the former needed to be taken seriously, controlling as he did much of Transbaikalia and the strategic Baikal tunnels. A diplomatic, sugary but serious response was telegraphed back to Semenov insisting that the Czechs had been misunderstood, even maligned, for all they desired was to take their leave of Siberia. Such a message was beyond the composition of the plumpish former architect Syrový. It had been drafted by Janin.

On Christmas Eve, Kolchak's seven trains steamed into Nizhne Udinsk. A Czech storm battalion under command of Major Hásek had the task of protecting the Admiral's entourage from the growing unrest developing throughout the region. Kolchak did not budge from his carriage for the entire two weeks the train remained in the sidings. The blinds of his carriage stayed down. Outside on the platform his soldiers faced the beguiling attention, promises, and threats of Bolshevik emissaries. Janin had let it be known that absolute liberty should be afforded to Kolchak's retinue. In a little over a week, none of the soldiers remained. After the officers were permitted to choose their destiny, forty opted to stay with the Admiral. Janin also suggested that Kolchak should be permitted to make his escape. In a typical demonstration of *noblesse oblige*, the chivalrous but none the less obstinate Supreme Ruler refused to abandon those who had chosen to remain. The messages Janin sent to the Russians via Czech intermediaries at Nizhne Udinsk was entirely one-way traffic. The efforts of Kolchak's staff to initiate a dialogue with the Frenchman always failed. 'The general impression was that neither the Czechs nor Irkutsk desired to hold converse with us,' commented a Russian officer.

The state and condition of Kolchak and his officers in the claustrophobic carriages can be imagined. Almost six weeks had elapsed since they departed Omsk, and Irkutsk was still 300 miles away to the east. Frustration, self-doubt, fear, disillusionment, strained loyalties and sheer anger were all evident as some sought solace in alcohol. It is possible that it was here at Nizhne Udinsk that Kolchak, inspired by one of those moments of uncontrollable rage which underlined his unsuitability to govern, sent out a message which would place his relationship with the Czechs beyond reconciliation. He ordered Semenov and Horvath to stop the Czech withdrawal by any means available including, if necessary, blowing up the Baikal tunnels and bridges. When the content of the signal was decoded, but more importantly relayed by Syrový to his angry troops, the breach had become irreparable. On quiet reflection both Semenov and Horvath must have recognized the damage that the severance of the rail link would cause to White interests. Consequently the order was never put into effect but, unfortunately for Kolchak, his ill-advised, damaging tit for tat signal confirmed in Czech minds the Admiral's dispensability.

In Irkutsk there had been significant developments. On 23 December, the political centre comprising the town's Social Revolutionaries and Mensheviks sought to polarize the existing nexus of authorities by staging an uprising. The Socialists were only partly successful. They seized control of northern Irkutsk, but in so doing, lost seventeen of their leaders to the clutches of secret police still loyal to Kolchak. On 24 December, the Fifty-Third Siberian Regiment accommodated to the northwest of Glaskov station declared their support for the political centre. On 25 December, Kolchak's Commander in Irkutsk announced his intention of shelling the barracks of the mutinous infantry lying on the other side of the frozen Angara. This proposal concentrated the minds and spoiled the Christmas celebrations of the allied High Commissioners. Theirs as well as Czech trains were by now firmly frozen into the sidings close to the walls of the renegade camp. Janin intervened by declaring the station area to be neutral territory, thereby frustrating the White plans. While the secret police continued surveillance and arrested thirty-one radicals among whom was a 28-year-old woman, help was sought from other quarters.

On 27 December, news was received from a small station 20 miles south of Glaskov that Semenov had sent a force along the railway to relieve Irkutsk. While the worried politicians and allies discussed what was to be done, the local railway workers demonstrated the value in taking direct action. They despatched an unmanned railway engine down the line with the throttle wide open. The leading armoured engine of Semenov's nominee, Colonel Skipterov, was derailed and the line wrecked. The now cautious advance continued on foot, but, lacking cohesion, the attack was easily defeated. Those not captured or killed withdrew over the ice of the half-mile-wide Angara to the centre of Irkutsk and the White lines. After a rest of two days, Skipterov's men set off to return to base. In order to guarantee their safe passage, they took with them thirty-one political prisoners released to their care by order of the garrison commander.

On 31 December, Major Hásek wired his headquarters. The local partisans demanded that he should hand over Kolchak and disband his staff and bodyguard. Worse still, several thousand Bolsheviks camped to the north of Nizhne Udinsk were now marching on the station, drawn by the gold like bees to a honey pot. What, asked the major, should he do? Hásek's storm battalion or, to use its correct title, the Sixth Czech Regiment, comprised 1,300 men, 8 guns and *Orlík* the armoured train. It was felt politic to move the Czechs out rather than face a threat to the railway and an undesirable clash with a larger body of Bolsheviks. Prompted by Hásek's question, a meeting of allied High Commissioners was hurriedly convened and presided over by Janin. On 1 January 1920, the allies drafted a directive to Janin giving him two courses of action depending on whether Kolchak wished to accept or decline allied protection. If the latter, then this became a matter of 'Russian internal politics'. Since Kolchak had now accepted allied protection Janin's relevant instructions were:

> All measures should be taken to assure the personal safety of Admiral Kolchak within the limits possible. If Admiral Kolchak should find himself obliged to appeal for the protection of the Allied forces there is no doubt that these forces should take Admiral Kolchak under their protection and take all measures necessary to assure his transfer to whatever destination the Allied Governments may decide.

The foregoing is an extract from the final draft. Janin scrapped the original and had it replaced by something he found more acceptable. It was Fleming who described the Frenchman's strange behaviour towards the Admiral as 'equivocal'.

Hásek awaited a reply to his question. Instead of sending to him the allied direction verbatim, Janin sent a vague response with regard to Kolchak's disposal but one of absolute clarity in relation to the gold. On 4 January, six copies of the relevant declaration were signed by delegates at the station representing Kolchak, the Russian bank and the Czechs before the allies took the bullion train on to Irkutsk. It was at Nizhne Udinsk that the Czechs made an informal though optimistic proposal that Kolchak might consider sledging the 250 miles south to Mongolia and safety. The scheme was rejected, the Russians keeping faith with the promised allied protection. As a means of indicating the fact that the Admiral had the benefit of such protection, Janin gave orders that the Admiral's carriage was to fly the flags of the Czech and allied guarantors. Further instructions from Janin relating to this special train was the requirement that Kolchak should abandon the six trains still comprising his entourage and for the party to continue in a second class carriage attached to a Czech train. The extent of Kolchak's rage and protestation at this affront to his dignity was relayed by his Quarter Master General to the allied High Commissioners. The requirement as to the size of the accommodation however, as opposed to its quality, had been correctly judged. It seemed that the authorities at Irkutsk were better informed as to Kolchak's situation than Kolchak. It may be that he did not wish to acknowledge the disintegration of the support surrounding him, but it would have been difficult not to have noticed, particularly when his personal band absconded to the partisans playing the Marseillaise.

The best efforts of the High Commissioners to administer a wobbly truce between Kolchak's ministers and the insurgents came to a climactic end during the evening of 4 January. On that night the garrison commander attempted to abscond with the contents of the vaults of the State Bank. The political centre took full advantage of the ensuing mayhem to take control of all of Irkutsk. Their declaration promised something for all. At first, they would form a representative Siberian Council as an essential preliminary to the long-promised Constituent Assembly. On 6 January, Kolchak accepted the *fait accompli*, advising Janin that he would resign his powers as Supreme Ruler in favour of General Denikin. He said that the formal instrument of resignation would not be signed until he arrived at Verkhne Udinsk which lay to the east of Irkutsk. Obviously, Kolchak had an eye on the personal safety of himself, Anna Timireva, and his dwindling band of followers.

Now that the regime to which they were accredited had ceased to exist, the High Commissioners began to take their leave of Siberia, commencing on 4 January. It had been assumed by the High Commissioners that Janin would remain in Irkutsk until that half of the Czech army still to the west of the city had passed safely through to the east. There was no doubt what was expected of him in pursuing the letter of their New Year's Day Directive. As soon as all the High Commissioners had taken their leave of Irkutsk, Janin felt no personal obligation to remain and he too departed on 8 January. The only allied flags now still flying in the area were attached to a solitary train which had set off the previous day from Nizhne Udinsk station to take Kolchak on the last part of his journey. The irony of his total abandonment was thus complete; the so-called allied protection now represented by nothing more than pieces of coloured linen, cracking in the freezing wind.

12

THE REPUBLIC OF THE USHAKOVKA

The First Czech Battalion's train had barely come to a halt at Nizhne Udinsk station before its Commander, Major Gustav Bečvář, leapt down on to the platform and hurried into the station master's office. He was quite used to having to argue about movement priorities and the special importance of his own battalion getting on towards the east. It was therefore a somewhat suspicious and surprised Bečvář who found himself overwhelmed by cordiality and the total absence of the usual difficulties. 'Yes, the sooner you go ahead the better we shall be pleased. Two engines are waiting for you with full steam up.' It all seemed a little too straightforward, particularly the allocation of not just one but two precious engines. 'What's the joke?' Bečvář demanded of the movements officer. 'Ah then, you don't know your good fortune. Well, my friend, you are to take Admiral Kolchak with you to Irkutsk.' 'So,' reflected Bečvář, 'the man who hated the Legionaries, who dismissed Gajda, and who could never utter an approving word of the Czechs, is now glad to accept our protection.'

The battalion train took on two additional coaches; one allocated to Kolchak and his staff and the other, a guard's van, to Prime Minister Pepelyayev. After the coaches had been examined to ensure that Kolchak was indeed aboard, something which irritated the Admiral intensely, the train pulled out. This apparent alliance between Czechs and Whites caused Bečvář considerable trouble *en route* to Irkutsk. The Siberians vented their anger on the Czechs, accusing them of providing Kolchak with safe passage and running off with the national treasure. Every station along the way had its own angry mob, demanding that Kolchak should be handed over, otherwise the Czechs could expect persistent acts of sabotage along the route, including the denial of coal. At first Czech diplomacy prevailed, if only because the revolutionaries were told that their orders from Syrový were to escort Kolchak only as far as Irkutsk. Besides, the revolutionaries lacked the co-ordination and strength to attack the Czechs, who went on their way preceded by inflammatory partisan proclamations. All this served to raise the political temperature in Irkutsk, where the political centre had eight days (the time taken for Bečvář's train to travel from Nizhne Udinsk to Irkutsk) to contemplate their next move.

One act more than any other would serve to colour any prospect Kolchak might have anticipated of a sympathetic and humanitarian reception. He, like all leaders, could not escape the ultimate responsibility for the behaviour of subordinates, no matter how tenuous the link or remote from the scene of action. How ironic that an incommunicado Kolchak, overseen as he was in Nizhne Udinsk by impassive Czech guards, should now be about to be brought to account for the misconduct of Semenov's men at Irkutsk. The massacres conducted by Dutov at Ufa, the killings of the Omsk prisoners by Krassilnikov, were all chickens coming home to roost in anticipation of final judgement at Irkutsk.[15]

The thirty-one hostages taken by Skipterov represented a significant number of the political centre's active leadership. Not unnaturally, the question of the fate of these thirty men and one woman gave rise to considerable interest as well as intensive speculation. The group was last seen on 5 January, bound together, being taken aboard the ice-breaker *Angara* on Lake Baikal. Inside the ship they had been thrown into cramped, basic accommodation alongside the engine room. After dusk, the vessel weighed anchor and headed up one of the short channels kept free of ice by warm springs. Accompanying Skipterov were two men with equally unsavoury sadistic reputations, Colonel Sipailov and an English mercenary, Captain Grant. This group had taken over the first-class saloon and settled into an evening of heavy drinking. It was dawn before their befuddled minds turned to their captives. One by one the prisoners were called into the saloon where they were obliged to forfeit their possessions, undress, and put on what was alleged to be prison uniform. Their acquiescent behaviour — only one man resisted — would suggest that they did believe they were not to be harmed. They may well have been deceived by an impossible undertaking they were obliged to sign to the effect that they would leave Russia within three days. From the warmth of the stuffy saloon the prisoners were led individually out on to the bitterly cold upper deck to be bludgeoned to death by a mallet-wielding man by the name of Godlevski. The woman was the last to die, suffering the same fate as the men before her. Her body was tossed over the side, falling between the broken ice floes and into the depths of Lake Baikal.

It was not long before the rumours of these killings circulated throughout Irkutsk. Confirmation of the deed appeared in a Czech newspaper published in the city. The sense of outrage among the partisans caused representatives to converge angrily upon Irkutsk, thereby placing intense pressure on the political centre to take positive, acceptable action. Their failure to take anything other than firm action to assuage the spontaneous, universal clamour for revenge would only lead to their own political demise. This, therefore, was the situation as Kolchak's train drew into Glaskov station during the early evening of 15 January 1920. Any reassurance the White entourage may have derived from being part of a Czech echelon under allied protection would have been tempered by the persistent, repetitive displays of threatened mob violence confronting them all along the way. Some strength could have been drawn from the presence in Kolchak's carriage of four Czech guards, a number which was doubled at night. But, as the train drew nearer to Irkutsk, the demands of the revolutionaries became that much more difficult for the Czechs to appease. An engine broke down. A condition for its replacement was for a revolutionary guard to travel in Kolchak's carriage. When it became evident that the Reds were adamant and no room existed for compromise, Bečvář reluctantly agreed to twelve armed, red-rosetted guards taking over duties from the Czechs. The status of the Whites had thus dramatically changed from that of men under escort to prisoners of the revolutionaries.

As Kolchak's train drew up alongside its appointed platform, a hundred or so Red Guards jostled to position themselves on either side of his carriage. In a very short time, the recently arrived train had been closed in by fifteen trains on one side and ten on the other. Nevertheless there were signs which when interpreted optimistically, could give comfort to those in desperate straits. Despite the presence of the Red Guard inside Kolchak's carriage, his close protection was still provided by Czechs. Out on the platform there was evidence of Colonel Fukuda's Japanese troops as well as an occasional Frenchman. Perhaps, after all, the allied guarantees were not valueless. While this assessment was being made from the train,

Major Bečvář and a colleague, Major Krása, picked their way gingerly over the thin ice of the Angara towards the Legion's Headquarters in central Irkutsk. Their mission was to seek approval to be released from the responsibility of guarding Kolchak and his gold. Later that night they returned to Glaskov having secured nothing. Kolchak's fate hinged on the as yet unannounced decision of General Janin.[16]

The air of gloom and despondency pervading the station during the evening percolated through the Admiral's carriage. The loyalty of the majority of officers who thus far had shared Kolchak's adventures had come to an end. Before very long, a formal Bolshevik guard could be expected to take over from the self-appointed, self-important irregulars. The opportunity to creep away into the darkness had to be taken now, or never. One by one, the officers slipped anonymously through the busy, crowded platforms into the cold night, their coloured epaulettes lying discarded in the snow. Little excited anger among the revolutionaries more than the sight of these large, gaudy and ostentatious signs of reaction, rank and position.[17] The standard Red procedure for dealing with those captured White officers still found to be wearing the offending epaulettes was to drive 6-inch nails through the officer's shoulder, one for each star.[18] In the light of morning it was possible to see among the badges of rank discarded in the discoloured snow the colour purple – a colour reserved for Kolchak's personal staff.

At breakfast time Major Krása received his orders to return to Headquarters. He went immediately, leaving Bečvář to tend to matters at the station. Krása was left dumbfounded by Janin's decision that Kolchak should be handed over to the Social Revolutionaries with the gold. That was the price demanded to guarantee a free Czech passage to the east. Up until that stage the Bolsheviks too had insisted on a Czech surrender without concession. Subsequent tenacious rearguard actions convinced the Bolsheviks that the Czechs would not surrender and concluded accordingly an Armistice on what proved to be a day of tragedy, 7 February 1920. Krása did not return to Glaskov station until late that evening. 'His face told us at once,' wrote Bečvář, 'that the interview from which he had come had been unpleasant in the extreme. He said little but each word was to the point, and they told a tale of tragedy.' Voices of protest arose from the gathered throng of Czech soldiers but these were quickly silenced by Krása: 'Those are our orders; there is nothing to be said,' and with that he turned away. Later Bečvář was called to Krása's office. Both men decided that Kolchak and Pepelyayev should be informed what their fate was to be.

Just before midnight, Bečvář set off to convey the grim news to the Admiral and his Prime Minister. Feeling sad and miserable Bečvář passed through successive lines of guards, his thoughts disrupted by a series of challenges until reaching the one unlocked door of Kolchak's corridor carriage. As he stepped up, he could sense the suspicious stares of the Russians on the platform. Inside the first two compartments he found half-awake Staff Officers. The Czech asked to see Kolchak. An Adjutant presented himself and after introductions set off down the carriage. The Russian returned and escorted the Czech into a dimly lit compartment where Kolchak stood. 'His face was pale but composed,' recorded Bečvář. 'He was a dignified figure. A handsome man, he looked magnificent in his uniform.' 'Sit down,' invited the Admiral pointing to a seat. 'Well, what is it?' he asked looking down at the ill at ease and perspiring Czech. 'We have just received orders to hand over both yourself and Minister Pepelyayev to the Political Centre tomorrow morning. The Government representatives will arrive at dawn.' Kolchak questioned Bečvář. Had the news, he asked, come from Czech Headquarters? When the reply came in the affirmative the Admiral said in an air of resignation, 'This means that the Allies have betrayed me.' When he spoke again his voice was calm. 'I should like to speak to General Syrový.' Bečvář pointed out that it had already passed midnight, but Kolchak insisted. Bečvář got up, saluted, and left to convey the message. Syrový proved to be equally as elusive as Janin. Consequently the message was never passed. A duty officer responded to the request by saying, 'It is too late.'

Meanwhile, Bečvář had gone off to relay the news to Pepelyayev whose carriage was next to Kolchak's. The Prime Minister was already on record as having said: 'Our case is lost but the Bolsheviks won't suceed either.' He did not strike a favourable impression in Bečvář's eyes. 'Pepelyayev had little of the dignity which characterised Kolchak. He was corpulent, and a smile, constant and weak, hung upon his bulky face. He continued smiling when I told him of our orders. It seemed to me that the message did not come as a great surprise.' By the time Bečvář returned to his unit the 'too late' reply had been received from Syrový's headquarters.

Immediately, he turned about to take the latest information to Kolchak. The Admiral was still up and dressed in full uniform. He would not sleep that night. Bečvář reported the exact words to the Admiral; words that stuck in his throat as he said slowly, 'It is too late.' 'What do you mean?' the Admiral wanted to know. 'Too late at night or too late as regards the situation?' Bečvář was unable to enlighten the Admiral, who just stood there in the half light, an ironical smile upon his lips. The Czech, feeling uneasy in the silence, felt the need to say something reassuring. He suggested that the Japanese might assist Kolchak. The Admiral turned sharply on his visitor. 'You are not misleading me?' Bečvář retreated, admitting that he could 'vouch for nothing'. After a further period of taxing silence, the interview ended.

In the early morning, while it was still dark, the guard arrived to take the Admiral and Pepelyayev over the river to Irkutsk. A receipt was given to the Czechs. There was some commotion and some wild firing during which the last of Kolchak's officers to make their escape got away uninjured. Timireva appeared in a nurse's uniform, the strain and tiredness evident on her face. She was close to complete collapse but refused to be separated from Kolchak. It was a simple matter to step over the rails between the carriages, straight over the river bank and onto the ice covering the Angara. The moon provided adequate light to guide the small party over the rugged ice avoiding the sharp pinnacles met along the way. As Bečvář and Krása had discovered earlier, the ice was still thin in places, particularly where it had been holed by recent shelling. In one such place, the Admiral's foot went through, his felt boot filling with icy water. The rest of the journey was uneventful. The group made rendezvous on the far bank with their transport, a staff car and a lorry which, once loaded, drove off at slow speed with a mounted escort. Their destination lay a quarter of a mile distant, the long squat white-painted prison building set on a bank overlooking a tributary of the Angara – the Ushakovka. The standard of quarters provided for the important prisoners was substantially better than that enjoyed by inmates elsewhere in the gaol. Their wing of the prison, thought to have been the sick bay, was secured but inside, the prisoners, Kolchak, Timireva and Pepelyayev, had adjoining but open cells.

On 16 January, representatives of the political centre made a routine call on Janin in his train, now positioned at Verkhne Udinsk.[19] They discussed matters of a general nature during the course of which the Frenchman made a casual enquiry after Admiral Kolchak. On being told, he pursued the discussion no further. He was not slow to insist that less fuss had been made when Tsar Nicholas had been killed. His chain of command was to the Prague Government and the Allied Council in Paris whose joint instruction to him was to secure the safe evacuation of the Czech army. He was emphatic in his determination that he would not risk 'the destruction of the Czechoslovak Army for the sake of that man'.

Two days after the prisoners' incarceration, the political centre was dissolved and replaced by Revkom, a Bolshevik Revolutionary Committee. On 21 January, the interrogation of Kolchak by an Extraordinary Investigating Committee began in the Irkutsk gaol. The convening of the Committee had been the last act of the political centre. It was for this reason that the composition of the Committee reflected its parentage. Three of the five-man team were liberal Socialists – two Social Revolutionaries and one Menshevik. Revkom established a *Cheka* for the Irkutsk *guberniya* but quite deliberately did not replace these men who brought to the proceedings a calming, non-confrontational atmosphere, permitting Kolchak to talk freely. Real power resided in the hands of the two Bolsheviks on the Committee, Chairman S. Chudnovsky and his deputy. The deputy, a lawyer named K.A. Popov, was not only the most interesting but also the most influential man on the Committee. Had he not been suffering from typhus while in Omsk prison he would most surely have been killed alongside his political associates. He opened the interrogation as no friend of the Admiral's but towards the end, there occurred a perceptive change and the development of a grudging respect for the man whose life he now controlled.

Among Popov's aims was to prove Kolchak a monarchist. He became intensely frustrated at what he described as the Admiral's refusal to recognize himself as a monarchist. 'He throws a veil of democratic tendencies' over his monarchism. The fault here was Popov's because he was unable to accept that many of those who had served under imperial colours had indeed rejected the monarchy. What the Committee did discover was the Whites now in prison 'all of them, to a man, were complete political nonentities; and so was their head Kolchak. ... Politically speaking, he had no personality; he was a mere plaything of the Entente powers.' What did separate Kolchak from his fellow prisoners, and what made him dangerous to the Reds, was his leadership and self-assurance. Popov described his bearing while under examination thus:

> It was that of the captive commander of a defeated army; and from this standpoint it was entirely dignified. In this he differed sharply from most of his ministers with whom I had to deal as investigator in the trial of the Kolchak Government. In the cases of those men, there was with rare exception, cowardice, a desire to represent themselves as involuntary participants in a dirty business initiated by somebody else, even a desire to paint themselves as having opposed these others; from yesterday's lords they became transfigured into flunkeys of the victorious foe. There was none of this in Kolchak's demeanour.

All along, the Admiral knew what fate was awaiting him. The manner in which he replied with encyclopaedic detail to the daily questioning of the Committee was not for their benefit but rather a straightening of the record before his inevitable death. This unintentional filibuster served to frustrate the Committee's desired aim of determining both Kolchak's life history and the history of his regime. Circumstances would intervene to prevent the completion of an examination which had few parallels; it was certainly no Judgement at Nuremberg. No charges were ever presented, no witnesses called; Moscow had removed capital punishment from the list of awards available to judges and, to add to the irregularity of the situation, the war was still continuing to the west of Irkutsk. The closest available comparison was with the events leading up to the murder of Nicholas II and his family.

On 20 January, elements of the Second and Third White Siberian armies under the determined leadership of General Kappel, captured Nizhne Udinsk. They now numbered less than 10,000, of which a high proportion were officers. It was here that they heard of Kolchak's imprisonment. The passage of this army against great adversity, extremes of weather, and an uncompromising enemy is an heroic record. Kappel's men reached Nizhne Udinsk in a state of utter exhaustion, having suffered from shortages of food and transportation as well as the ever persistent typhus. 'Great was the distress of these miserable men,' wrote an observer, 'wandering through the forests, some on wretched horses, most of them on foot.' To have paused here to rest awhile on their laurels would have been an understandable action, but Kappel would have none of it.

He, and only he, had the ability to pick his men up and lead them out into the Siberian blizzards to force a way through the enemy's lines to rescue their Commander. Frostbite, which afflicted many of the Whites, had so affected Kappel's legs that he was unable to ride his horse. At 39 years of age he was obliged to take to a sledge with the reluctance of an elderly person taking to a wheelchair for the first time. A Czech doctor pleaded with Kappel to abandon his quest, for otherwise his life would most certainly be at risk. The Czechs did not hold Kappel's challenge to Syrový against him, preferring to remember him not only as a brave Russian, but also as one of the Legion's founder members. Space was offered to him aboard a warm, well-provisioned ambulance train. He refused. He could permit no accommodation with those who had betrayed Kolchak. The Czechs did retain the capacity to look after those to whom they were indebted. At the eleventh hour they spirited General Zinovich out of Kolchak's railway carriage, if only because his brother had fought and died with the Czechs during their eastern campaign.

The onward deployment of the Whites moved in tandem with the rearmost of the Czech trains from which provisions were purchased for gold. Repeatedly the Czechs, as well as his own staff, pleaded with Kappel to go aboard one of the Czech trains. The frostbite moved up through his body and only morphine could provide comfort from the infliction and jarring of the sledge along the frozen, rutted *trakt*. On 27 January, when it was clear that Kappel would not survive the day, General Voytsekhovsky assumed command. After Kappel had breathed his last, his body was received with due ceremony aboard a Czech train and taken on to Chita for burial.

Reports of the White Army's successes and the resumption of its advance eastward caused grave concern among a none-too-secure Revkom. Kolchak's urbane autobiography continued its patient evolution from 21 January, the opening day of the formal examination. In these the early days up to Kappel's death, polite discussion touched on the Admiral's early life, the Russo-Japanese and First World Wars, his American mission, and his negotiations to serve in the British armed forces. Attempts to lead Kolchak into agreeing that the villains of the piece had been the Tsar and the political leadership were all deflected by a man batting with consummate ease and confidence and – unusually for Kolchak – calmness and patience. Thus the examination would continue with its essentially autobiographical ramble, failing until the morning of 6 February to come to grips with the serious accusations of atrocities.

Meanwhile, Voytsekhovsky was making gains. Zuria fell, followed by the coal mining area of Cheremkhovo and on 2 February, the Whites had taken Innokentieveskaia five miles to the west of Glaskov. On 29 January the nervous Revkom declared Martial Law, upgraded to Siege Law when it was discovered that the Whites were in Innokentieveskaia. Ongoing negotiations between interested Irkutsk parties and Voytsekhovsky led to the formulation of the Whites' terms, duly passed to Irkutsk over the telephone. It was agreed that Revkom's rule would not be contested and the city by-passed, subject to three conditions. First, Kolchak and his co-prisoners were to be released to the allies; second, an indemnity (equivalent to the Imperial bullion) was to be paid to the Whites, and, lastly, certain Red Cross ambulance trains were to be permitted free and safe passage through Irkutsk. Revkom was in no position to accept these terms – to have done so would have brought the whole weight of Bolshevik opprobrium upon them. As a concession, Revkom agreed to allow Voytsekhovsky and his men to pass through Irkutsk on condition they surrendered their arms. Both sides had reached an impasse. Accordingly, on 4/5 February, the White advance resumed, bringing the advanced forces to Glaskov's suburbs in a matter of hours. From the east came rumours of the move of Semenov's army towards Irkutsk, a city Revkom was convinced was riddled with White underground forces. The masses were as unsettled as a herd of corralled cattle awaiting the looming storm. There was also the fact of a Czech presence in the city. A swing of the power pendulum, or reflection of what they had done to Kolchak could have served to produce an undesirable reaction from an opportunist army. All these circumstances had convinced Revkom that Kolchak should be executed.

Not unnaturally, Kolchak's future had been discussed in Moscow. Trotsky pressed, as he had in the case of Nicholas II, for a show trial. Lenin also agreed that Kolchak should be sent to Moscow, but his mood was one of caution.

> It is pretty unintelligent to blame Kolchak merely because he practises violence against workers and even flogs women teachers for sympathising with the Bolsheviks. This is a vulgar defence of democracy; this is a foolish way of accusing Kolchak. Kolchak acts by such methods as he finds handy.

Lenin emphasized that the Admiral was not to be executed. Revkom was quick to point to the real difficulties in moving Kolchak westward, without apparently considering moving him, albeit temporarily, eastward. Stung by Lenin's implied criticism, Popov suggested that Kolchak was Siberia's problem. With the Whites banging at the very door of Irkutsk, having a doubtful army of their own and the Fifth Red Army too distant to be of any assistance, Revkom transmitted a message on 4/5 February to Smirnov, who commanded the Fifth Red Army. Permission was sought to execute Kolchak and Pepelyayev in Irkutsk. It was with reluctance that Smirnov signalled his concurrence. The death of two prisoners was a small price in comparison with the upheaval their rescue and survival would cause.

The final examination of Kolchak occurred on 6 February, by which time his execution had been agreed but no decision promulgated. The Admiral was aware of Voytsekhovsky's ultimatum. From the prison, the rumble of guns could be heard growing louder each day, telling their own story of the approach of the White forces. No longer did the prisoners enjoy their earlier freedom. Communication was by written message, passed secretly. What, Timireva asked of Kolchak, were the implications of Voytsekhovsky's ultimatum? In his reply, intercepted by his captors, Kolchak admitted to being sceptical, forecasting that the march on Irkutsk would only hasten the inevitable end. On this, the last day of interrogation, both sides were noticeably tense. The Admiral recognized that he was close to the end. His composure and self-control had given way to the nervousness which had been such a feature of his behaviour over the recent months. The Committee recognized that they had nothing more than a detailed but incomplete autobiography. For them, too, time had run out as they sought to push on with the questioning, sacrificing system and method through 'the necessity of fixing a few of the more colourful aspects of this dictatorship'. The pace became frenetic. Orlov, now impatient, took over the lead from Alekseyevsky, the asker of the blandest and most unimportant of questions. The previous daily average of questions leapt sixfold as the Committee sought to put on paper some justification for the action they were about to take. Despite the enormous strain, Kolchak parried the questions with caution and consideration:

> He steered clear of even the least chance of supplying material for the indictment of persons who had already fallen, or might fall, into the power of the re-established Soviet rule, and of any possibility of revealing the fact that his own rule – eager

as it was to combat the hell-born Bolsheviks whose very life breath is violence and despotism – that that government of his could in its turn act outside all law. He feared that the examination might tear away the cloak with which he tried to shield that rule throughout his testimony, a cloak of consistent adherence to legality and order.

If the Committee had anticipated some last-minute admission of guilt by Kolchak for White atrocities, they were disappointed. The attempt to blame Kolchak for the massacres at Omsk of which Popov had first-hand knowledge, was deflected by the fact of the Admiral's genuine indisposition due to a severe attack of pneumonia. To other claims Kolchak merely replied, perhaps honestly, that he had not heard of the alleged atrocity. When confronted with evidence of three villages being razed to the ground, the Admiral replied: 'They were insurgents' bases; and so long as a base is taken it must be destroyed so as to make impossible its subsequent use.' When Alekseyevsky suggested that the villages could have been secured by a garrison, Kolchak swung into the offensive by describing an event which clearly demonstrated that neither side was blameless of committing atrocities. Kolchak recounted that whilst on the Ural Front he had cause to hold a conversation with a captured member of a Revolutionary Committee. The Red asked the Admiral whether he was aware of atrocities perpetrated by specific White units. Kolchak said he did not know of those cases described but was prepared to admit that such activities did happen. 'When I came to one village with the insurgents,' the man had said to Kolchak, 'I found several persons with ears and noses cut off by your troops. I reacted to it in such a way that I cut off the foot of one prisoner, tied it to him with a string and in such a shape let him go back to your side, "eye for eye, tooth for tooth" '. Kolchak explained to the Committee that all he could say to this man was: 'Next time, possibly, people, on seeing one of their own with a foot hacked off, will burn down a village and massacre its people. This is usually done in war and in a struggle.' These were the last words spoken by Kolchak to his interrogators. He had made his point. The session closed and he was taken back to his cell for the last time.

On 7 February 1920, before first light, the firing squad arrived at the prison. With them was Chudnovsky, Chairman of the Examining Committee, and the commander of Irkutsk garrison. Kolchak was up and already dressed in warm clothing. He was calm and composed and bore himself according to one witness, 'like an

Englishman'. He and Pepelyayev were taken handcuffed from their cells, leaving behind the distraught Timireva. Kolchak walked proud and upright. Poor Pepelyayev's courage had deserted him as he was half carried into the cold darkness of early morning for an appointment with his executioners. Both men had 100 yards to walk along the bank of the Ushakovka. They could see the firing squad ahead, drawn up on either side of the lorry that had brought them from Irkutsk. Next to the lorry and down the short bank, prison staff stood on the firm ice, prodding at a persistent film of transparent ice which threatened to seal a hole affording access to the fast-flowing river. The two men were taken into the converging beam of the lorry's headlamps. Their eyes reacted to the light. Kolchak was offered a blindfold, but refused. By some accounts they were administered by a priest to whom they said their prayers aloud. The Admiral's last request was that his wife in Paris should be told that he had blessed his 9-year-old son Rostislav. Chudnovsky half promised to pass on the message but in the event, failed to do so.

'Prepare, aim, fire.' A ragged volley sent both men to the icy ground. A second volley made certain. The bodies were kicked over the bank and onto the ice at the lip of the hole. With one final effort, the corpses were nudged by boots over the slippery ice, disappearing from view for ever. The first light of dawn illuminated the scene as the firing squad returned to their lorry. All that remained of Kolchak were freezing bloodstains on the ice while below, his body, submerged in the darkness, and tugged at by the current, was taken away into the depths of the Republic of the Ushakovka.

EPILOGUE

After hearing of Kolchak's execution, Voytsekhovsky's White Army bypassed Irkutsk, crossing over frozen Lake Baikal into the east and eventual obscurity. As for the rest of the assorted leadership, Baron Ungern von Sternberg suffered the ignominy of being surrendered to the Reds by his own troops. He made a reasonably favourable impression on his interrogators. When first addressed as 'Ungern' he bellowed back his full title 'Baron Ungern von Sternberg!' Still, his pedantic persistence did not save him.

Semenov had already discerned an unsettled atmosphere among his own ranks, even before it became clear that the Japanese were soon to abandon Chita. Prior to departing for the coast, the Japanese transported the Ataman's ill-gotten gains to his new home in Manchuria. From here, Semenov continued his agency in support of Japanese aspirations in Manchuria. For over two decades he enjoyed a comfortable, cosy and safe existence under the umbrella of Japanese patronage. There was more than a touch of irony to the circumstances which brought Semenov's good life to a sudden, climactic conclusion. The Soviet forces sweeping the Japanese out of Manchuria at the end of World War II fell upon Semenov in the smart town of Dalny (Dairen). He was taken back to Moscow where he stood trial in 1946. His reputation and the quality of the evidence, some of which was provided by captured Japanese officers, sealed his fate. He was found guilty of his crimes and hanged.

General Graves took his leave of Vladivostok on 1 April 1920, sailing in the last trooper, the *Great Northern*. As the ship left the quay, a band from the Japanese army bid the Americans farewell. On 30 June 1920, Graves reverted to his substantive, post-war rank of Brigadier-General. He served in a number of appointments in the

171

United States commanding brigades, a division and the Sixth Corps area. His final post was in the Panama Canal Zone, from where he was ordered home on 1 April 1928 to await retirement. After over 40 years of service, he retired at his own request as a Major-General on 4 September 1928. Graves was not destined to fade away for, in 1931 he published a book, *America's Siberian Adventure*. Graves gives two reasons for writing what is a dull, repetitive and whimpering book in which he attempts, despite assertions to the contrary, to justify his conduct in Siberia. The first reason given was to rectify 'an erroneous impression, not only in the United States but elsewhere, as to the orders under which American troops operated in Siberia'. The core reason, however, was as a rebuttal to a damaging book published in 1920 by Colonel John Ward, *With the Die-Hards in Siberia*. In his book, Ward accused Graves and his officers of colluding with the Reds, 'maintaining that more than one understanding had been arrived at between them'. Moreover, Ward alleged that American protection had made it possible for two Red divisions to embark upon wholesale murder and robbery, destroying 'every substance of order which the Supreme Governor and Allies had with so much labour attempted to set up'. Graves maintained that Ward's book

> gives and, in my judgement, is intended to give, erroneous impressions as to the conduct and faithful performance of American troops in Siberia. This book can be found in American libraries, and I do not believe it is just to the Americans whom I had the honour to command, to let such unjust implications be handed down to posterity without refutation.

The arguments and accusations rumbled on. The enigma of Graves remains; was he saint, sinner or a mixture of both?

The Czech Legion succeeded in saving itself. Its evacuation – a total of 95,000 troops, camp followers, and their booty – was completed on 30 November 1920. Many of those returning to their recently freed homeland had been absent for over six years. Now they converged on their new republic to stake their own future. Some went overland via Canada, while the majority passed a contemplative sea journey via China, India, the Suez to Trieste.

General Rudolf Gajda was of course already in Europe. Perhaps he had taken heed of Kolchak's damning allegation that he had not had the benefit of a formal military education. He took himself off to Paris where he was evidently prepared to eat humble pie by enrolling at l'Ecole Supérieure de Guerre, the French Army Staff College. Not unnaturally, the General excelled among his classmates of senior Captains and junior Majors, although he was not greatly older than they. At the end of course examinations, Gajda protested that he should not be tested by a mere Colonel, but by one of equivalent rank. The Czech was thereupon examined by a French general officer who passed him with flying colours. As the French student officers departed the Course for company command or the monotony of routine Grade 2 staff work, Gajda established an unique record for a student passing out of Staff College. He assumed command of the army corps at Košice. From this point, his career went from strength to strength, until his turbulent right-wing beliefs brought him into conflict with the Czech leadership. His reputation was one factor contributing towards his acquittal at his treason trial. In 1926 he joined the Fascists, a move which was to be instrumental in his committal to prison when the war ended in 1945.

The one-eyed General Syrový had found no such problem in finding accommodation with the new, leftward-leaning government of Czechoslovakia. When in 1938 Chamberlain uttered his notoriously dismissive statement of Czechoslovakia, Syrový had risen to become the country's War Minister. In 1945 he was sentenced to life imprisonment for collaborating with the Germans. He shared the same gaol as Gajda.

When the French Government heard the reports of Janin's behaviour towards Kolchak, he was sacked on the spot and ordered to return to Paris. An account by Dr George Montandon suggests that this had not been an overreaction by Paris, but rather a punishment to fit the unpardonable crime of damaging French prestige. 'This betrayal of Kolchak destroyed France in the esteem of her remaining Russian supporters. During the two whole years we were travelling widely in Russia, we did not hear a single Russian speak well of France.' Before leaving Harbin in April 1920, Janin took delivery of a chest and three suitcases placed in his care by General Dieterichs. Janin hoped the contents of this luggage would be a sweetener, a form of homage to be taken to Paris. In this matter Janin had neglected to consult his government on a mission which he regarded as, 'a solemn duty that fell to me personally.' Packed neatly inside the containers were the mortal remains and minor accoutrements of Tsar Nicholas II and his family, recovered from the scene of butchery and pyres near Ekaterinburg. 'There were no teeth,' noted the General, 'the heads having been severed from the bodies and taken who knows where and the cases filled with sawdust by a man named Axelbaum.' If Janin hoped this festering smoke-screen would divert attention from his conduct in Siberia, he would be disappointed. The packages were supposed to be presented to Grand Duke Nicholas, the senior surviving Romanov but he, being underwhelmed by the nauseous offer, declined to accept the gift. From here, in a wide-ranging game of pass the parcel, other would-be recipients sought to dodge the remains lest they be caught in possession when the music stopped. So complete was the desire not to be associated with Janin's gesture, that the packages eventually disappeared for ever. The reward for the self-professed 'political general' was the frostiest of receptions in Paris. At the Ministry of Foreign Affairs he learnt of the Minister's displeasure, to be confirmed by a personal reprimand from Prime Minister Millerand. From this point, Janin's career failed to progress. Anticipated appointments did not come his way. Indeed, he was fortunate to have avoided an official enquiry into his conduct. During the course of subsequent mundane appointments, Janin took to his pen, seeking to explain to an uncomprehending world, in *Ma Mission en Sibérie*, exactly what had taken place.

When the last notes of the Japanese band's rendition of 'Hard Times Come Again No More' faded, and the last American trooper had slipped her ties from the Vladivostok quay, it was Japan's clear intention to remain in Siberia. The Japanese national ego had already been bruised, however, by the March massacre of 700 Japanese residing in Nikolaievsk. Rather than increase the resolve to withdraw, the incident had the opposite effect, and was taken as a clear indication that Japan should remain as a stabilizing influence. The resolute pressure for Japan to leave came not so much from Russia but rather from the United States. The germ of the fatal rivalry that had been evident at the 1905 Treaty of Portsmouth had continued to grow and now, in 1921, the possibility of conflict between the two nations could not be discounted. The Washington Naval Treaty of 1922 was designed to control the size of the world's growing fleet of warships. The agreed ratios did not favour Japan. It was international pressure such as this, and the sustained American effort, which eventually encouraged an unforgiving and reluctant Japan out of Siberia on 25 October 1922. In November 1922 the so-called Far Eastern Republic, a post-Kolchak phenomenon, dissolved itself and made way for the Bolsheviks to lay claim, with the exception of the Baltic States,[20] to all that continental territory[21] now known as the Union of Soviet Socialist Republics.

What distinguishes Major-General Sir Alfred William Fortescue Knox among the key survivors of this period is that he was the only one not to write a book of his exploits in Siberia. This is all the more curious because he was the one important allied officer in Siberia who had already established himself as a military writer. His two-volume record of the performance of Russian forces in the First World War, *With the Russian Army 1914–1917*, is a valuable record. It is possible to conclude that the unsatisfactory outcome of the Intervention had a dulling effect on Knox; something he did not wish to share with a wider public. On returning from Siberia in 1920 he retired from the army and from 1924–45 was Conservative Member of Parliament for the Wycombe Division of Buckinghamshire. He died on 9 March 1964 in his 94th year.

John Ward resumed his seat as Member for Stoke-on-Trent. He established a new family home in 1920 on the outskirts of his beloved Appleshaw in Hampshire, naming the new house Omsk. Commuting between London and the north created its own pressures. In 1926 his wife died, followed in 1928 by the death of his son, a doctor, whom he idolized. The young man's body was originally laid to rest in the garden of Omsk so that father and son would never again be separated. Bureaucracy intervened, and the body was exhumed and removed to a cemetery. In 1929 Ward forsook his Socialist origins, contesting Stoke-on-Trent as a Liberal. The Labour Party chose as their candidate Lady Cynthia, Sir Oswald Mosley's first wife, and daughter of Lord Curzon. Ward was defeated and settled into quiet retirement, involving himself more completely in village life until his death in 1934. His home is now derelict, vandalized and strangled by a tangle of undergrowth. All that remains to tell of this man and his involvement in the history of Russia are a few words on an outbuilding, partly hidden from view by spreading ivy:

OMSK
LT COL JOHN WARD CB CMG
MP STOKE-ON-TRENT
1920

Of the unhappy, 'highly discreditable enterprise' in which he had found himself embroiled, Ward wrote: 'The Statesman and the soldier rarely write history; it is their misfortune to make it.'

APPENDIX

PRESIDENT WILSON'S *AIDE-MEMOIRE*

The whole heart of the people of the United States is in the winning of this war. The controlling purpose of the Government of the United States is to do everything that is necessary and effective to win it. It wishes to co-operate in every practicable way with the Allied Governments, and to co-operate ungrudgingly; for it has no ends of its own to serve and believes that the war can be won only by common counsel and intimate concert of action. It has sought to study every proposed policy or action in which its co-operation has been asked in this spirit, and states the following conclusions in the confidence that, if it finds itself obliged to decline participation in any undertaking or course of action, it will be understood that it does so only because it deems itself precluded from participating by imperative considerations either of policy or of fact.

In full agreement with the Allied Governments and upon the unanimous advice of the Supreme War Council, the Government of the United States adopted upon its entrance into the war, a plan for taking part in fighting on the western front into which all its resources of men and material were to be put, and put as rapidly as possible, and it has carried out that plan with energy and success, pressing its execution more and more rapidly forward and literally putting into it the entire energy and executive force of the nation. This was its response, its very willing and hearty response, to what was the unhesitating judgment alike of its own military advisers and of the advisers of the Allied Governments. It is now considering, at the suggestion of the Supreme War Council, the possibility of making very considerable additions even to this immense program which, if they should prove feasible at all, will tax the industrial processes of the United States and the shipping facilities of the

177

whole group of associated nations to the utmost. It has thus concentrated all its plans and all its resources upon this single absolutely necessary object.

In such circumstances it feels it to be its duty to say that it cannot, so long as the military situation on the western front remains critical, consent to break or slacken the force of its present effort by diverting any part of its military force to other points or objectives. The United States is at a great distance from the field of action on the western front; it is at a much greater distance from any other field of action. The instrumentalities by which it is to handle its armies and its stores have at great cost and with great difficulty been created in France. They do not exist elsewhere. It is practicable for her to do a great deal in France: it is not practicable for her to do anything of importance or on a large scale upon any other field. The American Government, therefore, very respectfully requests its associates to accept its deliberate judgment that it should not dissipate its force by attempting important operations elsewhere.

It regards the Italian front as closely co-ordinated with the western front, however, and is willing to divert a portion of its military forces from France to Italy if it is the judgment and wish of the Supreme Command that it should do so. It wished to defer to the decision of the Commander-in-Chief in this matter, as it would wish to defer in all others, particularly because it considers these two fronts so closely related as to be practically but separate parts of a single line and because it would be necessary that any American troops sent to Italy should be subtracted from the number used in France and actually transported across French territory from the ports now used by the armies of the United States.

It is the clear and fixed judgment of the Government of the United States, arrived at after repeated and very searching reconsiderations of the whole situation in Russia, that military intervention there would add to the present sad confusion in Russia rather than cure it, injure her rather than help her, and that it would be of no advantage in the prosecution of our main design, to win the war against Germany. It cannot, therefore, take part in such intervention or sanction it in principle. Military intervention would, in its judgment, even supposing it to be efficacious in its immediate avowed object of delivering an attack upon Germany from the east, be merely a method of making use of Russia, not a method of serving her. Her people could not profit by it, if they profited by it at all, in time to save them from their present distresses, and their substance would be used to maintain foreign armies, not to reconstitute their own. Military action is admissible in Russia, as the Government of the United States sees the circumstances, only to help the Czecho-Slovaks consolidate their forces and get into successful co-operation with their Slavic kinsmen and to steady any efforts at self-government or self-defense in which the Russians themselves may be willing to accept assistance. Whether from Vladivostok or from Murmansk and Archangel, the only legitimate object for which American or Allied troops can be employed, it submits, is to guard military stores which may subsequently be needed by the Russian forces and to render such aid as may be acceptable to the Russians in the organization of their own self-defense. For helping the Czecho-Slovaks there is immediate necessity and sufficient justification. Recent developments have made it evident that that is in the interest of what the Russian people themselves desire, and the Government of the United States is glad to contribute the small force at its disposal for that purpose. It yields, also, to the judgment of Supreme Command in the matter of establishing a small force at Murmansk, to guard the military stores at Kola, and to make it safe for Russian forces to come together in organized bodies in the north. But it owes it to frank counsel to say that it can go no further than these modest and experimental plans. It is not in a position, and has no expectations of being in a position, to take part in organized intervention in adequate force from either Vladivostok or Murmansk and Archangel. It feels that it ought to add, also, that it will feel at liberty to use the few troops it can spare only for the purposes here stated and shall feel obliged to withdraw those forces, in order to add them to the forces at the western front, if the plans in whose execution it is now intended that they should co-operate should develop into others inconsistent with the policy to which the Government of the United States feels constrained to restrict itself.

At the same time the Government of the United States wishes to say with the utmost cordiality and good will that none of the conclusions here stated is meant to wear the least color of criticism of what the other governments associated against Germany may think it wise to undertake. It wishes in no way to embarrass their choices of policy. All that is intended here is a perfectly frank and definite statement of the policy which the United States feels obliged to adopt for herself and in the use of her own military forces. The Government of the United States does not wish it to be understood that in so restricting its own activities it is seeking, even by implication, to set limits to the action or to define the policies of its associates.

It hopes to carry out the plans for safeguarding the rear of the Czecho-Slovaks operating from Vladivostok in a way that will place it and keep it in close co-operation with a small military force like its own from Japan, and if necessary from the other Allies, and that will assure it of the cordial accord of all the Allied powers; and it proposes to ask all associated in this course of action to unite in assuring the people of Russia in the most public and solemn manner that none of the governments uniting in action either in Siberia or in northern Russia contemplates any interference of any kind with the political sovereignty of Russia, any intervention in her internal affairs, or any impairment of her territorial integrity either now or hereafter, but that each of the associated powers has the single object of affording such aid as shall be acceptable, and only such aid as shall be acceptable, to the Russian people in their endeavour to regain control of their own affairs, their own territory, and their own destiny.

It is the hope and purpose of the Government of the United States to take advantage of the earliest opportunity to send to Siberia a commission of merchants, agricultural experts, labor advisers, Red Cross representatives, and agents of the Young Men's Christian Association accustomed to organizing the best methods of spreading useful information and rendering educational help of a modest sort, in order in some systematic manner to relieve the immediate economic necessities of the people there in every way for which opportunity may open. The execution of this plan will follow and will not be permitted to embarrass the military assistance rendered in the rear of the westward-moving forces of the Czechoslovaks.

Washington, July 17, 1918

(From *Foreign Relations*, 1918, *Russia*, II, 287–90)

NOTES

1. As a result of the Portsmouth peace talks, the northern half of Sakhalin was returned to Russia, but not until 1925.
2. Petrograd was the new name for the capital in preference to the Germanic-sounding St Petersburg. It was again renamed as Leningrad in 1924.
3. Variations of this story exist. Grondijs's account is similar to a number of other plausible minority reports: 'A few weeks later, the Admiral, beaten, was summoned to the bridge of his flagship to surrender to his ship's company. He maintained an attitude of great dignity, refusing to relinquish his sword, which he threw overboard into the sea: a fine gesture which would be celebrated in both patriotic poetry and in caricature'.
4. According to Kerensky's War Minister Verkhorsky.
5. An echelon was an 80-axle train made up of 40 × 2-axle cars or carriages.
6. See Appendix.
7. The same report gave the untruth that 'The wife and son of Nicholas Romanov were sent to a safe place.'
8. The Twelfth Division was the first division to go ashore in Korea in the opening round of the war on land in Japan's war against Russia 1904–1905.
9. The Japanese Army had been trained by Germany 1870–1914.
10. 222 American soldiers were killed in north Russia and 36 in Siberia.
11. A State Department plan is alleged to be in the archives of the Soviet Ministry of Foreign Affairs. If it does exist, it remains as a lasting legacy to what Kennan described as 'philosophical and intellectual congenital shallowness' in the US approach to world problems. The plan supposedly recommended that Russia should be divided into economic zones but none large enough to permit the formation of a strong, independent state.
12. Under the terms of the Railway Agreement, China dispossessed Japan of the complete control of the Chinese Eastern Railway. China therefore had to police exactly half the 2,500 miles of track for which Japan remained responsible. The United States was given 316 miles of track to guard in the Ussuri and Baikal regions.
13. Arthur Ruhl.
14. *The War of the Rising Sun and Tumbling Bear*, p. 91–8.
15. 'The White guard military dictatorship became transformed from a centralised dictatorship into one exercised by individual generals and Cossack Atamans, and from a tyranny firmly guided from a single centre into

violent practices all over Siberia by separate gangs which slipped from the control of the "Supreme Ruler".' Elena Varneck and H.H. Fisher, K.A. Popov, quoted in *The Testimony of Kolchak and Other Siberian Materials* (1935), p. 6.

16. According to the Bečvář account, the episode at Glaskov station spanned two nights whereas most other accounts suggest it had been of one night's duration. In view of Bečvář's close association with these events we have used his record. This coincides with Popov's account that the Czechs handed over Kolchak to the political centre on 17 January 1920.

17. During his interrogation, Kolchak was pressed by one of the Social Revolutionaries, A Lekseyevsky, to give his 'personal attitude to epaulettes'. Kolchak replied that he had been in favour but when it was suggested that soldiers at the front were opposed, he responded: 'During my trips to the army this question was not raised. I met soldiers and officers on front positions who were clothed in a perfectly fantastic way – could there be any talk about epaulettes? One was lucky if he had anything to put on'.

18. The Soviet Government reintroduced epaulettes in 1942 to distinguish between the various grades in a classless society.

19. Verkhne Udinsk lay within the United States Army's controlled railway zone. They, like the Japanese, remained supremely disinterested in the fate of Admiral Kolchak.

20. The Baltic States were taken in to the Russian Empire in 1939.

21. Japan did not return northern Sakhalin to Russia until 1925. Russia acquired all of Sakhalin in 1945 as part of an agreement with the allies for her last-minute entry into the war against Japan.

BIBLIOGRAPHY

Alioshin, Dmitri (1940) *Asian Odyssey*, New York, Henry Holt.
Baerlin, Henry (1926) *The March of the Seventy Thousand*, Leonard Parsons.
Bečvář, Gustav (1939) *The Lost Legion: A Czechoslovakian Epic*, London, Stanley Paul.
Bennett, Geoffrey (1964) *Cowan's War*, London, Collins.
Bradley, John (1968) *Allied Intervention in Russia*, London, Weidenfeld & Nicolson.
Bullitt, William C. (1919) *The Bullitt Mission to Russia: Testimony Before the Committee on Foreign Relations of the United States Senate*, New York, Huebsch.
Carr, E.H. (1953) *The Bolshevik Revolution, 1917–1923*, vol. iii, London, Macmillan.
Chamberlin, W.H. (1935) *The Russian Revolution, 1917–1921* 2 vols, London, Macmillan.
Churchill, Winston S. (1929) *The World Crisis, the Aftermath*, London, Thornton Butterworth.
Coates, W.P. and Zelda, K. (1935) *Armed Intervention in Russia 1918–1922*, London, Victor Gollancz.
Coleman, Frederic (1918) *Japan Moves North*, London, Cassell & Co. Ltd.
Deutscher, I. (1954) *The Prophet Armed: Trotsky 1879–1921*, Oxford, Oxford University Press.
Dobson, Christopher and Miller, John (1986) *The Day We Almost Bombed Moscow: The Allied War in Russia 1918–1920*, London, Hodder & Stoughton.
Dunsterville, L.C. (1920) *The Adventures of Dunsterforce*, Dunton Green, Edward Arnold.
Fischer, Louis (1951) *The Soviets in World Affairs* vol. i, Princeton, NJ, Princeton University Press.
Fleming, Peter (1963) *The Fate of Admiral Kolchak*, London, Rupert Hart-Davis.
Footman, David (1961) *Civil War in Russia*, London, Faber & Faber.
Graves, William S. (1931) *America's Siberian Adventure, 1918–1920*, London, Jonathan Cape.
Grondijs, Ludovic-H. (1922) *La Guerre en Russie et en Sibérie*, Paris, Bossard.
Halliday, E.M. (1961) *The Ignorant Armies*, London, Weidenfeld & Nicolson.
Hodges, Phelps (1931) *Britmis*, London, Jonathan Cape.
Hoffman, Max (1929) *War Diaries and Other Papers* 2 vols, London, Martin Secker.
Horrocks, Brian (1960) *A Full Life*, London, Collins.
Hoyt, Edwin P. (1967) *The Army Without a Country*, London, Macmillan.
Ironside, Lord (1953) *Archangel, 1918–1919*, London, Constable.

183

THE REPUBLIC OF THE USHAKOVKA

Janin, P.T.C. Maurice (1933) *Ma Mission en Sibérie, 1918–1920*, Paris, Payot.
Kennan, George F. (1956–8) *Soviet American Relations, 1917–1920* 2 vols:
   i *Russia Leaves the War*; ii: *The Decision to Intervene*, London, Faber & Faber.
Keynes, John Maynard (1919) *Economic Consequences of the Peace*, London,
   Macmillan.
Kindall, Sylvian G. (1945) *American Soldiers in Siberia*, Richard R. Smith.
Knox, Alfred (1921) *With the Russian Army, 1914–1917* 2 vols, London,
   Hutchinson.
Lloyd George, D. (1938) *The Truth About The Peace Treaties*, 2 vols, London,
   Victor Gollancz.
Lockhart, R.H. Bruce (1932) *Memoirs of a British Agent*, New York, Putnam.
Luckett, Richard (1971) *The White Generals*, London, Routledge & Kegan Paul.
McCullagh, F. (1921) *A Prisoner of the Reds: The Story of a British Officer Captured in
   Siberia*, London, John Murray.
Manning, Clarence A. (1952) *The Siberian Fiasco*, New York.
Markovits, Rodion (1929) *Siberian Garrison*, Peter Davies.
Montandon, George (1923) *Deux Ans Chez Koltchak et Chez les Bolchéviques*,
   Librairie Félix Alcan.
Morley, James William (1954) *The Japanese Thrust into Siberia, 1918*, New York,
   Columbia University Press.
Noulens, Joseph (1933) *Mon Ambassade en Russie Soviétique, 1917–1919*, 2 vols,
   Paris, Librairie Plon,
Rouquerol, J. (1929) *L'Aventure de L'Amiral Koltchak*, Paris, Payot.
Silverlight, John (1970) *The Victors' Dilemma*, London, Barrie & Jenkins.
Smith, Hedrick (1976) *The Russians*, London, Times Books.
Snow, Russell E. (1977) *The Bolsheviks in Siberia, 1917–1918*, London, Associated
   University Presses.
Stewart, George (1933) *The White Armies of Russia*, London, Macmillan.
Swettenham, John (1967) *Allied Intervention in Russia 1918–1919 And the Part
   Played by Canada*, London, George Allen & Unwin.
Trotsky, Leon (1934) *The History of the Russian Revolution*, London, Victor
   Gollancz.
Ullman, Richard H. (1961–8) *Anglo Soviet Relations, 1917–1921* 2 vols: i
   Intervention and the War; ii *Britain and the Russian Civil War*, Princeton, NJ,
   Princeton University Press.
Unterberger, Betty Miller (1956) *America's Siberian Expedition*, Durham, NC, Duke
   University Press.
Varneck, Elena and Fisher, H.H. (1935) *The Testimony of Kolchak and Other Siberian
   Materials*, Stanford, CA, Stanford University Press.
Vining, L.E. (1924) *Held by the Bolsheviks*, The Saint Catherine Press.
Ward, John (1920) *With the 'Die Hards' in Siberia*, London, Cassell.
White, D. Fedotoff (1939) *Survival Through War and Revolution in Russia*, Oxford,
   Oxford University Press.

INDEX

185